World
Politics
and the
Evolution
of War

World Politics and the Evolution of War

JOHN J. WELTMAN

THE JOHNS HOPKINS UNIVERSITY PRESS
BALTIMORE AND LONDON

Published 1995

Printed in the United
States of America on
acid-free paper

04 03 02 01 00
99 98 97 96 95
5 4 3 2 1

The Johns Hopkins
University Press
2715 North Charles Street
Baltimore, Maryland
21218-4319

The Johns Hopkins Press
Ltd., London

LIBRARY OF CONGRESS
CATALOGING-IN-
PUBLICATION DATA

Weltman, John J.
    World politics and the
evolution of war / John J.
Weltman.
        p.   cm.
    Includes bibliographical
references and index.
    ISBN 0-8018-4948-9
(hc : acid-free paper). —
ISBN 0-8018-4949-7 (pbk. :
acid-free paper)
    1. International rela-
tions.   2. War (Inter-
national law)   3. World
politics—1989–   I. Title.
JX1391.W45   1995
327.1'17—dc20 94-13024

A catalog record for this
book is available from the
British Library.

For T.S.C., with love and thanks, sine qua non

Contents

Preface and Acknowledgments

The end of the cold war has left many students of international politics at a loss as to what might come next. This has come about because so much of the analysis with which the past two generations have grown up has been dominated by the concerns of the cold war. In particular the role of war in international politics is uncertain. Thinking runs the gamut from the view that rampant nationalism, religious enthusiasm, and growing strategic multipolarity will make the coming decades at least as dangerous as those we have just experienced, to the view that common interests in economic and ecological questions, and the absence of a universalistic philosophy capable of challenging the new orthodoxies of liberal democratic capitalism, herald a world order of unprecedented peace.

Rather than speculate about the future on the basis of ideas dominated by the cold war, this study treats the role of warfare in international politics as a historical process, in which the conditions of the cold war are understood as unusual. It attempts to understand the broad range of influences that have affected the incidence and character of warfare throughout modern history, and to apply that understanding to the world in which we are now living. It insists throughout that understanding of the particular character of warfare in a given period cannot be obtained by concentrating upon either the general influences of the international system or the attitudes and idiosyncrasies of the individual players of the game. Neither element can conclusively establish the degree or manner in which warfare will intrude on social and political life. Such factors, though important, are not sufficient. To these must be added matters related to warfare itself: the weapons at the disposal of those who would fight, and the social organization through which they would organize themselves for fighting.

This combination of factors—weapons and organization, as well as international influences and individual attitudes—produces expectations about the character and usefulness of warfare to those who might contemplate embarking upon it. They may regard warfare as a useful and efficient tool for achieving their objectives, or as an unpredictable and uncontrollable process that could well impose costs far greater than any gains. These expectations are not always fulfilled. Indeed, modern history is replete with situations in which the players of the game experienced profound, and often catastrophic, surprise. But if we wish to begin speculating about the circumstances that await us, we must consider the present period in light of those influences that have affected the role of war in international politics in the past.

To that end, this book begins by surveying theories of the causes of war in international politics. It explores the reasons for the prominence historically given to war and the means of war in international politics. It deals with the effects of political, economic, and technological change upon the prevalence of war in modern history; the patterns of conflict in international relations; and the manner in which war has been carried on. It introduces the reader to the development of thought about "strategy," the study of the organization and use of force, and the threat of force as a means of achieving policy goals in international politics. It considers attempts to eliminate international war or to mitigate its effects. Finally, it surveys the emerging scene after the end of the cold war and speculates about the effects that contemporary developments will have on international conflict, including the question of whether war has undergone a fundamental decline in importance. The historical circumstances in which these issues are raised enable the student to place today's events and their implications in a context that analyses dominated by the bipolar structures and ideological contests of the cold war lack.

The work casts doubt on the notion that the number of players in the international system yields definitive conclusions about the incidence or the character of war. I suggest instead that the social, material, and intellectual context within which conflicts occur is far more influential, although I do not accept another piece of the prevailing wisdom, that democracies are inherently peaceful and autocracies inherently warlike.

Rather the propensity to war, and the effects of war, are largely products of the character of prevailing expectations about war: whether war offers a means for the cheap, easy, and decisive accomplishment of governmental objectives.

The book is critical of the view that conflict, and especially violent conflict, is necessarily a product of some psychological pathology or abnormality, some malformation of the perceptual process. This view is dealt with most directly in chapters 5 and 6, where the outbreak and character of World War I are understood as a reasonable extrapolation from political and strategic experience, however horrendous a miscalculation that extrapolation would prove itself to be in the light of later events.

The work draws on the contrast between two traditions in strategic thought: Jomini's search for autonomous, objective, and calculable laws of war, laws that would yield predictive conclusions; and Clausewitz's emphasis on the overriding importance of the intangibles of the political context. This contrast is carried forward to the nuclear debate, with the ambitions of the dominant school of nuclear strategists presented as profoundly Jominian in approach and aspiration. This Jominian approach, I suggest, is at the root of the frustrations of the nuclear strategists and their inability to find ways to make nuclear weapons serve the ends of policy.

The book draws on the distinction, from Clausewitz via the historian Delbrück, between wars of *annihilation* and wars of *attrition,* and makes the argument that a secular trend against the former, and in the direction of warfare's increasing costliness and disutility, is apparent. I do not attribute this trend, as have others, to fashion, to a growing civility, to a changing aesthetic, or to an emergent ideological homogeneity, but largely to a growing lack of utility in getting desired results. The discussion of World War II, a conflict usually interpreted as heralding a new decisiveness in warfare, emphasizes instead its attritional character. This interpretation is carried forward into the cold war and post–cold war period.

I conclude by arguing that we are likely to see a continuation of this trend toward attrition in warfare. The recent war in the Persian Gulf was unique, not a harbinger. The trend toward attrition may not suggest the end of warfare, still less the "end of history." It does imply the localization of conflict and the minimization of the danger of global conflagration. The world will be far from peaceful, but the conflicts that will arise, because of their particularist character, will be slow-burning and difficult to spread.

An appointment in the Department of Political Science of the Johns Hopkins University gave me an occasion to develop my ideas and to test them in the crucible of the classroom. I am grateful to Matthew A. Crenson and Steven A. David, who served successively as department chair during my residence, for this opportunity. An affiliation with the Graduate School of International Studies of the University of Denver, kindly offered me by its dean, E. Thomas Rowe, facilitated the completion of the work. Among those who have read the manuscript, in whole or in part, and offered valuable commentary, are Steven A. David, Michael Nacht, Lawrence Scheinman, John Spanier, Roderick S. C. Tang, Robert W. Tucker, and George H. Quester. I am especially grateful to my teacher and friend, Robert W. Tucker, for support and encouragement over more than three decades, and to Roderick S. C. Tang for wisdom and support in recent years. Needless to say I have not always accepted the wise advice of these friends. The inadequacies remaining in the work must, alas, therefore be laid at my door alone.

World
Politics
and the
Evolution
of War

_____

The Role of War in International Politics

1

The greatest war in the past was the Persian War; yet in this war the decision was reached quickly. . . . The Peloponnesian War, on the other hand, not only lasted for a long time, but throughout its course brought with it unprecedented suffering. . . . Never before had so many cities been captured and then devastated. . . . Never had there been so many exiles; never such loss of life—both in the actual warfare and in internal revolutions. . . . War began when the Athenians and the Peloponnesians broke the . . . truce. . . . But the real reason for the war is . . . disguised by such an argument. What made war inevitable was the growth of Athenian power and the fear which this caused in Sparta.—Thucydides (trans. Rex Warner)

Twenty-five hundred years ago Thucydides, the greatest of Greek historians, felt compelled to probe the causes of wars and the differences among wars. In order to understand the conflict that had ravaged his civilization, he raised a series of questions that continue to intrigue us. Why do some wars end quickly and cheaply, whereas others are lengthy and exhausting in blood and treasure? Why do some wars remain confined to their original participants but others draw in the initially uninvolved? Why do some conflicts threaten the social order within societies, while others leave it intact?

The use of force, and the threat of its use, are pervasive in the history of relations among organized political units and have taken many forms. Over the past five centuries alone, war has been "present three times more frequently than it [has been] absent."[1] Some would say that the effective use of force has been the principal reason for the rise and fall of governments— indeed of whole civilizations—and their ability to exercise influence over others. Some would argue further that the tools of major violence, and the organizations that have evolved for managing its use, have been unequaled as influences on the social, cultural, and intellectual development of human beings throughout history.[2]

The causes of war, the many forms war has taken, and the various effects it has had on the societies among which it has occurred[3] are especially compelling questions at the present moment. An era dominated by the great Soviet-American conflict that came to be known as the cold war has ended, but the patterns of international conflict and cooperation that will take the place of the cold war are still uncertain.

INTERNATIONAL POLITICS AND DOMESTIC POLITICS

When we think about politics, we implicitly have as our model the sort of politics with which we are familiar in everyday life. The modern, territory-based, centralized state that has dominated Western civilization for three centuries has come to dominate the rest of the world as the institutions of Western civilization have spread around the globe. When we think of politics, we think of hierarchical institutions with power to decide on matters of common interest and to enforce those decisions with effective coercion, if need be. Politics is debate over those decisions, and the struggle to control the institutions that make the decisions.

Our historical experience over the past few centuries gives us some justification for looking on this sort of politics with a certain degree of optimism.[4] The political process within modern states has allowed change in the influence that different groups in society can exert over governmental decisions. Newly important groups, such as industrial workers or manufacturers, have acquired political influence where previously they had little or none. Various groups have been able to use the political process to acquire greater access to material advantages. In the nineteenth and twentieth centuries industrial workers have been able to use the political process in America and Europe to improve the conditions of their employment and to gain access to medical care and old-age insurance. Through the political process, undesirable social practices have been curbed or eliminated. Child labor has been limited, for example, and sanitary conditions improved.

To be sure, the political process within the state has also produced great horrors, persecutions, catastrophes. Nazism, communism, and other totalitarian regimes have come to power through domestic political change, at the cost of the lives and freedom of millions, within the totalitarian states and outside of them. Conversely, it is often argued that those changes that have occurred within some modern states are still inadequate. Some feel that the workers or the poor or ethnic minorities are still at an unfair disadvantage. Arguments that radical change is still necessary if inequities are to be eliminated are common. But we can believe that progress in desired directions, through the mechanism of the domestic political process, is at least possible. If and when major violence occurs in domestic society, we tend to regard it as pathological, abnormal, unusual. When major violence becomes a part of the domestic political process, we regard it as a sign that the process has broken down.

Politics is also found beyond the boundaries of states. Struggles between states, those that cross state frontiers, occur over material resources and over how issues of mutual interest should be resolved. They arise over religious principles and social doctrines. They erupt over the possession of pieces of territory and mineral resources. They develop over the rules of international trade and over how best to deal with environmental or ecological challenges. Such struggles were endemic well before the arrival of the modern state, when empires, nomadic tribes, and other sorts of political units dominated the scene. Yet in contrast to the domestic political process, the international political process attracts less optimism about its potential to resolve problems or make changes. International politics has had a certain sameness about it over the years, and few developments can truly be called "progress."

The means and methods of force that human groups employ toward one another have changed vastly over the centuries. Nuclear weapons and laser beams differ dramatically from hatchets and clubs in the extent and character of their physical effects, but they, too, represent ways to employ or threaten to employ physical violence against other groups in order to achieve some goal. The presence of such violence, and the constant possibility of its use even when not actually present, have pervaded the political relations among human societies. Indeed, war—organized collective violence among human groups—is for many not only *typical* of international politics; the constant possibility of war *defines* international politics.

In domestic politics, the questions for debate have centered on conceptions of *justice*. What principles should define the relationships among persons and groups and how can they be ascertained? What is the good state and how can it be constructed? Can citizens make existing institutions better, more just? Should governmental institutions be involved in all issues or should some be the concern of only private persons?

When we turn to that form of politics that takes place between societies, we find that we can concern ourselves with these questions of justice only intermittently and fleetingly. The problems imposed by the presence of organized violence intrude themselves with an urgency that requires us to deal with them immediately, before we can have any hope of considering the pursuit of justice. The eruption of warfare may put at risk any scheme for achieving international political change or progress through nonviolent means. The intractably unprogressive, static character of international politics makes it a subject that many—even those who believe politics can offer change for the better—prefer to overlook.

THE CAUSES OF WAR

Under what conditions do wars occur, and what conditions cause them to be more or less nasty, ferocious, costly, or widespread? These sobering questions have dominated the concerns of those who have been drawn to the study of politics among states and nations.

A useful way to organize our ideas about the causes of wars is to sort them out in order of importance. In Kenneth Waltz's terms, we may see the causes of war in human nature itself, in the particular ways in which particular societies are organized, or in how those societies are organized in relation to one another.[5]

Human Nature

Perhaps bad people cause wars. Wars may be attributed to acquisitiveness, to a universal human lust to dominate, to anger. Thus, the key to alleviating war—if there is any key at all—lies in keeping those who have these undesirable traits from getting power over others, or perhaps in reforming those with bad characters so they will no longer cause trouble. Some of those who have taken this approach have traced war to some defect in human nature itself. War comes from a lust for power or domination embedded in the human personality.[6] Theologians in the tradition of Saint Augustine approach the problem of war from such a perspective. This is a profoundly pessimistic view.[7] If this lust for power can be alleviated or controlled at all, it is only through counterpoising the aggressive instincts of one with those of others, and hoping they may each keep the other under control.

If, however, war is truly a product of an inevitable human nature, how then can periods of peace, which must be produced by the same human nature, be explained? Many of those who trace war to human nature respond by saying that the defects responsible for war are not universal, that they are found only in some human beings, and even those with such a defective character might still be cured.

Thus, wars are attributed to individuals whose characters are warped to the point of insanity—Hitler, Napoleon, or Kaiser Wilhelm II are often cited—or to "normal" individuals who are suffering from some psychological defect. People may see enemies where there are none. They may see weakness and opportunity in the camp of others, rather than resolution. They may perceive the goals of another as in conflict with their own when in fact they are not. When an overwhelming amount of conflicting interpretations about a situation or an opponent is available, decision makers may simplify their problems by choosing the interpretations that confirm what they already expect to happen, or that are consistent with policies to which they are already committed.[8]

If wars are caused by bad people, how do we explain the involvement in wars of good people? How do we explain it when those with the best of intentions, those who seem admirably well balanced, those who are not given to seeing hostility and enmity where there is none, those who are averse to taking risks—people such as the American presidents James Madison, Abraham Lincoln and Woodrow Wilson—nevertheless find themselves involved in wars they did not desire? How do we explain the role of human nature in those who are warlike at some periods but apostles of peace at others, such as the nineteenth-century German statesman Otto von Bismarck?

Some would argue that war fulfills an instinctive need, found primarily among young males, for activities involving great emotional excitement and physical exertion.[9] This instinctive need, perhaps a function of the male sex hormones, might explain the wars of Alexander the Great, who conquered most of the civilized world as known to the ancient Greeks while still in his twenties. But most wars, while fought by young men, have been fought at the orders of older men, in whom the fires of raging hormones have declined. Some wars in the past may have fulfilled needs for emotional release, just as riots or athletic contests, two activities in which young males commonly participate with relish, may do today. But what of modern wars, where one may never see one's opponent, and one "fights" by performing actions that require little physical effort, actions that may be no more emotionally charged than word processing or calculating problems in trigonometry? If the roots of wars are to be found in the emotional needs they fulfill, whether for leaders or followers or both, how can periods without war be explained, periods during which we have no reason to believe that the emotional makeup of the individuals involved has changed in any important way from what it was during periods of violent hostilities?

Either we insist that any leader who becomes involved in a war must, by definition, have had something pathological or defective about him or her—whether that defect can easily be observed or not—or we must go further in our search for an explanation of war. Perhaps human nastiness or aggressiveness or paranoia, or even hormones, may form part of the explanation for some wars, but for a more general explanation we must look to a level other than that of individual human beings.

Internal Organization

This brings us to the proposition that the causes of wars lie in how human groups organize themselves domestically. Societies, states, or political units that are organized internally in the "wrong" way fight wars; those that are organized according to "correct" principles do not. Thus, some have argued that democratic states tend not to fight (and when they do fight, they rarely fight each other), whereas authoritarian states oftentimes do; or that capitalist states fight, and socialist states do not; or that capitalist states do not fight, but communist states do. It is difficult, however, to choose among statements such as these. There is no agreement on what constitutes a "good" state, or on the principles of domestic organization that will produce a society inclined to peaceful relations with its neighbors. Indeed, there are diametrically opposed views on this question.

Thus, Marxists have said that wars come from the inherent need of capitalism to produce surpluses of goods and capital. The resulting struggle for markets causes capitalists to induce their governments to back them up with military force. Capitalism, however, is a recent historical development; Europe cannot be said to have been dominated by a capitalist economic system much before the sixteenth century. The phenomenon of war, however, is as ancient as the earliest historical records of civilization. The Marxist explanation for war fails to account for all those wars that antedate the emergence of capitalism. It is as if Newton had proposed a theory of gravity that only applied from the seventeenth century on.[10]

Even if the Marxist account is plausible, how are we to explain the many occasions where the *reverse* of the Marxist notion of cause and effect occurred? Thus, in the late nineteenth century, a newly united Germany acquired colonies in Africa and the Pacific. This German imperial expansion was not produced by the pressure of capitalists forcing the German government to expand. Rather, the German government drove imperial expansion, motivated by a desire to catch up to the British and the French, who had acquired *their* empires earlier.[11] The German government often prevailed upon businessmen to embark on projects that were not otherwise attractive economically, although some groups may, in the end, have benefited economically from these transactions. To admit that, however, is not to prove that the groups that benefited *caused* the government to act in the manner it did.

Whereas Marxists have argued that capitalism is inherently aggressive, others have suggested the opposite, that capitalism is inherently inclined to peaceful behavior.[12] As the great Austrian economist Joseph Schumpeter put it: "In a purely capitalist world, . . . wars of conquest and adventurism in foreign policy in general are bound to be regarded as troublesome distractions."[13] Capitalists, it is argued, want to maximize order and predictability. The last thing they want is a fight in which their capital, their goods, and their commercial relationships could be destroyed or disrupted. Mention a war and the first thing the stock market does is crash.

Marxists assume that, while the capitalists are warlike, the workers are inherently peaceful. In 1914, when World War I began, most European Marxists expected the workers and the labor unions of all European countries to line up against the war. They were shocked instead when the workers in each European country enthusiastically went to war against the workers of other European countries. More recently, followers of Marx have asserted that the world capitalist economic system as a whole reinforces and widens the division between rich and poor, producing conflict in its train.[14] This is to overlook, however, the widely differing abilities of poor nations to change their relative positions in the global economy. Thus, Singapore and South Korea have been much more successful in improving their economic position in today's world than Bangladesh or Somalia.

Whereas Marxists trace war to the *economic* organization of the state, liberals trace it to its *political* organization: democratic states are peaceful, but authoritarian states are inherently warlike. Such a conclusion may have seemed compelling when World War II broke out in 1939. Germany, Italy, and Japan were all governed by authoritarian regimes of one sort or another. Germany and Italy were ruled by fascist regimes and Japan was dominated by its military leadership. These governments all pursued domestic policies of violent repression. All three states had embarked upon campaigns of external territorial expansion, using military force or the threat of military force. The great democracies in Britain, France, and the United States, on the other hand, pursued pacific policies and attempted to avoid the use of force.

The Soviet Union, however, governed by Joseph Stalin's Communist regime, was as authoritarian as Hitler's Germany, and engaged in a horrendously bloody repression of its own people in which millions perished. Yet Stalin pursued a pacific policy externally, until attacked by Hitler in 1941. Similarly, while fascist Germany and Italy were entering World War II, fascist Spain under the dictator Francisco Franco remained neutral.

It is comforting to believe that democracies are inherently peaceful, that only nasty militarists make war, but is this inevitably the case? Some wars have drawn immense and wide support in democratic societies. In the Spanish-American conflict in 1898, perhaps an America less driven by popular emotion might not have been so quick to fight. Similarly, during World War I it was difficult for many of the European governments involved to try to bring the war to a halt even after it had become obvious to them that the war had turned into a vast killing field serving no meaningful purpose. They faced this difficulty precisely because public opinion was so important in these states.[15] Political leaders in Britain, France, and Germany all felt that to talk about accepting a compromise peace would be to commit political suicide.

Thus, no clear or simple connection exists between "good" states and peace, and "bad" states and war. However we define "good" and "bad"—and there are violent disagreements about that—we often find "good" states going to war and "bad" states keeping the peace. Perhaps the internal organization of states may provide part of the explanation for some wars, but we must search still further for a more general understanding of the causes of war.

The International System

If neither human nature nor the domestic organization of human political groups provides us with an adequate explanation for the causes and prevalence of war, we must turn next to explanations cast in what Kenneth Waltz has called the "third image" of the causes of war.[16] This is the condition of states in their relationship to one another. The internal characteristics of the units or of the human beings composing those units are less important here than how the units deal with one another. In domestic politics a hierarchy exists. Political units serve specialized roles. Some units, such as legislatures and courts, make and enforce rules for others.[17] In international politics, political units are not subordinated to one another in this way but can rely only on their own efforts. If there is conflict or differences of view, there is no guarantee that the issue can be settled peacefully. Of course, all issues in dispute, or even most issues, in international politics are not settled only by the resort to force. But one cannot *rely* on the assumption that force, or the threat of force, will not be appealed to by a party dissatisfied with how a dispute might otherwise be peacefully settled.

I do not normally worry, according to this view, that others might use force to settle a disagreement in everyday life, largely because government imposes a system of rules on us all, including the rule that the use of force is forbidden as a means to settle private disputes. Usually I assume that others will not use force because of this system of rules and the known disposition of the government to back those rules forcibly if need be; and for the same reason others will not fear that I would use force. This is what we commonly assume in the marketplace. We may disagree about property rights or contract requirements, but we carry on our interactions without worrying that physical violence will be used to settle such a dispute. We do not fear that the physically stronger party will overpower the other and simply *take* that which is in dispute.

In international politics, no institution can make and enforce rules for states, as a government does for individuals and groups subordinate to it. All varieties of rules are to be found in international politics, rules that are discussed widely, often agreed upon widely, and often widely followed, but there is no reliable assurance that they *will* be so followed.[18] In their actions those in charge of the external relationships of states will tend to consider the possibility that violence may come into play at some time or another. Not that violence necessarily *will* occur, but that it *might.* In this environment statesmen are still free to act as if violence were impossible, but they may be taking a grave risk. If they guess wrong, they may suffer great losses and even threaten the survival of the institutions they control.

In the seventeenth century, political philosophers used the device of a "thought experiment" to imagine the nature of the problems that would arise without government, and how the creation of government could alleviate or eliminate these problems. Thomas Hobbes and John Locke both imagined a "state of nature," an intellectual construct from which to begin their reasoning about government.[19] Both imagined a situation in which people capable of reason existed without government. They then asked what problems people in such a state of nature would face.

For Locke, the problems produced by the state of nature would not be overwhelming. Most of the time, rational people would be able to avoid conflict simply by following the rules of justice that they are capable of ascertaining and applying through their own powers of reasoning. Problems would arise only occasionally, principally when the rules were ambiguous, or susceptible to diverse interpretations. Where alternative interpretations were possible, the parties to a dispute might each err in the direction of their own interests. Each might choose the interpretation that gives him an advantage. In such situations, the need is simply for some third party, disinterested in the specific matter in contention, to interpose itself. What is needed is, simply, a *judge,* who can apply the rules impartially between the disputants.

For Hobbes the problems that arise in the state of nature are much more severe. Each person attempts to maximize the likelihood of his survival. Each person is capable of rationally calculating the best means to accomplish this. But each must make such calculations in an extremely dangerous environment. Each person in the state of nature possesses the capacity to end the existence of any other. This does not mean that each possesses this capacity to an equal degree. Obviously, some will be stronger than others; some will possess more alertness or physical skill than others. But given favorable circumstances—one could surprise another while asleep, perhaps—the weakest could kill the strongest.

Each seeks to increase his chance for survival. He may build walls, acquire weapons, take up residence in high places with long views. Whatever actions each takes, however, no matter how much his motives are defensive, these actions nevertheless make him seem more threatening in the eyes of his neighbors. If I build walls or a moat around my house, for example, this new construction not only protects me and mine from you. It also makes it easier for me to surprise you and yours. So my behavior, even if motivated solely by my desire to increase my chances for survival and to give myself greater security, lowers your security; since it lowers your security, it increases the likelihood that you will adopt behavior similar to mine and, in the process, lower my security.

I may promise to obey the rules: not to trick or cheat you, or use force against you. There is no reason, however, for you to believe that I am likely to keep my promise if it should be to my immediate advantage to break it, since I do not think punishment by some third-party judge for breaking the rules is likely. You know that punishment is unlikely, and I know that you know it. Each of us must look to his own immediate security and guard against betrayal by others, even though we may see quite well that everyone's security is decreased if everyone behaves like this. The actual use of violence may not be constantly present. "The nature of war consisteth not in actual fighting; but in the known disposition thereto, during all the time there is no assurance to the contrary."[20] The potential for its use can never be ruled out, however, and all who wish to survive must adjust their behavior accordingly. If there were some institution possessing so great a capacity to use force that we were all confident we would be compelled to obey its rules and keep our promises, we could all desist from the search for security. Without such an institution we cannot.

We may take this "state of nature" among individuals as an analogy to the situation that prevails among states that coexist, but in the absence of any institution above them capable of making and reliably enforcing systems of rules for the behavior of those states. "Kings, and persons of sovereign authority, because of their independency, are in continual jeal- . ousies, and in the state and posture of gladiators; having their weapons pointing, and their eyes fixed on one another; that is, their forts, garrisons, and guns upon the frontiers of their kingdoms; and continual spies upon their neighbours; which is a posture of war."[21]

Such a situation imposes a psychology of its own on the players. What is considered sensible behavior, and what is considered irrational, depends upon the context. The American "Wild West" literary genre, and its representation in "Western" movies, illustrate this contrast in psychology. In the Westerns, the behavior of characters is constantly conditioned by concern for their physical safety against violent attack by others. They assess the landscape and plan their movements in terms of the potential that violence might be employed against them. They carry guns. They stay close to cover and peer around corners carefully. They avoid being silhouetted against the sunset or being seated at poker games with their backs to the door. In an environment where the capacity for violence is widespread and the presence of institutions of law enforcement weak or nonexistent, such behavior is only prudent. In our everyday life today, however, someone who insists on taking such precautions is considered paranoid. The absence of constant concern with precautions against physical attack is considered a sign of vigorous mental health in our everyday life. In the Old West such an attitude was seen as tantamount to suicide.

Not only is the possibility of violence present in the state of nature as in the international system within which states exist, but cooperative behavior is difficult. Even if all parties are inclined to behave in a socially correct and cooperative fashion, powerful pressures operate for each to seek his immediate advantage, because each knows that the others are similarly tempted, as long as there is no one to prevent them from doing so.

The eighteenth-century French philosopher Rousseau told a fable about a "stag hunt."[22] Several men are hunting a large animal, a stag. If they succeed in killing the stag, they will all be fed. However, the cooperation of all of them is necessary for them to be successful. At this point, they catch sight of a small animal, a hare. Any of them could kill the hare alone, and the hare would be sufficient to satisfy the hunger of that one, but not of the others. If one of them kills the hare and satisfies his hunger, he may no longer be motivated to cooperate with the others in killing the stag. Lacking sufficient numbers to cooperate successfully to hunt the stag, all those except the one who had killed the hare would go hungry. Each person in the fable is sorely tempted to abandon cooperation with the others and seek his own advantage by killing the hare, precisely because he knows the others are making the same calculation, and he has no reliable assurance that one of the others will not preempt him by abandoning the course of cooperation.

This sort of situation does not depend upon the people in question being egotistical or narrowly self-interested. Even if all the players strongly preferred to act according to the requirements of cooperation, they would each experience powerful constraints in favor of acting for themselves, because they could not be certain that all the others would also choose the cooperative course if they did. This is a metaphor for the "security dilemma" that is found in international politics.[23] What I do, or may reasonably do, simply to increase the likelihood of my survival, may appear with equal reason to you as an increased danger to your survival. The potential for violence in a world of independent states is present, even if all the states are only concerned about their own self-preservation, as long as there is no government-like institution above them capable of giving them all reliable assurance that common rules of behavior will be enforced upon all.

In an important sense, then, wars occur because there is nothing to prevent them from occurring. A general explanation for international war arises from the condition of states coexisting together, but without a government among them capable of coercing them to maintain cooperative, peaceful behavior among themselves. In the absence of such a central institution, from time to time differences in interest or perspective between states may arise, and violent conflict may result, simply because there may be no other way to resolve the differences.[24]

Even if the international condition is the general explanation for the problem of war in international politics, why does a particular war happen at a specific time, between specific governments? The international condition does little to help us understand why particular wars were fought in the manner they were, why some remained confined to a few states and others spread widely, why their effect on the people and societies fighting them and on the arena within which they were fighting ranged from minimal to overwhelming, or why some wars served the purposes of those who started them but others brought catastrophe. To answer such questions, it is necessary to return to the levels of explanation that were examined earlier in this chapter—the individual, internal political organization, and the security dilemma in international politics—and consider how they interact to produce specific wars with particular features at particular times among particular political units. By looking at international warfare and the conditions surrounding it concretely we can understand why specific conflicts took on the precise features that they did. By tracing how warfare changed over time we can come to understand the role of politics, ideology, and technology in producing that change.

In coming chapters, international war will be considered historically, concentrating on the types of political organizations that prevailed in given periods: their domestic makeup; the motivations and ambitions of those who governed them; the economic and technological capabilities they had at their disposal; and the specifically military effects that resulted from the application of those capabilities. If the weapons, military organization, and ideas about deploying armies and navies seemed to make it easy and cheap to use military force to achieve political goals, it was tempting to make war. If war seemed costly, unpredictable, or less than useful in accomplishing political ambitions, then war would not be undertaken lightly.

As Europe emerged from the medieval period, it underwent a confused period in which wars were waged for a mix of religious motives and the ambitions of secular rulers. Disputes over religious issues of transcendent importance to the participants ensured that warfare would become especially ferocious and dangerous to civil populations. But the inability of armies to attack successfully and destroy one another, and the inability of governments to control their military forces once put into the field, meant that governments were unable to ensure that the results of military action bore any relation to the purposes for which it had initially been undertaken. Armies wreaked far more havoc on civilians than they did on the military forces of their enemies. As the governments of Europe consolidated their control over their territory in the eighteenth century, their military forces remained unable to achieve decisive results against external opponents. This was due not only to the cost of weapons, the inability of armies to move rapidly, and the great advantages that the defense held in an era of elaborate fortifications but also to the cumbersome organizational structure of armies, a structure that followed directly from the authoritarian domestic political structure of European states. Armies were largely composed of men who had to be constantly watched over and coerced, lest they desert. It was thus difficult to achieve decisive advantage in warfare for technical reasons, and dangerous to existing political structures to attempt to do so. Governments came to assume that wars, while frequent, would have marginal consequences. Events on the battlefield would not suddenly threaten major change in the relationships among European powers.

These assumptions changed rapidly at the end of the century. In the wake of the French Revolution, warfare took on a new and threatening character, in which sudden change in the fortunes, and even the existence, of European governments could come about as a result of the clash of armies on the battlefield. But the physical means for waging war changed little in this period. The new, threatening character of warfare was due instead to the introduction of new forms of political organization, and the spread of new popular ideas governing the motives of men and governments. Soldiers who thought they had a personal stake in the outcome of the wars they fought could be trusted to fight without being forced to do so. Europe divided along lines of politics and ideology produced an intensification of conflict, just as Europe divided along lines of religion had done in the seventeenth century.

The dramatic character of revolutionary and Napoleonic Wars mesmerized governments and generals in the nineteenth century, blinding them to the effects of accelerating technological change, which was making easy and decisive victory in the clash of armies on the battlefield an increasingly elusive goal. In the burgeoning new study of strategy, attempts to understand the role of the political context in influencing the course and outcome of wars were ignored in favor of claims to provide infallible rules for the production of military success. This blindness to the implications of technology and political context, and the self-serving erroneous interpretations that were conveniently drawn from the wars of the mid-nineteenth century, would lead directly to the carnage of World War I. The quest for the decisive battle continued despite the growing evidence that such a quest could lead only to bloody slaughter.

That our historical examination concentrates on the development of international politics and war in the West should not in any way be taken to imply any general superiority of Western civilization to others, or the lack of important lessons that might be learned by studying those other civilizations directly. Nor, conversely, should it be taken to imply that organized violence has been more prevalent or pervasive in the West than elsewhere. This concentration is justified simply by the observation that over the past five centuries or so Western civilization physically and militarily overwhelmed the other civilizations of the planet, many of them arguably superior to the West in diverse aspects of human culture.

> For in large measure the "rise of the West" depended upon the exercise of force, upon the fact that the military balance between the Europeans and their adversaries overseas was steadily tilting in favour of the former. . . . With them they took their new military methods and, as these steadily improved, they gradually gained superiority over all their opponents: over the Americans in the sixteenth century, over most Indonesians in the seventeenth, over many Indians and Africans in the eighteenth. In the end, only Korea, China and Japan held out against the West until the Industrial Revolution in Europe and America forged some new tools of empire . . . to which even East Asia at first possessed no effective reply.[25]

In this process of expansion the West spread to those other civilizations the ideas, forms of organization, and material means that had enabled the West to overwhelm them. If we wish to speculate about the role that war will play, we must recognize that the ideas, institutions, and material means now connected with war and international conflict worldwide are largely Western in origin.

As the wars of Napoleon mesmerized statesmen and generals, so too were they mesmerized by World War I, and with equally disastrous results. Expecting another long, drawn out conflict fought between static positions, in which the offensive would be suicidal, they found themselves once more in a war in which quick and sudden military movements caused the collapse of governments and transformed political relationships in Europe and Asia at a stroke. With the memory of the butchery of World War I fresh, governments felt that they could easily manipulate the fear of a repetition of such carnage to achieve their aims without fighting. When tried, however, this manipulation neither prevented war nor ensured desired objectives.

Weapons and military organization themselves did not determine how those weapons would be employed. To the material and social factors bearing upon the development of war—political organization, motivation, and capability—must be added the development of strategy and strategic thought. "Strategy" has been defined by the twentieth-century British writer Sir Basil Liddell Hart as "the art of distributing and applying military means to fulfill ends of policy."[26] The study of strategic ideas helps us to understand how people at different times and places thought about and organized themselves for using force internationally. It helps us to understand what the relationship was between these ideas and the results that followed. Were the wars that occurred frequent or infrequent? Were they small or large, controllable or uncontrollable? Did the strategists predict the sorts of wars that would come or were they surprised by their character? Looking at questions such as these enables us to put today's world in some perspective and helps us to speculate about the direction in which we are now heading, about the shape of war and conflict in the world after the cold war. It even helps us to ask whether war itself, for so long a fundamental defining feature of world politics, has been rendered obsolete by history.

A world driven by the ideologies of communism and democracy, each claiming universal dominion, has now apparently been replaced by one in which political goals seem confined to the achievement of limited and local objectives. A world given order by one great conflict has been replaced by an environment in which many lesser conflicts have arisen. A shifting multitude of national and ethnic conflicts dominates the headlines and provides the motivation for governments and other political groups to fight or threaten to fight.

These changes have occurred while technology has continued to offer governments, in the form of nuclear weapons and other weapons of mass destruction, instruments of organized violence beyond all historical parallel in their capacity to wreak destruction. But the military technology that seemed to offer so much to the nuclear strategists was paralyzed by its very potential. Nuclear weapons in the cold war have proved to be weapons so horrendous that their possessors shrank from their use. These "absolute weapons" proved themselves largely useless in helping governments to accomplish their desires. The utility of nuclear weapons was confined to the threat of their use. And even that threat was of questionable utility in accomplishing the goals for which the threat was made. In this declining usefulness, nuclear weapons were not unique. They represented the culmination of a historical process that has operated over the past five centuries, dramatically at times, fitfully at others. Often this process has been hidden. It has even seemed on occasion to reverse itself. Over time, however, the large-scale use of force has become increasingly ineffective as an instrument of policy. The almost bloodless (for the victors) war in the Persian Gulf that inaugurated the first post–cold war decade is a unique case, with few lessons to teach about the shape of future conflicts.

The ineffectiveness of force, however, has not eliminated the implications of the security dilemma that has been the principal consequence of the international condition. The ineffectiveness of force has not been accompanied by a new political structure for the organization of international politics. Issues that formerly could only find resolution through violence remain unresolved. War has therefore changed its character, but it has not disappeared from the international scene. Warfare has come to approximate its character in the eighteenth century, as a costly tool for the realization of limited purposes. It is resorted to only with growing reluctance and in peculiar and unique circumstances. Although we shall not see the end of the horrors of warfare for those immediately caught up in it, conflict no longer threatens global conflagration or the sudden catastrophic demise of existing political arrangements. Outsiders can afford to be relaxed in the face of such wars, and the high costs of intervening in them.

The general condition of states existing in a state of nature without an authority above them may explain why states tend to behave in the manner of denizens of the Old West, why they tend to think in terms of their own security, why they fear betrayal and violence, why they tend to find cooperation difficult, and why they tend continually to foster and develop the means to use violence in international affairs. To assist us toward understanding whether a given disagreement will erupt in violent conflict and, if so, what consequences that violent conflict will have for protagonists and onlookers, however, more is required. It is necessary to consider the idiosyncratic aspects of individuals in particular places and times; the specific manner in which states are organized internally; the qualities of the capabilities that they have at their disposal; and the ideas entertained within and among states about the uses of organized violence externally. It is necessary to consider how change in all these factors was reflected in change in the character of warfare. Against this light we should not expect that the world after the cold war will at last be a world at peace. There will be many violent conflicts, but these conflicts will be slow-burning and localized. The new world order will not carry with it the dangers to civilization that we have come to associate with warfare itself in the twentieth century.

The Rise of Modern World Politics

2

At the beginning of the period loyalties were often to ideas or to men, not to States, and both the ideas and the men were often international. At the end the conflicting forces of the mêlée were to a great extent polarized about the States. . . . The statesmen had gone far towards establishing public monopolies of force and a reliable machinery of diplomatic intercourse between the monopolists.—George Clark, *War and Society in the Seventeenth Century*

The rise of the modern territorial state brought to an end an era of European history in which the structures of political authority were confused and localized. The new states competed with one another in developing potent coercive instruments with which to ensure their authority internally and to advance their desires externally. In attempts to resolve disputes among religious sects, however, these instruments soon slipped out from under the control of the governments that had created them. As religious fervor subsided and politics became dominated by more limited goals, governments regained control over the instruments of violence, and international war, while frequent, came to be regarded as a stylized and eminently manageable tool for those who ruled European states.

THE MEDIEVAL HERITAGE

The seventeenth century saw the formal demise of the medieval political order in Europe and its replacement by a political pattern based on territorial political units. The medieval political order had sustained the fiction that Europe was politically unified, as it had been under the Roman Empire. The reality that lay behind this fiction was something different. Europe was far from political unity. The pattern of politics in medieval Europe was instead a crazy quilt of multiple and overlapping feudal authorities and reciprocal allegiances. A feudal lord might give rights to a piece of land to another member of the aristocracy, in return for an obligation on the part of the latter to perform services for the lord. Usually the subordinate, or "vassal," provided military assistance, either personally or through a specified number of men-at-arms, for a given period. The lord in turn might hold his own land in return for an obligation to provide such service for someone else. At the bottom of the social pyramid were the serfs, peasants who were regarded as a form of property tied to the land in a way not dissimilar to the buildings on it. A few people in the towns were not directly part of this system of mutual obligations, supporting themselves by commercial or craft activity. Kings theoretically held their kingdoms without obligation to provide service to someone else. Except for these three groups, everyone owed obligations to someone else, in return for tenure of his land. In turn they were owed reciprocal obligations by others.

To make the situation more confusing the structure of obligations differed from one piece of land to another. Thus, a lord could be the superior of another in regard to one piece of territory, while being subordinate to him in regard to another plot of land. Even kings might hold some land outside their own kingdoms in the capacity of vassal to some other ruler. For many centuries, for example, the kings of England held Normandy and other vast territories in France, for the tenure of which they were theoretically subordinate to the French king. In fact powerful subordinates were often far more influential than the rulers who were in theory their superiors. Central governments, when they existed at all, were consequently very weak. A king depended on his subordinates to provide the military capabilities that enabled him to exercise influence. If his principal subordinates held vast territories, however, they might well be able to field military forces far larger than those of their supposed superior. The situation was a very confused one, and obligations were often ambiguous or easily evaded. A landowner might have obligations regarding one of his territories that were in direct contradiction to those required of him with respect to another piece of land.

The major activity of the knightly landholding aristocratic class was stylized disputation over the ownership of particular pieces of property.

These conflicts were waged through a very localized military structure. Armies rarely could move very far or very fast. The agricultural economy yielded little more than subsistence. The labor of large numbers of peasants was required to produce a small surplus that could be appropriated by the aristocracy. It was difficult to force large numbers of peasants into military service, or to keep them in service for long periods, since to do so would destroy the fragile productive basis of the economy. Available supplies and transportation were insufficient to provision large numbers of men for long periods.

Military forces were dominated by mounted and armored knights drawn from the landowning class. Men on foot could rarely withstand onslaught by mounted knights. Archers could, on occasion, successfully attack knights at a distance. However, the social and economic basis for maintaining and training large groups of military specialists was usually lacking, and only the knights could afford to train extensively. Most of the other members of medieval armies were peasants who could be spared from their labors on the land for brief periods. Medieval military forces were ad hoc organizations created for specific purposes. Since feudal obligations restricted military obligations to short periods of service, and since it was difficult to keep large groups supplied, medieval warfare typically involved localized sieges of castles and other fortified strong points. Because it was difficult to maintain a besieging army in the field for very long, these fortified positions were difficult to overwhelm.[1]

THE NEW STATES AND THE WARS OF RELIGION

This medieval political and military order was gradually eroded in the late Middle Ages by economic developments in western Europe that favored central political institutions. As commercial and manufacturing activities in the towns gained in importance and profitability, a tacit alliance arose between the royal central governments and the rising middle classes of the towns to challenge the old feudal nobility. In return for protection against the arbitrary demands of the nobility, the towns increasingly agreed to regular taxation by the central governments. These governments were in turn able to use their new-found sources of revenue to create standing armies, military forces that would remain permanently at the disposal of governments throughout the year. The central governments were also able to employ their new revenues to encourage the nobility to exchange their old feudal military service obligations for regularized positions as officials in the central government and salaried commanders in the new armies.

Accompanying these economic changes were new military technologies that threatened the dominance of the knight on horseback and the impregnability of the medieval castle.[2] The use of gunpowder in siege artillery enabled the castle's high stone walls to be swiftly breached. Powerful and accurate battlefield weapons, such as the crossbow and then firearms, rendered the position of the armored knight on horseback highly vulnerable. Increasingly, only the royal central governments could afford the new weapons, as well as the construction and maintenance of the new fortifications systems that could resist artillery. As these new military technologies came into play, they gradually increased the effective size of political units, giving more importance to the territorial monarchies and less to the smaller political units that had previously dominated political life.[3]

These technological developments should be set against the immense religious quarrels of the period. The Reformation had set off a variety of Protestant movements, as well as a Catholic Counter-Reformation. A new motive was added to political conflict. Governments attempted to advance the cause of the religious views to which they subscribed by gaining more territory and people and recapturing territory that had fallen under the sway of rulers professing opposing religious outlooks. These ideological motives became mixed up with the ambitions of rulers for greater territorial dominance.

The Thirty Years' War (1618–48) began as a struggle for control over Germany, then a mere geographical expression for territories in which hundreds of political units of various size existed. The struggle originally pitted the Catholic Hapsburg rulers of Austria (who still held the title of Holy Roman Emperor, a carryover from earlier times and the medieval fiction of political unity) against the Protestant princes of northern Germany. Into this conflict the Protestant Swedish king Gustavus Adolphus intruded himself, ostensibly on the Protestant side, but fired primarily by ambition to acquire new territory for his dynasty. And the Catholic French monarchy entered the war also, but on the side of the Protestants, and against the Catholic Hapsburgs, in hopes of advancing its dynastic family interests against those of its ancient rivals.

There emerged from this mix of motives what a great historian of the period has called a "general mêlée," or "collision of peoples."[4] The Thirty Years' War devastated the territory in which it was fought. Parts of Germany were almost depopulated. Some estimates say half or more of the German population may have been lost.[5] While most of the major governments intentionally got themselves into the war, the fighting quickly went beyond their control. Armed bands rampaged across the countryside, usually wreaking far more havoc on the civilian populations than they did upon opposing armies. Governments were too weak, financially, economically, and organizationally, to control, pay, or supply their armies once they had been put in motion.

Many circumstances contributed to this result. Recall first that the war had begun as a religious conflict. Combatants on all sides thought that their opponents were, in a literal sense, instruments of the devil, who could and should be exterminated, whether they were soldiers or not. Indeed extermination of civilians was often preferred, precisely because it was easier to do away with civilians, and civilians would offer greater prospects for loot.

Soldiers normally had no loyalty or attachment to the governments for whom they were fighting. They were usually mercenaries, attracted by the prospect of pay and booty. Typically, governments found themselves unable to deliver on their promises of pay. Road and transport systems were poor; once an army went into the field, effective supply was questionable, and the army plundered the countryside as it went along. Governments quickly discovered that once they had acquired a military force, their best hope was to send it away from home territory as quickly as possible and to keep it there. If armies stayed home, they would likely plunder the people and government in whose interests they were supposedly acting.

The Thirty Years' War was not only an international conflict. It was also a multitude of civil wars inside the many political units then existing. In many places, parties fought among themselves over religion, and each called upon outside powers to help them against their domestic enemies. In others, the outsiders took it upon themselves to assist their coreligionists without prior invitation.

Once begun, the religious wars of the seventeenth century proved very difficult to stop. Their effect, in those places unlucky enough to be in the path of the armies, was catastrophic. The depopulation that Germany experienced was probably a crucial factor in stunting economic growth in central Europe for the next century. In spite of this widespread destruction, no party could achieve a clear-cut victory on the battlefield, a victory that might enable it to eliminate opposing armies or impose a settlement to its liking. All the factors that made armies so dangerous to civilians—their lack of mobility, the difficulty in supplying them, the lack of discipline of the troops, and the use of cumbersome, slow, and inaccurate weapons—made them less dangerous to other armies.

For those not in the path of the armies, however, and for those who had not been kidnapped or dragged off to be soldiers, seventeenth-century wars were largely irrelevancies. Indeed, in those countries that managed to avoid being the scene of the fighting, the wars may well have stimulated economic activity and technological development. As the century wore on, the stimulus of effectively waging war caused these governments to grow more centralized and more powerful.

The intrusion of nonreligious motives, the repeatedly demonstrated inability to exterminate one's religious enemies, and the exhaustion brought on by the attempt gradually produced a general willingness to coexist with that which could not be destroyed. The Treaty of Westphalia, which ended the Thirty Years' War in 1648, legitimized the notion that territorial governments could freely decide questions of religion for the inhabitants of their own domains, and that these governments did not owe some kind of allegiance to higher powers. The confusing political structure inherited from medieval times became more rational. The medieval crazy quilt of authority in which individual landowners owed reciprocal loyalties to one another in a complex and often contradictory pattern was succeeded by growing acceptance of the notion of a smaller number of rulers, each legally supreme in his own territory and answerable to no other earthly power for his actions there.

STATE SUPREMACY AND LIMITED WAR

As the seventeenth century grew to a close, reality gradually came to conform more closely to this notion of state sovereignty. All states were of course not equal. Huge differences existed between them in size, population, territory, and resources. The political units residing on the territory that we now know as Germany ranged from the states of Prussia and Austria, which exercised control over populations in the millions, to many others whose territory barely stretched for a few square miles and whose authority extended to a few thousand persons. All states, however, could claim complete control over a piece of territory, however extensive or minuscule that territory might be. For most of the eighteenth century, a pattern of international politics and international conflict was to prevail that was very different from that which had marked the previous century.

Governments became richer and stronger. They developed administrative mechanisms that enabled them to gather revenues efficiently and collect them in central treasuries. The last vestiges of the old medieval armies—collected on an ad hoc basis in fulfillment of feudal personal service obligations—were gone. Armies were paid regularly and supplied efficiently by governments. Bureaucracies were developed to procure supplies and to get those supplies to the troops. The roads in Europe improved to the point where at the end of the century land transportation had become about as rapid and as reliable as it had been during the Roman Empire, a millennium and a half previously.

Eighteenth-century governments and social orders on the European continent were, with a few exceptions, hereditary monarchies. For these governments, the interests of the ruling families were paramount. Typically, these dynastic interests were defined in terms of the acquisition of wealth, and a state's territory and its population were among the prime indicators of its wealth. The more of these a monarch possessed, the better off he was considered to be.

Few if any of these governments were now motivated to any significant degree by the ambition of exterminating heresy or heretics. It was an age of skepticism for those at the top of society. Religious "enthusiasm" was suspect. Governments had the fresh experience of the wars of religion of the seventeenth century to draw upon, an experience that suggested the extermination of heretics would likely prove to be both highly expensive and extremely difficult to achieve. International political rivalries during this period turned upon territorial conflict. States attempted to enlarge their territory at the expense of their neighbors and to prevent their neighbors from doing the same to them in return. Occasionally some ruler appeared with larger ambitions: to eliminate other states or to turn them into permanent dependencies. Territorial expansion, not the cure of souls or fundamental change in the way of life of the populace, was the goal. Those in charge of governments rarely thought questions of belief, or of political or social organization, were worth fighting wars to settle.

In most European states, especially those in western Europe, the royal central governments had in effect concluded a tacit bargain with the rising middle classes in the towns, at the expense of the old landed aristocracy. The newly prosperous urban commercial classes would pay regular taxes to the kings, who in return would have the resources and the motivation to keep the local nobility from interfering in these burgeoning commercial activities, which were the source of that new revenue. Kings would allow the middle classes to get on with the business of making money without their having to worry that some noble landowner might impose restrictions on the free flow of trade, or that some violent feud between members of the nobility might disrupt life and commerce. The new wealth at the disposal of the central governments allowed them increasingly to monopolize the instruments of organized violence within their territories, and to remove from the hands of the nobility the means to carry on the private wars that had been the main vocational interest of the aristocracy since medieval times.

The new wealth also gave the central governments more resources for the defense of their territories against military invasion. Governments constructed elaborate belts of fortifications on their frontiers and encouraged the emerging professions of architecture and engineering to design even better systems of fortifications. New theories were propounded by the growing number of military fortification specialists, many of whom were paid salaries out of the state treasury to do this work full-time. Indeed these specialists were among the first members of the officer corps of the armies that we would today consider professionals. These were people whose whole career consisted of building and planning fortifications, and devising schemes to attack the fortifications of other governments successfully.

Full-time military professionals were also employed in the artillery. The sciences of ballistics and metallurgy were pressed into service to develop artillery pieces that could fire projectiles further and more accurately. Armies required people who could maintain these devices and knew the mathematics necessary to aim them in the right direction.

Officers in the infantry and the cavalry, who still tended to be drawn from the nobility, rarely received any specialized training for their roles.

Increasingly they too, however, were becoming salaried servants of the government, rather than people who took up arms simply because that was what one did if one was a male of noble blood. This was perhaps an unintended part of the bargain between the central governments and the middle classes. If the sons of the nobility were kept busy in the army, they were less likely to complicate the commercial life of the towns.

The lower ranks of the armies, conversely, were predominantly drawn from the dregs of society. The gainfully employed were left free from military service. Petty thieves, drunks, misfits, troublemakers—or men who were just unlucky enough to be caught not doing anything obviously productive when kidnapped by recruiting gangs—were the raw material out of which soldiers were made. Mostly they were less than overjoyed to find themselves in the military. They were normally required to remain in the service for long periods. Discipline was brutal, and those in charge of discipline saw it as their role to make their charges more afraid of their superiors than they were of the enemy. Soldiers in most armies were not imbued with love of country, or anxious to sacrifice for their homeland. If they should be wounded, their prospects were scarcely better than being killed outright. Medical care was practically nonexistent.

In Voltaire's *Candide*, the protagonist makes the mistake of accepting a drink in a tavern from some strangers who, unknown to him, are in fact collecting recruits for the army. Candide's unfortunate experiences scarcely exaggerate the actuality of eighteenth-century military recruitment and disciplinary practices:

> And with that they clapped him into irons and hauled him off to the barracks. There he was taught "right turn," "left turn," and "quick march," "slope arms" and "order arms," how to aim and how to fire, and was given thirty strokes of the "cat." Next day his performance on parade was a little better, and he was given only twenty strokes. The following day he received a mere ten and was thought a prodigy by his comrades.[6]

Yet considerable expense had been borne by governments to clothe and feed the soldiers and to teach them these rudimentary skills. Soldiers left to themselves would desert, it was feared. To guard against this, soldiers were kept together in large groups. While marching from place to place and even on the battlefield itself, they were carefully and precisely controlled. Officers extensively and repetitively drilled them in a variety of movements, in order to get them where and when their leaders desired without opportunities for escape.

The elaborate parade-ground maneuvers that we often see military units performing on ceremonial occasions today are the descendants of the maneuvers in which eighteenth-century soldiers were drilled every day for years. This was how they moved about, even on the battlefield under fire. Soldiers also had to perform elaborate and time-consuming contortions, involving many steps, to fire the personal weapons of the day. The performance of these contortions in unison was the object of another set of drills. Oddly enough, actual firing at something was not an activity in which eighteenth-century armies were typically drilled. Because bullets and ammunition were expensive and the muskets of the time were highly inaccurate, soldiers were drilled only in the maneuvers necessary to get their muskets ready to fire and pointed in front of them on command. On the battlefield, the favored formation for infantry was the line abreast, which allowed a maximum number of soldiers a clear field of fire in front, making simultaneous massed volleys possible, but at the cost of rendering further movement, once the line of battle had been formed, all the more difficult to control.

While necessary to keep armies from disappearing, the emphasis on formations made armies cumbersome and slow. Since troops would desert if allowed to forage in the countryside, eighteenth-century armies were supplied from central stockpiles amassed by government bureaucracies in advance. Because huge fleets of supply wagons moved even more slowly than the men marched, it became difficult for an army to move very far from its base of supplies fast. Artillery and fortifications further compounded the problem. Artillery was cumbersome and slow to move, and fortification systems were often among the largest and most complex construction projects undertaken in these countries.

Cost was also a consideration. Artillery and fortifications were frightfully expensive. And because it took a long time to acquire all this capital equipment and train men in its use, keeping the army fed and equipped was a great expense. In the eighteenth century, armies—and in some cases navies—consumed the vast bulk of government revenues. Thus, at the middle of the century, the Prussian king Frederick the

Great spent nine-tenths of his revenues for military purposes. In 1784, the French devoted about two-thirds of government income to their army.[7]

The townspeople who paid the taxes were not especially involved emotionally in the objects for which military campaigns were commonly fought. They cared little whether the king increased his glory by adding a few provinces to his territory, and they were not likely to be happy about any developments that might result in higher taxes. Although governments were now much more efficient and possessed a more reliable source of revenue, that revenue was distinctly limited. This meant that armies became highly valued commodities, precious bundles of capital goods that governments and generals did not like to risk losing or damaging.

Warfare in the eighteenth century became a formal, stylized business. Because armies were slow, and because systems of frontier fortifications tended to block what might otherwise have been natural transportation corridors, much of the warfare of this period involved placing fortifications under siege. The process of siege involved the construction of elaborate systems of tunnels and trenches, themselves major construction projects, which often rivaled in complexity the forts they surrounded. A successful siege might take weeks or months to force surrender. If the surrender of a fortification was forced, however, this usually meant only that the army could advance a few miles, until it came to the next fortress belt where the process of siege had to be repeated.

Even when fortifications did not block the way or supply trains hinder their advance, armies might prefer to move slowly. Because armies had become commodities so dear in terms of resources available, generals were distinctly leery about pitting them against one another in battle. It was exceedingly difficult to move sufficient forces quickly enough to concentrate a clearly superior force against an opposing army. Then again, one could never predict what might happen in a battle. Discipline could break down, the army could disintegrate, the king could lose his precious artillery. If a general won a battle, he was not likely to go very far, because even a victorious army would still have the problems of maintaining discipline and supply. Armies that had won a battle were rarely able to pursue their opponents effectively enough to eliminate them as militarily significant forces.

In warfare at sea, decisive battles between fleets were equally rare.[8] The inaccuracy of naval gunnery combined with the ability of the wooden ships of the period to absorb much punishment and still stay afloat. Fleets approached one another in long lines, parallel or at a narrow angle. Emphasis was placed upon keeping these cumbersome ships in line, so that the maximum number of their guns could bear in the direction of the opponent. Initiative was discouraged. Officers who risked their ships by breaking the line suffered severe punishment. Major battles tended to become long-range gunnery duels, in which ships were rarely sunk, and in which the disadvantaged side had ample opportunity to break off action well before serious damage could be inflicted.

On land and at sea, it came to be regarded as much more the mark of the brilliant commander to outwit his opponent, to lure him out of the way by clever maneuvers that might gain small advantages without risking the uncertainties of battle. Generals preferred to threaten each other's flanks, or make elegant moves against each other's supply lines, their object being to induce the opposing army to withdraw, rather than to bring it to battle. A military operation might have as its aim the occupation of territory in one place, not for its own sake but as a scheme to enhance bargaining leverage in diplomatic negotiations about a separate issue. When battles did take place, they could be awfully bloody, but they tended to be regarded as evidence of a lack of finesse on the part of generals. Eighteenth-century wars usually led to marginal gains or losses of territory. This was not because governments did not have extensive ambitions. Some did. But it was exceedingly difficult to realize those ambitions, owing to the difficulty of swift and decisive movement.[9]

While the competitive development of the instruments of warfare was rendering decisive encounters more difficult in Europe, a different result was occurring as Europeans met other peoples. When confronting other civilizations, Europeans became progressively more capable (even when armed Europeans went abroad in numbers trifling by the standards of European wars) of overwhelming the military forces of African, Asian, and American civilizations. On land, European military superiority was due not only to the Europeans' exploitation of firearms but also to their development of techniques of military organization, fortification, supply, and drill that others could not match. At sea, the Europeans outfitted large sailing vessels with new navigational aids and cannon batteries, a combination that enabled them to move swiftly and accurately over great distances and to project force ashore in a fashion previously unknown.[10] By the end of the eighteenth century only the great states of East Asia remained free of European dominance.

In Europe itself, the international environment within which eighteenth-century states operated reinforced the constraints imposed by their difficulty in achieving decisive results on the battlefield. The European international system also tended in its own way to produce wars involving relatively small gains and losses.[11] There were five major military powers in Europe, plus many more minor ones. While each preferred to be friendly to some and tended to be hostile to others, none of the major powers was an eternal opponent to another or irrevocably tied to its allies. In a pinch, each would be prepared to ally with those with whom it had a long-standing feud or to betray a long-term friend.[12]

The large powers all watched developments throughout Europe carefully. Those in charge of their governments believed that they could measure relative gains and losses accurately by calculating the population gained or lost by an exchange of territory. Statesmen typically were optimistic about their ability to predict the diplomatic attitude of other states toward questions that might arise, and thus to predict the diplomatic combinations that would be formed on the various sides of such issues. But the large number of the other players, and the further consideration that each calculated its attitude on the basis of expectations about how the actions of others might affect its own position in the future, meant that such predictions were continually upset, with states often encountering unexpected behavior on the part of other governments.

Each might harbor desires to acquire more territory and resources for itself at the expense of any or all the others. Each might, from time to time, act on those desires. But none wished to see anyone else gain significantly. Each worried that a power making major gains might some day threaten its own interests. Each was prepared to be fluid in its alignments, shifting partners now and then as its advantage seemed to dictate.

A power that enjoyed some success was likely to find that it acquired unexpected opponents as it went along, making further gains progressively more difficult and threatening reversal of gains already made.

Either more governments would join in war against the successful power (as usually happened in western Europe), or they would demand that they be given equal gains at the expense of some third party, usually a small state (as tended to occur in eastern Europe, most notably to Poland, which was successively partitioned out of existence by its neighbors during the eighteenth century). An unanticipated shift in the position of another government might lead to war instead of an expected pacific resolution of a question. Diplomatic surprise was not uncommon. States might find themselves fighting others whom they had not expected to fight. Indeed surprises of this sort may account in large part for the relative frequency of wars during this period. Governments neither expected nor feared major change in their relative position, however. The tendency of European states to balance militarily and diplomatically against a successful power meant that even if major advances occurred in war, there was little risk that the outcome of military campaigns might give to such a power the ability to dominate or eliminate the others.

Because wars no longer were fought to defend or advance religious doctrines, governments and peoples lacked motivations for extensive effort or sacrifice, and governments thus found themselves unable easily to make major gains in war. If they expected little more than the acquisition of a few more miles of territory, they feared little more than losses of a similar extent if a campaign went badly. It became a general conception among statesmen that war was a game in which both the gains and the risks could and would be kept limited. Since they had military forces at their disposal and easily to hand, and since war could be carried on in such a fashion as not to put these very expensive resources at risk, governments went to war easily and frequently. We might say that the "flash point" of war was low.

A dispute might arise, usually over title to territory. Parties directly and indirectly interested might hold diplomatic discussions. If the dispute could not quickly be resolved by diplomacy, it would be tested by a season of military operations. Once at war, matters went slowly. Typically movement became impossible during the winter, so military campaigns were largely confined to the warmer months of the year. A pattern emerged in which belligerents would fight in the summer and negotiate about the fighting in the winter. They would conduct a military campaign and assess its effects upon the relative bargaining positions of the parties, to see if an agreement could be reached. If a settlement could still not be arrived at, another season of campaigning might follow, and then another attempt at negotiation. In the major states at least, statesmen were not worried that any very dramatic changes might occur as a result of military actions, before they had a chance to consider those results at the conference table.

The emergence of the postmedieval modern state began in a period in which ideological motivations were high. Political conflict among the states was mixed up with widespread belief that profoundly important issues were at stake. With such matters as the nature of society and the nature of man's relationship to God at issue, conflict was carried on under few restraints. Even though it was difficult to deal decisively with an enemy's armed forces, or to defeat or destroy his armies in battle, horrendous destruction was visited upon those parts of his society, the civil populace, which could be reached. Because of the passions unleashed as well as their inability to keep the military instruments that they had created subject to their will, governments found that they could not control the organized violence that they had set in motion. A long period of violent conflict resulted, a period that did not gain for any of the belligerent parties what they wished, which laid waste much of the countryside, and which the parties found very difficult to bring to an end.

During the century that followed, the motives of political action were moderated and governments gained greater control over their resources, agents, policies, and territories. Still it remained difficult to produce quick or decisive advantage in warfare. The technology of warfare made it difficult to destroy an enemy army on the battlefield. The nature of the social order within states made leaders reluctant to put costly armies and weapons at risk. The European international order of the eighteenth century tended to produce combinations of states that restrained the powerful among them from achieving substantial gains. All these factors coalesced to produce a period in which wars were begun and ended frequently and easily, in which wars were limited in their purposes and in their impact on society. Those who oversaw the policies of European governments came to feel that the use of organized violence in their external relations did not threaten those domestic and international relationships with which they were so familiar and from which they derived so many benefits.

Nationalism and Savagery: The Wars of the French Revolution

3

Since Bonaparte, then, war, first among the French and subsequently among their enemies, again became the concern of the people as a whole, took on an entirely different character, or rather approached its true character, its absolute perfection. There seemed no end to the resources mobilized; all limits disappeared in the vigor and enthusiasm shown by governments and their subjects. . . . War, untrammeled by any conventional restraints, had broken loose in all its elemental fury.—Clausewitz, *On War*

All the assumptions about warfare that had prevailed among European political leaders in the eighteenth century—that war was controllable, that it was slow, that it was easily manageable—were to change in a few years at the end of the century. The wars of the French Revolution began as an attempt by a coalition of European powers in 1792 to put the French king back in power.[1] A revolution had disrupted French life, and the monarch had been reduced to the position of a figurehead, doing the bidding of the newly empowered French legislature. The throne was later to be abolished altogether and its former occupant put to death. Members of the aristocracy were purged from positions of power and many executed. The centralized bureaucracy, which had been the means by which the royal government had exercised its control, was in disarray. The army was split. "Of the 9,000 officers of the old army, two-thirds . . . had left the colors; of the old generals, only three . . . remained, and all three of them were guillotined."[2]

The members of the coalition thought it would be an easy business to accomplish their aims. In a mistake that would be repeated under similar circumstances many times thereafter, the allies assumed that the effect of the Revolution had been to weaken France seriously as a military power. Before the Revolution France had been the richest of the continental powers, its armies widely considered the most powerful in Europe. Many of the wars of the previous two centuries had been contests between French attempts at expansion and attempts by France's neighbors and other powers to curb that expansion. The coalition allies thought that the disintegration of French governmental and military structures would make a victorious march on Paris possible in short order. They hoped not only to restore the French king to his throne but also to take advantage of the situation to garner for themselves some of those small territorial gains that had been the spoils of most international conflicts during the eighteenth century.

THE REVOLUTION AND MILITARY POWER

The outcome of the first coalition campaign was to be quite different from what the allies had expected. Not only were the French able to stop the allied invasion of French territory but they went on the offensive themselves, carrying the war into the territory of their enemies. In 1792 the French revolutionary armies were to begin a career of military expansion that was to result in territorial conquest without precedent in the experience of all those involved, and that was to last for a decade and a half.

The initial French military success had been due in part to the ineptness of the coalition commanders. Supremely confident of success, they advanced leisurely. Rather than coordinating their efforts, they attacked the French piecemeal. Spared the full weight of the coalition armies, the French were able to meet and defeat one allied army, and then turn in time to meet another.

The inadequacies of their enemies formed only a small part of the explanation of French success, however. For what the allies soon discovered was that the Revolution, far from *reducing* the capacity of the French to support military power, had *enhanced* that capacity. All the old assumptions about military power and the possibilities of warfare had been based on the ancien régime, the prerevolutionary social order. The Revolution destroyed that social order within France and, with it, the material and psychological basis on which French military power had rested. In place of the ancien régime, the Revolution substituted a new set of social attitudes and beliefs, beliefs that were to make military power immensely more dangerous and unpredictable. In a fundamental sense, the effect of the Revolution was vastly to increase the willingness of civilians and soldiers to endure sacrifice in the service of military success.

The political and ideological homogeneity that had prevailed in Europe throughout the eighteenth century had disappeared. No longer was the domestic political order essentially similar within all states on the continent. The political and ideological basis of French society had shifted, while the domestic foundations of other governments remained as they had been. France's enemies were governed by hierarchical authorities who based their claims to power strictly on inherited status. After the Revolution, the French justified the authority of their governmental institutions on the basis of such ideas as equality and popular will. European states became divided again into different camps on the basis of the differing and incompatible principles governing their domestic political orders, in much the same way as they had been divided by their disputes over religious systems in the sixteenth and seventeenth centuries.

The Revolution culminated in a changed psychological and emotional relationship between the French government and large sections of the populace, persons whose relationship to the institutions of the state had previously been distant or nonexistent. These people came to subscribe to a new set of beliefs about politics and the social order. They came to believe that they had a connection to the state, to the government and the government's fortunes. From this sense of identification there followed a concern with the success or failure of French armies.

Middle-class townspeople were now more likely to feel that they had a stake in French military success. If the enemies of France were to prevail, they felt matters of value to themselves would be put at risk. Newly won social positions and property rights would be threatened. Previously, the fortunes of royal armies had been a matter of supreme indifference to people such as these, whose concerns were confined largely to whether military operations would threaten their commercial activities or require major new tax levies. With this new sense of identification these groups were now more willing to provide material resources in the form of taxes to support military operations. They were also more willing to supply human resources, soldiers, to the army in a fashion previously alien to the middle classes. The lower ranks of the army now came to include large numbers of volunteers, men with at least a minimal education and some knowledge of contemporary technical skills, men for whom physical coercion was no longer constantly required, either to bring them into the army or to keep them there.

Change in the social composition of the army implied change in its psychology. Soldiers were more likely to feel solidarity with their fellows, to feel that they were all part of a common effort. Commanders now had less fear of desertion. The rigid system of control of masses of men in large groups, the system that had been so characteristic of eighteenth-century armies, could now be relaxed. Commanders felt that they could experiment with smaller and more flexible formations, that they could dispense with those requirements for constant control over every movement that had characterized prerevolutionary armies.

Smaller formations meant that French armies could move about the countryside faster, operate independently, and proceed to common destinations as set by the commander but by separate routes. Because French armies could usually advance faster than their enemies could withdraw, the French could, at will, force their opponents to accept battle.[3] Reduced fear of desertion meant that French armies' former extreme dependence on supply columns from bases in their home territory was lessened. When in enemy territory, officers could expect their troops to live off the land, foraging for supplies locally, with less concern that soldiers might use the opportunity to slip away. While armies continued to require supply from the rear of such commodities as ammunition, they could now requisition most of their food from the unfortunate citizenry in their path.

Once they reached the battlefield, armies could maneuver in smaller and more flexible formations. No longer were they confined to long, slowly moving or static lines of battle.

> At first the new republican armies . . . sought to move in the traditional formations. But they were unable to accomplish what was required. They were lacking in the discipline and the drill necessary for the advance in line and the firing of salvos. Since it was impossible to hold the men together and move them in the thin lines, they were grouped in deep columns, and these columns were given firepower by having . . . marksmen or sharpshooters ahead and beside them.[4]

Troops attacking in column sacrificed the massed firepower of the line in which all troops could bring their weapons to bear on the enemy. In column only those in the front ranks were in a position to fire at their opponents. But by using the column the French substituted the speed and shock value obtained by throwing large numbers of attackers against weakly held portions of the opposing line. Troops could more easily move across country, to threaten the flanks and rear of enemy positions and generally to turn up in unexpected places. Irregular formations, "clouds of skirmishers," could approach the opposing army, with each soldier making his own decisions about firing and movement, taking advantage of features of the terrain to provide himself with cover.

The old armies of the allies found themselves faced with French armies that moved faster than prerevolutionary armies and could appear suddenly in places and in numbers that were not anticipated. On the battlefield, the French attacked from new and unexpected directions[5] and in more open formations. Because they presented such swiftly moving targets, the allies found that it was more difficult to fire with much effect at the French.

French generals came to be more audacious, an attitude encouraged by the conspicuous execution of those the revolutionary authorities deemed lacking in sufficient zeal. To appear cautious was to risk being labeled an enemy of the Revolution. Furthermore, the revolutionary authorities conveyed to the army's leaders confidence that, if an army or its expensive material were lost, an enthusiastic populace would quickly supply the resources and personnel to replace it.

To force an opponent to battle, a French general would attempt to deduce the position of his opponent's forces at some point in the future, split up his army, send it to its intended destination by different routes, expecting it to forage on the march ahead of the supply wagons, and aim to recombine the pieces of his army into a force superior to that available to his opponent just before the battle. On the battlefield, the French would try to attack their opponents on the flanks, or to surround them. If their enemies broke formation under attack, they would endeavor to pursue them until they were completely destroyed as an organized military force, or captured. Because of the new social solidarity in their army brought about in the wake of the Revolution, the French were little worried that their own troops would melt away into the countryside, if allowed loose to exploit opportunities that the fortunes of battle had created.

As a result, there were many more pitched battles than during the limited wars that had taken place previously. Many of these battles led to routs, in which losing armies simply disintegrated or were captured en masse. French armies tried to envelop and overwhelm their opponents by moving against them on the flanks or attacking them from the rear. Most of the great battles of the period were won by these envelopment tactics. Occasionally an army charged straight at the opposing line, but for the most part the French attempted to disconcert the enemy by attacking simultaneously from directions from which he did not expect to be attacked. The French generally had the advantage in such maneuvers because they could concentrate superior forces against their opponents faster than the latter could against the French. Even when the French lost battles, they were able to replace and reequip their armies in the field at a rate unprecedented in European experience. Knowing they possessed this advantage, and that their armies could move fast by living off the countryside, generals were encouraged simply to ignore fortified positions and to aim instead at the opposing armies, risking their own forces in battle.

THE REVOLUTION AND THE END OF LIMITED WAR

The developments that followed these battles startled Europe. Capital cities fell and entire countries were rendered defenseless following a few battles or a single season's campaigning. Dramatic and decisive results came about much more quickly than the experience of those in government suggested was possible. The clash of armies often created decisive change in political relationships, well before diplomats and statesmen had a chance to realize what had happened, much less to negotiate about its implications.

One of the Revolution's most prominent and successful generals, Napoleon Bonaparte, used his popularity to overthrow the republican institutions created by the Revolution and to put himself in a position of personal power. Eventually, he was to place himself on a new throne as emperor. He continued to claim, however, that the legitimacy of his position at the head of the state derived from the will of the people. With brief respites, Napoleon's wars continued until his final defeat at

Waterloo in 1815. During this period he defeated two formerly great powers—Austria and Prussia—and reduced them to the status of satellites. He almost overwhelmed Russia, occupying Moscow for a brief period.

Clearly the character of war had changed. It now seemed no longer tame and controllable, as it had for much of the preceding century, no longer limited in the effects it could have on political relationships. How do we account for these changes? Our first instinct is to look to technical change in the instruments of warfare as the explanation for these changes in the character of war. Did the French develop new weapons, new tactics, or new means of organization that enabled them so suddenly to overwhelm their opponents? Indeed, some new developments in weaponry occurred toward the end of the eighteenth century, when, for example, artillery became progressively more standardized, more accurate, and easier to transport; and the French were at the forefront of technological advance in this field. But these changes were slow and incremental. And these incremental developments had mostly taken place *before* the outbreak of the French Revolution. Yet warfare had remained limited and formal.

Nor can we find an explanation for change in the character of warfare in new developments in military organization or tactics. Experimentation in the use of the column and in the use of light infantry in irregular formation as skirmishers can be found in military literature and practice in the last prerevolutionary decades. The revolutionary armies did not invent these techniques. Yet before the Revolution, these techniques had not produced any major change in the effects of warfare on politics or society.

We should not overestimate the significance of the changes in weapons and organization that did occur in the last decades of the eighteenth century. From a broad perspective the eighteenth century was a period of technological and organizational stability that lasted through the end of Napoleon's wars. An officer of the ancien régime would have found little to surprise him in Napoleon's armies, in how they were organized or in how they fought. If we cannot find in the tools, techniques, or tactics of war the causes of the drastic change in character that warfare underwent at the time of the Revolution, we must look instead to the realms of politics and mass psychology.

The French Revolution marked the emergence of popular nationalism as an influence on relations between governments in Europe.[6] In France one could now observe widespread identification with the activities of the government by groups of people in the middle and lower ranks of society who were previously indifferent to such activities. People came to describe themselves above all as French, rather than identifying themselves by their occupation or locality of residence. Even those enjoying positions of political power or influence now felt that they owed loyalty to the French nation as a group—to all those who identified themselves as French—and that this abstract group was embodied in the institutions of the state; no longer did they owe a personal loyalty to the monarch or to some superior in social status.

It was this *psychological* change—this popular sense of identification with the nation—that enabled the French to wage the new kind of war. With popular willingness to sacrifice resources, France could field larger and better equipped armies, and French generals now felt they could risk battle without risking their heads. With armies composed of men more highly motivated, and feeling group loyalty to one another, more open, flexible formations became possible, and armies could move faster, feed themselves on the move and still achieve their objectives. As a result, they could more often force battle and exploit battlefield victories to achieve political results.

War at sea developed some dramatic new characteristics that seemingly matched those of war on land.[7] During the revolutionary wars and Napoleonic Wars, some British admirals—the most notable of whom was perhaps Horatio Nelson—managed, by using more aggressive tactics, to break out of the indecisiveness that had characterized eighteenth-century naval battles. At the Battle of the Nile in 1798 and the Battle of Trafalgar in 1805 Nelson managed to sink or capture large portions of his opponent's fleets, by following the then startling practice of encouraging his captains to break the line and close with and attack portions of the enemy's fleet.

Although naval battles themselves might indeed yield more decisive results, their effects on the general course of the war remained limited and incremental. British naval victories eliminated the possibility that the French could swiftly defeat them by putting an army across the

Channel where the French would undoubtedly have overwhelmed the small British land forces. To prevent this happening, however, overwhelming naval victories were unnecessary. All that was required was that the British fleet remain intact. More important than the dramatic battles between the fleets was the belligerents' use of war at sea to attempt to destroy the commerce, and through that the economy, of their opponents. The British employed their navy to good effect to blockade ports under French control. But the effects of their naval superiority were slow and indirect. Since the French at their height controlled most of the European continent, the British were rarely able to deprive them of crucial supplies. Indeed, the British were far more dependent than the French on maintaining overseas trade. The French with their smaller navy found that their best use of it was not to attempt to meet the British fleet in pitched battle, but to play havoc with British trade by sending out, singly or in groups, smaller ships whose purpose was to attack and capture British commercial vessels and ships trading with the British.

The British could use their naval superiority to land troops at points they chose along the French-dominated coastline. When they did this to open a new front in Spain by supporting indigenous Spanish resistance to the French, they started a long process of slowly bleeding away French resources. In and of themselves, however, these actions were mere pinpricks. Naval power had the potential to reach behind the lines to affect the economies of the states waging war, but as of yet this was little more than potential. Navies could only play a subordinate role in affecting wars whose results were primarily determined by clashes of armies on land.

Given the superiority of French arms on land and the subordinate role played by sea power in British hands, how can we account for the eventual French defeat? We may look first to the behavior and personality of Napoleon himself and how his behavior impacted upon French domestic politics. His appetite for conquest apparently knew no bounds. We cannot know for certain whether his attitudes derived primarily from his personal psychology, or from a belief that his power, having been established on the basis of military success, required continual further successes to sustain itself. For whatever motive, he recruited army after army, flinging them at his enemies in campaigns that often produced huge casualties, until even the new French capacity for supporting military expenditure was exhausted and popular support for military adventures evaporated.

On several occasions, he could well have put an end to French military expansion, with every likelihood that France could have indefinitely retained the conquests already made. That he resisted such opportunities gave the British repeated opportunities to assemble and finance new military coalitions against him. The British remained throughout implacably opposed to his activities (although they were forced to accept one brief cessation in hostilities) owing to their traditional view that a power dominating the Continent must inevitably threaten their position. Britain's insular position limited its direct vulnerability to French military pressure. But this position would have been of little avail had Napoleon's policies not continually threatened continental states and induced them repeatedly to join the British in anti-French coalitions.

In supporting these coalitions, furthermore, the British were able to exploit the superior financial resources that were at their disposal. British dominance of world trade, and the beginnings of the industrial revolution in Britain in the latter part of the eighteenth century, led to the creation of considerable capital resources that in turn fueled an unparalleled expansion of credit markets in Britain. The British government now had access to capital in amounts an order of magnitude greater than that available to other governments. The ability of the British government to draw upon these resources for loans to finance its operations at home and abroad was the basis for the continued British ability to support anti-French coalitions.[8]

Napoleon's crucial mistake doubtless was his decision to invade Russia.[9] If he had kept the peace with the Russian tsar, the British would have been unable to find the materials to construct an effective military coalition against France. France might well have dominated the Continent indefinitely. Even after Napoleon had invaded Russia, if the Russians had taken the conventional view and assumed that they were beaten after Napoleon had captured Moscow, the French emperor might well have gotten away with even that bold adventure. Instead the Russians refused to do what other powers had done in similar circumstances—to accept defeat. Napoleon waited in Moscow, expecting that the tsar would sue for peace. The Russians, however, were able to exploit the advantages of their vast territory into which they were able to withdraw their defeated but still intact armies. Refusing to submit, they began a campaign of harassment of the long French supply lines. With winter approaching Napoleon realized too late that his position in Moscow was untenable and ordered a withdrawal. The much-chronicled destruction of his huge army on the road back from Moscow signaled the beginning of the end of French dominance in Europe. Of almost six hundred thousand men who crossed into Russia, less than thirty thousand returned.[10]

Napoleon's mistakes, and the ability of the British to capitalize on those mistakes, only provide us with a partial explanation for the ultimate French defeat, however. French military successes themselves created the conditions that led to their defeat. In the process of expansion the French unwittingly spread their social and cultural notions of nationalism to the peoples whom they conquered. When French armies crossed into foreign territories, they did more than advertise the virtues of French language and culture, or the benefits of organizing society according to the principles of "Liberty, Equality, and Fraternity." French armies of conquest made themselves hated in the countryside and united all social classes in German and other occupied territories in opposition to their depredations. Although some elites and literary groups in these territories may have developed an envy of French cultural dominance, the experience of conquest and defeat by the French revolutionary armies created national identifications among broader segments of the population in the defeated states. "Resistance to the French domination became an affair of the peoples themselves."[11] This phenomenon, in which other peoples were to emulate French popular sentiments of identification with a national group, began in those areas physically touched by French conquests, but spread beyond these areas and, indeed, by the end of the century was to go beyond Europe itself.

The humiliated and defeated Germans . . . responded . . . by lashing back and refusing to accept their alleged inferiority. They discovered in themselves qualities far superior to those of their tormentors. They contrasted their own deep, inner life of the spirit, their own profound humility, their selfless pursuit of true values . . . with the rich, worldly, successful, superficial, smooth, heartless, morally empty French. This mood rose to fever pitch during the national resistance to Napoleon, and was indeed the original exemplar of the reaction of many a backward, exploited, or at any rate patronised society, which, resentful of the apparent inferiority of its status, reacted by turning to real or imaginary triumphs and glories in its past, or enviable attributes of its own national or cultural character.[12]

Initially, governing elites among France's opponents felt that they dared not avail themselves of these new nationalist feelings. For it appeared that national sentiment must inevitably be tied to those egalitarian political doctrines with which the French Revolution was first associated. The governments of these French opponents were, for the most part, monarchical, and their leaders had little desire to embrace principles that would subvert the existing social order in their societies and threaten their own positions. They soon realized, however, that national feeling could be separated from democratic or popular sentiments and political institutions. It was often enough merely to be against the French. It proved quite feasible for governments that remained hierarchical and authoritarian to take advantage of national sentiments to mobilize new military forces that drew on popular attitudes similar to those which had contributed to French military success. Such monarchies could exploit newly available financial resources. They could form armies composed of men who had enlisted willingly and felt loyalty to the states in whose name they fought.

Governments in the coalition opposed to France were thus able in time to develop military forces that possessed those organizational and material features that had enabled the huge initial spurt in French military power after the Revolution to occur. Because of the spread of a form of popular group loyalty that had little precedent, coalition armies also could adopt open formations, execute rapid movements, seek battle, and attempt tactics aimed at the destruction of opposing forces. Driven by their felt need to compete militarily, governments fighting against the Revolution found ways to employ the tactics and organizational methods that had led to French successes on the battlefield.

WAR AND THE FEAR OF REVOLUTION

The legacy of the Napoleonic Wars was double-edged. On the one hand, war had become vastly more effective in its potential as a tool of foreign policy than it had been before the French Revolution. Statesmen now could anticipate decisive results from warfare. No longer were they limited to the incremental gains or losses typical of eighteenth-century warfare. On the other hand, they felt a great sense of foreboding that the institution of warfare in Europe could easily become uncontrollable and unpredictable. Matters of great moment could happen quickly and unexpectedly, and events could no longer be monitored in a timely fashion by politicians or diplomats. Not only could wars produce changes in international borders involving the shift of a province from one government to another. They also could cause the fall of governments, a change in political regimes, even transformation of the social fabric itself. Wars could sweep away institutions and political relationships that had been familiar features of the social order for centuries. As a result, those governing European states came to feel that the decision to make war had all the attraction of a leap in the dark.

It was this understanding of war as unpredictable, as possessed of a manifest potential to catalyze uncontrollable change, that was to dominate the attitudes of European statesmen in the decades following Napoleon's final defeat at the Battle of Waterloo. For a considerable time European governments were able to avoid wars in Europe, through a system of periodic international conferences that aimed at resolving controversies through consensus. If an issue arose among them, the attempt was made to bring all the great powers together in a common diplomatic forum, in hopes of producing a settlement. This process of diplomacy by conference became known as the European "Concert of Nations." The process placed a premium on statesmen capable of looking beyond the immediate interests of their states, and placing a high value on the common interest of all in avoiding violent new conflicts that could threaten the existing social order. The willingness of states to accept sacrifice to maintain consensus declined after the first decade of the Concert's existence, however, especially as the great powers increasingly came to disagree among themselves on the significance of outbreaks of domestic unrest in Europe, and the advisability of international military intervention to put down revolution.

Major war in Europe was nevertheless avoided through the mechanism of the Concert of Nations for almost forty years, until the outbreak of the Crimean War, which pitted Britain and France against Russia in 1854. In part this period of relatively benign relations among the great powers in Europe was achieved because, in an exceptional burst of sense and moderation, the powers victorious over Napoleon did not make a punitive peace against France.[13] They could have followed past practice, forcing France to give up all the territorial gains of the Revolution and even imposing further territorial losses. Instead, under the peace settlement agreed upon at the Congress of Vienna in 1815, the allies actually allowed the French to keep some of the territorial gains they had made in the early revolutionary period, and generally attempted to restore the French to the diplomatic process. Rather than ostracizing the French, their erstwhile enemies treated them as an acceptable diplomatic partner. Perhaps as a result of this, no government that was interested in pursuing renewed expansionist policies came to power in France for many decades.

The dominant motive in energizing the Concert system, however, was a mutually shared fear, among those who governed the great powers, of the potential consequences of war. All societies on the Continent were exhausted after the exertions of the Napoleonic Wars. All were worried about the potential that war among them could again be the harbinger of domestic revolution. These concerns dominated among Europe's governing elite until the middle of the century.

> The desire to avoid another European war was widespread among governments and deeply rooted in popular opinion. Aside from the distasteful memory of the Napoleonic Wars, the domestically conservative states (Russia, Austria, and Prussia) feared war because they feared revolution, especially if they had to fight a liberal state; while in Britain and France liberal bourgeois sentiment opposed the deflection of attention and expenditures from domestic to military purposes, thereby enforcing military retrenchment.[14]

While governments saw the potentially unpredictable character of war, military officers saw the experience of the Napoleonic period in a different and contradictory light. What the latter saw was the age of the decisive battle, in which warfare had changed from its former status as a formal, stylized activity to an enterprise that offered the prospect, through battle, of achieving clear-cut and dramatic results. Military professionals became obsessed by the victorious battle as the proper model for waging war. They studied Napoleon's campaigns, hoping to find in them principles and rules that could be applied to all wars, which could provide a manual for the conduct of war and the winning of battles.

The French Revolution unleashed tremendous changes in the political and social organization of European society, and equally momentous changes in the nature of the relationships between European populations and their governments. In the seventeenth century European warfare had appeared to governments and peoples as horrendous and uncontrollable carnage. In the next century warfare had been transformed into a limited, stylized, and manageable tool of foreign policy. Generals sought only marginal gains and avoided the risks of battle. Following the Revolution warfare again frightened governments with its potential for uncontrollable violence and incalculable impact upon social structure. It tantalized generals with the prospect of achieving decisive victories through battle. The character of revolutionary warfare can, in some small part, be traced to changes in the tools and methods of conducting war that appeared in the last decades of the eighteenth century. But to an overwhelming degree the explosively changed impact of war followed from the societal and intellectual effects of the Revolution. Political, social, and intellectual change provided the precondition for new weapons, military organizations, and military doctrines to transform the effects of warfare on European society and politics.

How governments and peoples were organized, and what the psychological bonds between them were, powerfully affected the sorts of wars they fought. A change in organization could vastly increase the military power of a state. Wars fought between societies that were different from one another—or *thought* they were—could be much more profound in their implications than wars fought between societies that were alike. It is well to note the importance of political organization and political attitudes, because Europe would shortly enter a period in which *technological* change in military matters was to be endemic and constant, in a manner never before experienced. The nineteenth century would combine technological change with political and social change. Because these different types of change occurred together and were intermixed, it would become increasingly difficult to sort out the effects of each on international conflict. The unsettling experience of the Revolution and its aftermath, the pervasive consciousness of change in all spheres of social life, was to prompt the burgeoning of new and systematic studies of war. In these studies attempts would be made to sort out the causes and extent of the changes in warfare, and to establish the degree to which human thought and effort could still ensure that international violence would remain the servant of human purposes.

The Genesis of Strategic Thought: Jomini and Clausewitz

4

There is one great principle underlying all the operations of war,—a principle which must be followed in all good combinations. . . . We will apply this great principle to the different cases of strategy and tactics, and then show . . . that, with few exceptions, the most brilliant successes and the greatest reverses resulted from an adherence to this principle in the one case, and from a neglect of it in the other.—Jomini, *The Art of War*

War should never be thought of as *something autonomous* but always as an *instrument of policy*. . . . This way of looking at it will show us how wars must vary with the nature of their motives and of the situations which give rise to them. The first, the supreme, the most far-reaching act of judgment that the statesman and commander have to make is to establish . . . the kind of war on which they are embarking; neither mistaking it for, nor trying to turn it into, something that is alien to its nature.—Clausewitz, *On War*

Out of the great upheavals of the Napoleonic period came a widespread impulse to understand the ordeals that European civilization had undergone. The early nineteenth century saw the appearance of a systematic body of thought about war. Writings in the eighteenth century had generally been little more than compendiums of anecdotes, tactical manuals, or simple chronologies of campaigns,[1] with little attempt to explain the phenomenon of war, the changes that it had undergone during the revolutionary period, or the factors that made the difference between victory or defeat. To find an earlier analysis linking the political context with military tactics and institutions, we must return to Machiavelli in the sixteenth century.[2] Practical motives also accounted for the emergence of military thought.

The revolutionary wars had the effect of enhancing professionalism in the officer corps of most states. Now officers in all specialties were mostly full-time salaried officials, appointed and promoted on the basis of some system of formal merit and seniority. There was increased demand that these professionals be given formal instruction as to how best they should carry out their duties. Were there secrets of success in war? Did Napoleon have some set of principles that guided him, and if so, could they be discovered and taught to others?

The mix of motives that accounted for the rise of strategic thinking was to lead to differing and often conflicting ways of approaching the problems of warfare and to the development of differing intellectual traditions. One approach sought educational maxims by which military operations could be guided and about which military officers could be taught, a set of rules that would provide predictability in the operations of warfare. The other approach emphasized the intimate and complex relationship between war and the political and social context within which it occurs, a tradition that denied that warfare has any fixed and immutable principles by which it can be understood and guided. We may take Antoine Henri de Jomini as the model for the first approach, and Carl Maria von Clausewitz as the model for the second.[3]

JOMINI: THE GEOMETRY OF WAR

Jomini was clearly the most influential military theorist of the nineteenth century. A Swiss citizen, Jomini went to revolutionary Paris as a young man to prepare for a career in banking. He managed instead to acquire a staff officer's position in Napoleon's army on the strength of some early commentaries on military affairs. He was to serve in both the French and the Russian armies until his death in 1869. His lasting popularity with military officers came about because "Jomini had given his audience what it obviously wanted."[4] This was an age impressed by science and scientists' claims to authority. Various social groups, especially those newly risen to status, attempted to establish some similar claim to expertise, to exclusive competence in a certain area. Such a claim was precisely what the newly professionalized military officer corps required. In a previous age, aristocratic officers did not require external support for their social standing. Nothing beyond noble birth was necessary to establish a position of influence and importance in society. But the role of the aristocracy had declined and more and more military officers were now drawn from the middle classes. These officers felt that, because of their social origins, their societal position and their influence on policy and on military organization were vulnerable. In addition, various political forces in European society were suspicious of the military and were determined to deny military officers the authority to instruct armies how best to organize themselves and carry out their functions.

The revolutionary and Napoleonic periods had dramatically shown those concerned with politics that there was a profound connection between military affairs and revolution, between the makeup of armies and the structure of domestic society. Military institutions became objects of suspicion from all points of the political spectrum. Conservative and more traditional quarters feared that armies might be used to create new revolutions and to replace authoritarian and hierarchical political orders with egalitarian institutions. These groups feared a repetition of the French Revolution, in which military force had been used to destroy the monarchy and the old social order, to export the Revolution, and in general to spread the unpleasant notions of "equality" and "liberty," if not of "fraternity."

Those who held conservative views had a sense that the social order over which they now presided, an order that had been cobbled back together in makeshift fashion after the disorder of the revolutionary decades, was a fragile one. Armies, precisely because they had demonstrated during the wars that they had the potential to mobilize and channel popular sentiment, were risky institutions that could again be used to foment revolution. Conservatives were determined to so organize armies that this could not happen again. Indeed, they wished to maintain only armies that could be relied upon to put down revolution whenever it should raise its ugly head in the future.

Those who looked back more positively upon the revolutionary period, however, were equally suspicious of the military. When liberals recalled the period Europe had just passed through, they saw laudable movements for popular control and equality put down by the use of force. Napoleon himself was seen as having, as it were, kidnapped the Revolution, using a popular army established by the republic to destroy that republic and then reestablishing a monarchy with himself on the throne and his cronies as a new class of aristocracy. The names of the characters had changed, but not the old plot, according to which a small class of rulers oppressed the disenfranchised masses. Those who held these liberal views wished to counteract the attempts by conservatives to shape militaries that were designed to suppress revolution and domestic dissent. The more radical among them even desired to facilitate the use of the military to foster new revolutions in the name of the people.

The disasters of the Napoleonic conquests produced military reform movements in states that had been victims of invasion and defeat by the French.[5] The reformers argued that to be effective in modern warfare armies had to consist of large bodies of troops. The new mobility and flexibility of warfare required that these formations rely heavily on enthusiasm and solidarity among the troops, not on sheer coercive discipline. The only practical way to acquire military formations of such size and character was to rely on mass conscription, and on major formations of militia or reservists, part-time soldiers drawn from the people at large. These reformers came under suspicion, both from those advocating renewed revolutionary social transformations and from those who wished somehow to return to the ancien régime. Liberals and radicals regarded the reformers as servants of the old regimes, determined to provide them with more effective instruments of social control. Conservatives in postwar governments regarded the reformers as dangerous. Royalists thought that the sort of armies military reformers advocated would create risks for their regimes. Thus, military reformers of the early nineteenth century, such as Scharnhorst and Gneisenau in Prussia (whose innovations were largely responsible for Prussia's ability to wage war effectively against Napoleon), found themselves removed from influence, and progressively ignored by their governments, in the years after the wars of the French Revolution.

Yet the reformers did not deserve the suspicion with which they and their proposals were regarded from either quarter. Their motives had little to do with domestic politics. They were instead driven fundamentally by their understanding of the requirements of military success in the new environment for warfare. They saw clearly that a return to armies like those of the ancien régime would lead to disaster if they should again be put to the test of war. Like it or not, they felt that old-style armies would suffer new defeats like those suffered by the coalition opposing the French Revolution in 1792, if such armies went to war again. Only mass armies could be successful in war. And mass armies could only be formed and operated by energizing the common people.

Against this background Jomini's ideas played an important role in supporting the position and influence of the military officer class, and the institutions that the military professionals were now developing. Jomini's works proclaimed that military affairs entail certain unique principles and laws known to those with expertise in the military profession, which can be taught to the young as they enter the profession. These principles and laws are independent of politics. Because of their claim to special authority, military professionals should therefore be allowed freedom to operate by themselves. The role of the political sector is simply to provide the revenue to support military institutions. How armies were to be organized and how they should fight wars were not proper concerns of politicians. External influences on matters of military organization and strategy were misguided and risked dangerous consequences, because such matters were areas over which only military professionals had competence.

Jomini claimed to have discovered these principles by analysis of the campaigns of Napoleon and other masters of the art of war, such as Frederick the Great of Prussia. Application of these principles had led to success. Failure to apply these principles had inevitably led to defeat in war and would do so in the future. The principles of war were timeless and immutable. No matter what changes in weapons or tactics might come about, the principles of war would always remain.

While making formal acknowledgment of the importance of the political and social environment, Jomini believed implicitly that the recent French successes were due to application of the principles he had discovered, not to changes in French political and social structure that had made the new armies and the new type of warfare possible.[6] Furthermore, these principles could easily and conveniently be formulated into maxims. Young officers and cadets in training could be taught these maxims, so that the entire officer corps could learn to apply them in a similar fashion.

Four maxims illustrated for Jomini the requirements of the "one great principle" by which military operations should be guided and which would ensure success if followed:

1. To throw by strategic movements the mass of an army, successively, upon the decisive points of a theater of war, and also upon the communications of the enemy as much as possible without compromising one's own.
2. To maneuver to engage fractions of the hostile army with the bulk of one's forces.
3. On the battlefield, to throw the mass of the forces upon the decisive point, or upon that portion of the hostile line which it is of the first importance to overthrow.
4. To so arrange that these masses shall not only be thrown upon the decisive point, but that they shall engage at the proper times and with energy.[7]

Much of this appears merely platitudinous, unless one could specify with precision where these "decisive points" were. Jomini believed, however, that the "decisive points" of the theater or the battlefield, against which military activity should be directed to assure success, could indeed be objectively determined. This could be done through determination of the correct "line of operations,"[8] which he defined as the direction of movement of a military formation from its "base of operations,"[9] the starting position from which it draws supplies and reinforcements, to its "objective point,"[10] which may be a geographical feature or the opponent's military forces. The commander's problem is to determine the lines along which the movement of his various forces from base to objective should be directed. Lines of operation are classified according to the geometrical relationship between them, and among the various classifications the most significant is the distinction between "interior" and "exterior" lines.

> *Interior lines of operations* are those adopted by one or two armies to oppose several hostile bodies, and having such a direction that the general can concentrate the masses and maneuver with his whole force in a shorter period of time than it would require for the enemy to oppose to them a greater force.
> *Exterior lines* lead to the opposite result, and are those formed by an army which operates at the same time on both flanks of the enemy, or against several of his masses.[11]

Much of Jomini's analysis is devoted to proving the superiority of "interior lines," which "*enable a general to bring into action . . . upon the important point, a stronger force than the enemy.*"[12] The advantage of interior lines was demonstrated by the extensive use of diagrams and by elaborate exercises involving ad hoc qualifications to his general principles. The benefits of interior lines were applicable to individual battles and engagements as well as to the general conduct of military campaigns over entire theaters of war.[13]

Throughout Jomini's work the importance of the decisive battle in warfare was emphasized. In such a battle one aimed to throw the bulk of one's force against an unconcentrated and still divided enemy, destroy his military forces, and put him at one's mercy. To be sure, Jomini qualified this view. He admitted that there were circumstances in which a general could achieve military success merely by occupying territory, without destroying the opposing military forces. Indeed Jomini has even been interpreted as the last proponent of a tradition of eighteenth-century warfare that emphasizes the importance of gaining favorable positions in a war of maneuver, over the mere destruction of enemy armies, as military objectives.[14]

Nineteenth-century militaries were largely to forget the qualifications, however, and to concentrate on the idea of the decisive battle as the preeminent means of success. In this, ample encouragement could be found in Jomini's work. Maneuver for the purpose of seeking decisive Napoleonic battles was taken as the normal model for waging war; military activity directed to different ends was considered the exception, justifiable only in special circumstances. "The system of rapid and continuous marches multiplies the effect of an army . . . but its effect will be quintupled if the marches be skillfully directed upon the decisive strategic points of the zone of operations, where the severest blows to the enemy can be given."[15] This was at bottom how all the great generals had fought. This was the secret of their success. Military experts, trained in the science of warfare, should be left free to fight future wars in this fashion, to make the destruction of enemy armies in battle their main objective.

Could this view of warfare be modified by the extensive changes in military technology that were taking place in the nineteenth century? Even though Jomini was to survive to see many of these changes, he denied that they would affect the manner in which wars would be fought.

> Improvements in fire-arms will not introduce any important change in the
> manner of taking troops into battle. . . . Two armies in a battle will not pass
> the day in firing at each other from a distance: it will always be necessary for

one of them to advance to the attack of the other. . . . Victory may with much certainty be expected by the party taking the offensive when the general in command possesses the talent of taking his troops into action . . . and of boldly attacking the enemy.[16]

Could the rise of popular passions and the involvement of populations in war put into doubt the validity of his rules for war? Here again, Jomini denied that such change would affect the conduct of war. He acknowledged the possibility of national uprisings, but only to deplore them and to hope that wars would be confined to those appropriate to the rules he had laid down. As to the military consequences should this not be possible, he is curiously silent.[17]

One can see why Jomini's approach had such a powerful appeal to military officers in the nineteenth century. It offered them authority against the outside forces that sought to direct them in the conduct of what, they now came to feel, was a profession unique to themselves. It claimed to have discovered eternal and teachable laws of warfare. It gave them a belief that warfare was an activity that could be mastered, be made predictable, and produce decisive results. Military officers had every personal and professional incentive to believe Jomini in all this, and they did.

CLAUSEWITZ: POLICY, CHANCE, AND VIOLENCE IN WAR

In contrast with the widespread celebrity that Jomini enjoyed, even during his lifetime, Clausewitz was largely unknown until late in the nineteenth century,[18] and even then was to be credited with views far different from those he actually propounded.[19] Whereas Jomini owed his prestige in military circles largely to his writings, Clausewitz pursued the conventional career of a professional army officer. He had seen his first combat in 1792 as a twelve-year-old military cadet. At his death in 1831 he was a major general and chief of staff of the principal Prussian field army command. The bulk of Clausewitz's writing was not published until after his death, although he was widely known in Berlin from the Napoleonic period as an important supporter of the military reform movement. During his career he received advancement somewhat ahead of his peers on the basis of his performance in combat missions and other normal military functions. After Prussia's defeat by Napoleon at the battles of Jena and Auerstadt in 1806 and its consequent reduction to the position of French satellite, Clausewitz left Prussian service. He then joined the Russian army, seeing combat during Napoleon's invasion of Russia in 1812. When Prussia scrapped the French alliance and resumed the war against Napoleon following the disastrous French retreat from Moscow, Clausewitz returned to Prussian service in 1813 and saw combat through the Waterloo campaign of 1815. Clausewitz thus had a distinguished conventional military career, but his writings were to have much less appeal to his professional colleagues than did those of Jomini. Then and now, the search for convenient slogans in Clausewitz's work is far more frequent in military analysis than serious attempts to understand the ideas pervading his work.

To some degree Clausewitz's relative lack of appeal for military professionals was a product of the complexity with which his ideas were expressed and his failure to revise fully his major work to reflect his mature views. Thus, a warped understanding of his views can result from selective quotation of unrevised portions of the work.[20] More fundamentally, however, Clausewitz's lack of appeal for the officer corps stemmed from his denial of two claims that were such prominent features of Jomini's approach: that war was predictable, and that it was possible to derive precise rules of action to guide the officer to practical military success.

Whereas Jomini argued that he had found principles for the conduct of war independent of change in political or social life, Clausewitz understood quite clearly that the fearful eruption of warfare that his generation had witnessed was a product of the political and social changes brought on by the Revolution. Central to understanding Clausewitz is his concept of the "dual nature of war":[21] "War can be of two kinds, in the sense that either the objective is to *overthrow the enemy*—to render him politically helpless or militarily impotent, thus forcing him to sign whatever peace we please; or *merely to occupy some of his frontier-districts* so that we can annex them or use them for bargaining at the peace negotiations. . . . The fact that the aims of the two types are quite different must be clear at all times." A war may be unlimited in its purpose, in the sense that a belligerent's goal is to impose physically its will on an opponent. But a war also may be limited in purpose, in that a belligerent aims to use combat to improve its negotiating position on some other issue, perhaps not directly related to the military events of the war. It is only in the light of war's "dual nature," that we can put into perspective what is Clausewitz's most frequently quoted statement: "That *war is nothing but the continuation of policy with other means.*"[22] We cannot understand a war without considering the larger purposes of those conducting it.

In the manner of the German Idealist tradition in philosophy of his day, Clausewitz approached war by attempting to define its essential character, that which distinguished it from other phenomena.[23] This essence Clausewitz found in violence. By defining "absolute war," that which is essential to the concept of war, as violence, Clausewitz sought to emphasize the inadequacies of those who still thought in terms of an eighteenth-century war of positions, in which the element of combat was subordinated to the chess game of maneuver and countermaneuver. "War is an act of force, and there is no logical limit to the application of that force. Each side, therefore, compels its opponent to follow suit; a reciprocal action is started which must lead, in theory, to extremes."[24]

Passages such as this have led some to interpret Clausewitz as an advocate in all cases of the use of force without limit. However, he only introduces the concept of "absolute war" in order to contrast that concept with "real" wars in history in which the extremes of violence are never reached. Although war's violent essence may indeed carry with it an internal dynamic that, unimpeded, would lead to uncontrolled violence, in reality this dynamic has always been impeded. Violent activity in all real wars is always constrained, to some extent, by one or more factors that Clausewitz collectively called "friction." Real wars are not isolated acts. They involve not abstract actors, but particular states, with specific cultures, institutions, and resources. They do not occur without background. They flow out of particular desires, histories of tension and dispute. "Absolute" war would consist of "one single decisive act." Real wars instead consist of individual actions separated by time and distance, and limited by the inertia of the individuals and institutions that wage them. The results of real wars are rarely final and irrevocable. Losers are rarely physically exterminated as a group. Both winners and losers anticipate that they will continue a relationship after the war, and this anticipation colors their conduct of the war.[25]

If the idea of absolute war, then, is introduced in order to distinguish war from those other human activities that are not defined by collective violence, real wars are played out through the interaction of three elements. "Its dominant tendencies always make war a remarkable trinity—composed of primordial violence, hatred and enmity, which are to be regarded as a blind natural force; of the play of chance and probability within which the creative spirit is free to roam; and of its element of subordination, as an instrument of policy, which makes it subject to reason alone."[26]

The violence that is a part of war can arouse intense emotions. War is not merely the exertion of force mechanically against an inanimate object. Force is employed against another animate organization, which responds in kind. Since war is a social relationship, with each side attempting to affect the behavior of the other, these emotions, once aroused, can spiral upward in intensity to produce still greater levels of violence.[27] Operating against this potential for violence to feed upon itself are the purposes of those who make war. Modern states go to war not primarily out of a visceral hatred of their enemies, but in order to achieve some result. Then again, fatigue and danger slow down operations and cool emotions. Information may be scarce, nonexistent, or wrong. The difficulties of coordinating the behavior of thousands of human beings and organizations mean that no plan will be carried out to perfection. Machines break down. Communications are garbled in transmission. A simple mistake produces a whole host of cascading errors in consequence. "Action in war is like movement in a resistant element. Just as the simplest and most natural of movements, walking, cannot easily be performed in water, so in war it is difficult for normal efforts to achieve even moderate results" (120). Violence will not be constant and unremitting. Pauses will occur in the progress of war. All those things that make action in warfare difficult, which conspire to make results less than plans call for, constitute "friction" in war (119–21). This friction inherent in military operations ensures that the unpredictable and the unanticipated will constantly arise in warfare. Friction keeps violence constrained to levels far below what might be imagined as possible in the abstract.

Above all else, real wars are fought by organized collectives to achieve certain goals. They are thus unavoidably political in character. The character a war will take is determined by the character and goals of the societies at war, and by the resources that they have at their disposal (585–94, 605–10). "Do political relations between peoples and between their governments stop when diplomatic notes are no longer exchanged?

Is war not just another expression of their thoughts, another form of speech or writing? Its grammar, indeed, may be its own, but not its logic" (605). Wars are won or lost because of correct or incorrect judgments about political capabilities and intentions. In Clausewitz's own time, the initial failures of the allies in the wars against the French were due not to technical military mistakes, but to a failure to realize the implications of the Revolution for the goals of both the French and their enemies, and for the military means they all now had at their disposal (610). From the primacy of policy, it follows that there can be no independently valid laws for the conduct of military operations. Therefore no sphere of military activity is outside the legitimate concern of those making policy. Clausewitz argues that political considerations will influence the conduct of war at all levels and indeed advises that the top military commander should be included in the highest policy-making bodies of the government, precisely to ensure that the conduct of war is unified with the broader purposes of the government (608).

Those who go to war should have clearly in mind the goals they wish to achieve through war, as well as the means by which they propose to get there. The goal of policy dictates the military means necessary to achieve the goal. The means necessary to achieve the goal are as much a function of the character of the societies waging the war as they are of the weapons and military institutions of the time. The price of failing to develop an understanding of the political character of the belligerents and their conflict may be defeat (585–94). Thus, the military means necessary to render a narrowly based authoritarian regime subject to one's will would be much less than what would be necessary to achieve the same goal with respect to a government with broad popular support. In the one case it may only be necessary to defeat some military units. In the other it may be necessary to occupy and garrison the entire country and remain there indefinitely. What may be feasible for one society in war may not be for others. The Romans may have been able to permanently garrison their conquered provinces. Other societies may not be able to support and sustain such an effort. The scale of effort necessary to render an enemy completely subservient may be much greater than that necessary merely to achieve leverage in diplomatic negotiations. If the military means are insufficient to achieve the goal of policy, we are left with the implication that either the goal or the means should be modified.

In spite of his emphasis on the subordination of strategy to policy, Clausewitz is not without detailed advice on the conduct of military operations. Thus, he generally favors offensive operations over passive defense.[28] He argues that military operations should be concentrated on a single object, and that this normally should be the destruction of the opponent's main armed forces. He praises speed and surprise in military operations. He favors the massive decisive blow over the slow accumulation of incremental advantages.[29] These injunctions are not offered as absolute rules, however, but merely as rules of prudence. Military decision making in his view is not a matter of deducing correct behavior from abstract rules, but of making pragmatic judgments about probabilities based on experience. Clausewitz presents his preferences as conditional generalizations about courses of action that, in most circumstances, have increased the probability of military success. But the conditions of particular conflicts may make it seem inadvisable to put his preferences into operation. If so, they can be, and should be, freely ignored. It was, however, the details of these conditional operational preferences, not his broader insistence on the primacy of political factors, that was to dominate the nineteenth-century military's understanding of Clausewitz. He was to be interpreted as if he had offered a set of universally valid rules for all circumstances, similar to those propounded by Jomini.

Clausewitz argued that the general must be intimately familiar with the political purposes of the war, so that he can fight it in a way that is consistent with those purposes. Equally, the policy makers should be familiar with their military tools and with what those tools can and cannot accomplish. Avoidance of failure requires that tools and purposes should be in harmony. Nothing could be further from the notion that the military can operate free from political interference.[30] But this aspect of Clausewitz was not something congenial to the officer corps. It threatened their claim to freedom from oversight by others and was largely to be ignored.

Clausewitz did not devote much attention to the potential for technological change in the means of warfare. The changes that he saw occurring in war in his own lifetime, and with which he was most highly concerned, emerged from the political environment, not from the availability of new types of weapon, new means of transportation, or new modes of communication.[31] Yet he admitted the possibility of technological change and the potential for such change to affect the larger shape of war. He indicated that changes in tactics—how wars are fought by individuals and small groups—could influence the overall character of a war and, by implication, even the purposes for which wars could or should be fought.[32] This view contrasts with the Jominian insistence that eternal principles of warfare had been deduced whose operations were unaffected by external change, either political or technological.

The Napoleonic convulsions led to the emergence of movements to understand the phenomenon of war and to train those who were to make preparation for its conduct their profession. But the demands of the new military professionals for social autonomy and simple, teachable rules were to cause them to adhere to intellectual schemes that made them increasingly unable to understand and control the very forces they now claimed the exclusive expertise to manage. Jomini led them to believe that maneuver and attack would forever provide the infallible key to decisions in war. He instructed them always to seek victory through the decisive battle. He argued that the political and social transformations they had witnessed during and after the French Revolution were unrelated to the newly decisive character of warfare. These beliefs would lead Jomini's followers to increasingly disastrous conclusions later in the century and early in the next. Just as they were about to move into a period in which the qualitative change in the machines and the methods that armed forces had at their disposal would increase exponentially, and the problem of the effect that this qualitative change would have upon warfare grew to be its most central question, military professionals largely deprived themselves of the intellectual capacity to consider the fundamental implications of change.

Clausewitz, however, did not fulfill the professional military officers' demand to find support for their claims in an autonomous knowledge of warfare, a knowledge that would give them the authority to resist the influence of societal forces outside the military. For this reason, the military used Clausewitz for the remainder of the century primarily as a source for dramatic slogans. When Clausewitz was appealed to at all, even in the land of his birth, it was as the apostle of maximum violence in war. Those who appealed to him ignored the implications of his analysis. But his recognition of the intimate connection between political purpose and military means in war, his insistence on the necessity to understand both ends and means fully, and his sense of the catastrophic consequences that failure to keep ends and means in balance could produce would be vindicated with increasingly tragic results in the years to come.

False Victories: The Wars of the Mid-Nineteenth Century

5

In the time I am writing, every stalk of corn in the northern and greater part of the field was cut as closely as with a knife, and the slain lay in rows precisely as they had stood in their ranks a few minutes before.—Union General Joseph Hooker at Antietam, September 17, 1862

After the Napoleonic Wars, major war in Europe was to be avoided for almost forty years, until the outbreak of the Crimean War in 1854. Fresh memories of the Napoleonic convulsions, and the mutual fear that new wars would unleash unpredictable domestic and international consequences similar to those of the Napoleonic era, impelled governments for decades to ensure that conflicts not be allowed to erupt into major violence. Paradoxically, it was to be a new outbreak of revolution at midcentury that was to destroy this European governmental consensus.[1] These revolutions convinced some governments that they could profitably use military power to harness popular national emotions to governmental interests. Once warfare between European powers had returned to the scene, European military experience seemed to support the Jominian optimism about the controllability and utility of war that had so come to dominate the thinking of those in the professional military. In an era dominated by rapid change in the tools of warfare, questions about the implications of change were answered with the firm assertion that Napoleonic victories remained possible and likely.[2] Evidence that such victories might in the future be less likely and more costly was ignored.

EUROPEAN WARS AND THE APPEARANCE OF VICTORY

The years following the Congress of Vienna had not been quiet ones. A variety of international disputes engaged the attention of the great powers, many of them arising out of the growing weakness of the Ottoman Empire in southeastern Europe. As Ottoman Turkey declined, other powers came to compete with one another for influence in the Balkan region and the eastern Mediterranean. Those not directly interested in acquiring Turkish territory were concerned that some new territorial arrangement in the region might be advantageous to a potential rival. European governments were threatened at home by repeated outbreaks of revolution. A new round of rebellions had occurred in 1848, many of which had in the end been put down with the powerful military assistance of the Russian tsar. One might have thought that this renewed reminder of the potential for revolution would have redoubled caution among European governments, and that the tsar's role as the friend and supporter of all those governments threatened by revolution would have made him the arbiter of Europe. Instead the Russians became increasingly isolated in Europe. The liberal parliamentary powers in the West, the British and the French, were not at all pleased with Russia's role in putting down revolution. Most significantly, the governments whom the tsar had assisted became equally suspicious of Russian motives. Neither the Prussians nor the Austrians looked favorably upon the growth of Russian influence in central Europe. The Austrians, who had received considerable support from the Russians in putting down a revolution in Hungary, became increasingly worried about the growth of Russian influence in the Balkans. Mutual suspicions about territorial ambition and security were aroused, suspicions that conflicted with the continued sense that these governments had common interests in cooperating against the threat of domestic revolution.

The consensus that had existed among European governments—that war carried more risks than advantages—began to come apart at mid-century. In France the great Napoleon's nephew was elected president of the republic that had come to power in the revolution of 1848. After a coup d'état in 1851, he was to reestablish his uncle's dynasty, taking the imperial title himself as Napoleon III. His regime was conspicuously dedicated to renewing France's martial tradition and to upsetting the territorial arrangements that had followed his uncle's defeat in 1815.

Italy was at this time divided up between a number of independent states (one of which was ruled by the pope), and the German-speaking Austrians, who ruled territories in the northeast. In northwestern Italy the Kingdom of Piedmont had come to see warfare as a tool by which it could ally itself with Italian national sentiment, throw the Austrians out of Italy, and gain territorial advantages for itself. Somewhat later the Prussian monarchy would come to see the potential advantages for itself of a similar policy, aimed at throwing the Austrians out of Germany.

The Russians found themselves involved in a dispute with the French and the British over Russian ambitions in Turkey and the straits linking the Black Sea and the Mediterranean. Revived Austrian concerns with Russian territorial ambitions caused Austria's Emperor Franz Josef to forget the tsar's recent assistance to him and to remain neutral, encouraging the Western powers to believe that they could achieve success in their dispute with Russia by war. The Western powers sent a military and naval expedition into the Black Sea, landed an army on Russia's Crimean peninsula, and besieged its port of Sevastopol. Although the mind-set of the aging generals in the Crimean War was fixated upon achieving the sort of great Napoleonic victories that many of them had witnessed in their youth, the war was not notable for great battles or great victories but for pervasive incompetence and maladministration. The war quickly bogged down into static and costly siege warfare, ending with the French and the British forcing the Russians to accept a settlement unfavorable to the latter.

The war was notable not for what happened, but for what did not happen. The great powers of Europe had fought a conflict, yet no governmental system was overthrown. The war set off no revolution. No drastic changes in political relationships occurred. The British and the French achieved their goal of defending the Turks against the Russians, although at a much higher human and material cost than they had anticipated. Russian ambitions in the area, for the moment, were humbled. The war remained limited to its original participants, however, and no great continent-wide political upheaval followed. One could reasonably infer from the experience of the Crimean War that international conflict once again could function as a useful and manageable tool for achieving political objectives.

This conclusion was not lost on governments in central and western Europe. In Germany, as in Italy, new political combinations began to emerge. At that time, Germany remained divided among many states, the Prussians and the Austrians being the largest among them. The Austrians were able to exercise the greater influence in this situation by exploiting the interests that they had in common with the rulers of the small German states against the Prussians. The Austrian dynasty was ethnically and linguistically German, but ruled a polyglot empire, composed of many nationalities in addition to the German-speaking Austrians. Neither the Austrian government nor the rulers of the small German princely states had any interest in encouraging German national sentiment. If the Austrians encouraged or legitimized national sentiment, their empire could fragment. Similarly the legitimacy of the small German princes depended on sentiments of dynastic loyalty. Appeal to broader German national sentiment would make the princes irrelevant, by submerging them in a bigger sea. For the German princes the major danger was Prussia, against whom they were happy to accept Austrian support.

Until midcentury, German national sentiment had been associated primarily with those on the political left, with liberals and partisans of parliamentary democracy. There had been an attempt at German unification during the revolutionary upheaval of 1848 advanced by liberal parliamentary institutions. The German princes as well as the Austrian rulers had seen in German unity a direct threat to their power. Indeed all monarchical governments had accepted the proposition that national sentiment would threaten their positions equally. In retrospect we may find it curious that the Prussian monarchy shared in this acceptance. For by cooperating with Austria and the small German governments to oppose German nationalism, Prussia accepted a situation in which Austria could keep Prussia subordinate to it in German affairs indefinitely. The Prussian monarchs and those advising them did not for many decades question the received wisdom on the topic, that nationalism inevitably led to republicanism and the unemployment of kings.

In the wake of the revolutions of 1848, however, some of those in the Prussian political elite began to question this automatic equation of nationalism with republicanism. They noted that many of the German nationalists of 1848, reacting against Austrian hostility, had called on the Prussian monarchy to establish German national political institutions. That the nationalists desired a liberal German political order, with all the institutions of parliamentary democracy, was of less importance than that those holding such national sentiments could call upon the Prussian king to oppose his fellow monarchs in the name of German unity. Against great resistance support grew, among partisans of the monarchy and the old social order, for a fundamental shift in the policy of the kings of Prussia. The argument was put forward that German national sentiment might, in the proper hands, prove useful to the Prussian monarchy. National sentiment was a given in political life: it could not be disinvented. If the Prussian monarchy were to put itself at the service of nationalism, it could reap important gains. It could use nationalism as a means to gain territory and influence, and to win out in the centuries-long contest between Austria and Prussia for primacy in central Europe.

When Otto von Bismarck came to power as the Prussian king's first minister in 1862,[3] he foresaw that, by taking the initiative rather than just reacting to events, it would be possible for the monarchy to break the automatic connection between national sentiment and liberal domestic institutions. The Prussian monarchy would be able to use nationalism not only to expand its territory at the expense of the Austrians and the small German princes, but to ensure that the new Prussian-dominated German polity would remain an authoritarian, hierarchical state dominated by a central monarchy, a state without powerful parliamentary institutions similar to the old, small Prussian state. Since those who would lose by such a program would clearly not give up their position voluntarily, Bismarck concluded that he could accomplish his goal only by warfare. The alternative was the emergence of some other political movement that would capitalize on nationalist sentiment and sweep away all monarchs alike.

With Bismarck in place, the governments in France, Piedmont, and Prussia now felt that they could achieve advantages by the use of force internationally. The Crimean War had convinced them all that war could occur between the great powers of Europe without threatening the domestic political and social order that these governments wished to defend. Even before Bismarck's accession, the French and the Piedmontese had combined to reduce the Austrian position in northern Italy. There followed a series of wars, all of which appeared to contemporaries to have a common character. In 1864, Prussia induced Austria to wage a joint war against the Danes in the name of German interests. In 1866, Prussia defeated Austria and gained unquestioned primacy in

Germany, while Piedmont was completing the expulsion of Austria from Italy.[4] Finally, in 1870 Prussia defeated France and eliminated the last obstacle to German unification under the Prussian monarchy. These wars were short and decisive: the important campaigns in each of them occupied only a matter of weeks. They featured climactic and victorious battles between armies. They ended cleanly with one side achieving its goals. And they did not produce unpleasant surprises in the form of social revolution. (To be sure, the Franco-Prussian War had produced the end of Napoleon III's regime and the restoration of the republic, but in social terms France was unchanged.) This neat picture of the effects of war was carried away from the battles by participants and observers alike. Suggestions that, but for chance, these wars could have had drastically different outcomes were largely ignored.

These wars were the first in which commanders had to cope with the effects of constant technological change in the means of warfare.[5] New forms of communication and transportation, the railroad and the telegraph, had emerged. Troops and supplies could now be moved great distances with a reliability and speed unheard of in previous decades. Orders and information could now be conveyed hundreds or even thousands of miles instantaneously. Weapons themselves were changing rapidly. Rifling and breech-loading weapons were introduced to the artillery and the infantry. The result of these and other technical developments was rapid improvement in the range, accuracy, and rate of fire of both combat arms. Seemingly trivial changes could produce large unanticipated effects. Thus for hundreds of years troops firing muzzle-loading weapons had been required to stand in order to reload. Although breech-loading weapons had been introduced primarily to increase the rate of fire, their effect was to enable soldiers to fire and reload while lying prone, or from behind low cover. Thus soldiers became much less vulnerable to enemy fire, while being able to increase the intensity of their own fire considerably.

What effects would these technological changes have on the character of wars fought under the new conditions? Would they encourage short wars or long wars? Would they allow armies to achieve decisive results that could be used quickly to achieve policy goals, or would they make for stalemate and frustration? Answering such questions seemed straightforward. All that was necessary was to examine the military campaigns that were waged during this period. Thus, both the Franco-Prussian

War and the Austro-Prussian War involved a few weeks' campaigning, some decisive battles, and a clear-cut conclusion. Most contemporary observers took this to mean that the new means of waging
war tended to produce quick and decisive results. But were results like
these the outcome of long-term trends produced by the evolution of
military technology, trends likely to continue, or were they the outcome
of chance or fortuitous factors that might not provide any guide to the
future? If a battle was won handily, was this because of the superiority
of the new weapons, or because of the incompetence of the generals?

Close examination of the wars of midcentury cast doubt on the adequacy of the simple images that prevailed at the time. The Austro-
Prussian War of 1866, which would establish Prussia's primacy in
Germany, began with Prussian armies converging on Austrian territory
from three directions. Helmuth von Moltke, the chief of the Prussian
general staff, felt it necessary to proceed in this way in order to get into
Austrian territory before the slow-moving Austrians could fully mobilize
and, most important, to forestall the possibility that the French (who
historically had favored a divided Germany) might intervene in favor of
the Austrians. Moltke violated Jomini's injunctions by advancing on
exterior, not *interior*, lines. Moltke's gamble paid off. His armies were
able to come together on the battlefield and defeat the Austrians at the
Battle of Sadowa.

The Prussians proved able to mobilize and move their armies faster
than the Austrians because of two interlinked factors: superior staff
work and the railroads. The Prussians had realized the importance that
the new means of transportation would have for military affairs. Prussian railways were planned to facilitate the quick movement of troops
and supplies to the frontiers at the beginning of a war. In their understanding of the importance of railroads to warfare, the Prussians were
ahead of the rest of Europe. They also were ahead of other powers in
realizing that, to take advantage of new developments like railroads,
meticulous, advance planning was required.

The Prussians had introduced into the military personnel structure
the innovative concept of a specialized body of officers trained for planning and staff functions.[6] These officers performed detailed studies of
the technical problems posed by the supply and movement of armies.
They attempted to examine systematically military problems that might
be encountered in the field, through various types of war games in

which campaigns could be simulated and alternative strategic approaches attempted and compared. Above all they prepared elaborate and detailed schedules for the myriad activities necessary to put the preferred strategies in motion in the event of war. As little as possible was to be left to chance or improvisation after the outbreak of war. These general staff officers served their entire careers performing such functions. They would receive their initial training at general staff headquarters and then serve as staff officers in army formations in the field, with some eventually returning to positions on the central general staff. Technically, general staff officers were subordinate to army commanders and did not actually command armies in the field, but their intimate knowledge of the problems of military operations and the terrain the advancing armies would encounter gave them great influence over the decisions of commanding generals.

In time many general staff officers, who had similar training and had often dealt in war games with the same problems, came to occupy positions of influence in various commands. They would come to react to situations encountered in the field in a manner that could be anticipated by colleagues in other formations, even when unable to communicate directly. The telegraph allowed communications between fixed positions, but once armies moved across the frontiers, commanders had to fall back upon old, unreliable and slow measures such as the dispatch of couriers on horseback. Once the campaign had been set in motion Moltke lost effective control of the movement of his armies.

While the Prussians benefited from superior staff work, advance planning, and superior exploitation of the railways, they also were the beneficiaries of Austrian mistakes. The Austrians were dilatory and cautious, not realizing the speed with which the Prussians were capable of moving. They failed to exploit opportunities that existed to attack Prussian formations at an early stage while the Prussians were still separated and vulnerable to defeat in detail.

The outcome of the great Battle of Sadowa itself was not the result of superior Prussian planning. The main armies basically blundered into one another, and outlying Prussian generals joined in the attack, even without orders. Some of the Prussian advantage may have been due to their infantry having been equipped with a superior breech-loading rifle, the "needle gun." Again, Austrian mistakes played a role. Balancing the Prussian needle gun was Austrian artillery that was superior to the Prussians' in range and accuracy. Aware of this, the Austrian commander, Benedek, planned his dispositions to subject advancing Prussian infantry to withering artillery fire, before the Austrians came within range of the Prussian needle gun. Benedek had the misfortune, however, to have serving under him as subordinate commanders aristocrats who considered themselves immensely more exalted than he in social status. Benedek's careful dispositions were cavalierly disregarded by these subordinates, exposing the Austrian flanks to Prussian infantry attack. The result was a catastrophic defeat after both of Benedek's flanks collapsed. Had this insubordination not occurred the battle could easily have had a much different outcome.

The message carried away from Sadowa, however, did not take account of these possibilities. The general conclusion was that the Prussians' new infantry weapon had enabled them to take offensive action in battle and overwhelm their opponents. That the battle could easily have produced stalemate or even a Prussian setback was largely ignored in the face of the overwhelming Prussian military victory, and the further circumstance that victory led to a political settlement of the war favorable to the Prussians only a few weeks later. Indeed, in those few cases during the war where the Austrians had been able to use their artillery effectively they were able to stop Prussian infantry attacks, causing the attackers to sustain very heavy casualties. The possibility that artillery could make infantry attacks impossible was never really tested at Sadowa, however, because of Austrian blunders.

The Franco-Prussian War that came four years later seemed to confirm what had become understood as the standard lessons of the Austro-Prussian War:[7] the superiority of the offensive, the centrality of decisive battles, and the controllability of wars. Bismarck provoked the French into a war designed to allow him to cement Prussian control over the other German states. He succeeded in this handsomely. The war saw the defeat and capture of the two main French field armies. Along with the French army captured at Sedan, the Prussians also acquired the person of the emperor Napoleon III, who had accompanied his armies in the forlorn hope of proving that he had inherited his uncle's martial genes. The Prussians created the new German empire while occupying the former French royal palace of Versailles. Germany acquired the territories of Alsace and Lorraine from the French, and a large financial indemnity. Again it appeared that the attacking Prussians had achieved a clear-cut advantage through a short and cheap war. War had been declared on July 15, and the French surrender at Sedan came on September 2.

As with the previous war, however, close examination of the conflict cast doubt on the simplicities that were suggested by the results. While winning the early battles of the war, the Prussians had consistently taken higher casualties than the losers. The French had learned what they took to be the lesson of 1866 and had given their infantry the chassepot, a weapon superior to the Prussian needle gun, with which they were able to subject formations of attacking Prussian infantry to horribly effective firepower.

The French had not learned equally well, however, the importance of the general staff and the use of the railroads. The Prussians again were able to mobilize and move faster than their opponents. The Prussian mobilization and railroad system was designed to expedite the movement of their armies to the frontiers. The French railway system centered on Paris, creating bottlenecks there of troops and supplies. The Prussians had worked out their plans for the initial movement of their armies in meticulous detail. The French had only the most general notions of what movements they would make once their armies were formed and, as with the Austrians before them, were slow and inept. Even though they proved capable of resisting the Prussians ferociously in detail, they allowed the Prussians to separate the main French armies and deal with them one at a time.

The war did not end once the French armies had been dealt with. The capture of the emperor caused the collapse of his government and the emergence in Paris of a new French republic, fired with enthusiasm for continuing the war. The republic raised new armies in the South, which forced the Germans to stretch their supply lines dangerously. It is not at all inconceivable that the French could have mounted a long, drawn out resistance in the countryside which might have bled the Germans indefinitely. This was a development with potentially ominous implications, which Bismarck recognized. It was to avoid the possibility of an extended war that he pressed Moltke to hasten the bombardment of the republican government, besieged in Paris. The surrender of Paris finally ended the war, but not until four months had passed after Sedan. As important as German military action was in producing the surrender, equally important was the fear on the part of moderate and conservative elements in Paris that they were threatened by social revolution. Putting an end to the war, even at the cost of accepting defeat, was finally thought advisable so the French could turn their energies to the business of putting down this domestic threat.

As with the Austro-Prussian conflict, matters could easily have gone differently. A less incompetent French command could well have stopped the Prussian invasion and forced a conflict whose costs the Prussians might have shrunk from accepting. These were not, however, the conclusions that were drawn. Victory does not encourage critical analysis of the methods of the winners. Instead the war was widely taken to confirm that the offensive would work under the new conditions, that infantry could effectively attack, that the new weapons worked in favor of the offense, that the presence of these weapons on the battlefield meant that future conflicts would be wars of quick movement and decisive results.

Yet a number of wars were fought during this period whose conduct could hardly be squared with the conclusions generally drawn from the wars of German unification. Some of these wars were fought in Europe, some elsewhere. At the end of the decade that had begun with the Franco-Prussian War, the Russians fought the Turks in a conflict characterized by the costly failure of infantry attacks against entrenched positions. Any claim that this war had lessons to teach was dismissed by the widely held view that both sides had competed with one another in the incompetence of their generalship. After the turn of the century, the Japanese—the first non-Western civilization to assimilate Western military organization and technology successfully—fought and defeated the Russians. Here again, infantry assaults proved extremely costly, the armies constructed extensive entrenchments, operations became static, and the land war was finally decided by the exhaustion of the parties. By the time of the Russo-Japanese War, of course, the machine gun was widely employed as an infantry weapon. This weapon is often singled out as having by itself put an end to the sort of wars the Europeans had fought in the middle of the nineteenth century. But the machine gun did not come into its own until after the Franco-Prussian War. (The French did possess a machine gun in 1870, the *mitrailleuse,* but they used it in limited numbers and behind their lines as an artillery piece; its potential effect against infantry attacks was thus lost.)

A war was fought before the advent of the machine gun, however, whose conduct clearly belied what became the mid-nineteenth century's conventional wisdom about warfare. Time would show that its conduct would predict the future of war with far greater clarity than had the wars fought in the center of Europe in the mid-nineteenth century. While technically not an international conflict, in most of its features it dwarfed those which were. It was fought between two societies able to employ the latest tools, weapons, and techniques. In terms of numbers engaged, length, and extent, it was the greatest war of the time. Furthermore, European officers studied it in large numbers.[8] Curiously, however, their examination of this war did not seriously affect the conclusions they were forming about the future conduct of war.

The American Civil War was the first war in which the railroad and the telegraph were put to significant military use.[9] On both sides, those who entered into it shared the expectation that it would be a quick and decisive romp. Lincoln's initial call for volunteers envisioned only ninety days' service. Generals anticipated fighting Napoleonic battles. Such expectations were summed up in the image of Washington civilians driving their carriages to what would be the first Battle of Bull Run in 1861, in the expectation of witnessing something like a theatrical entertainment, only to be driven back to the capital in panic when the Confederate army routed the Union forces. A war that was to last only ninety days instead lasted four years. The Confederacy was able to resist for this long, and repeatedly to best Union forces militarily, even though the North possessed overwhelming superiority in manpower and in all forms of industrial development. Casualties were immense. More than 600,000 soldiers died on both sides.[10] The South was devastated for a generation.

What had happened to frustrate these initial expectations? In spite of the generals' orientation to fighting great battles, soldiers early on in the fighting learned the advantages of digging in. It had become very difficult to launch successful frontal attacks against entrenched infantry, even a force protected by only makeshift field entrenchments. From behind this protection the defenders could lay down a murderous fire against infantry attackers, who of necessity had to be standing up. The attackers were equally vulnerable to the defenders' artillery fire even

before they came within range of the defending infantry. The vulnera-
bilities faced by attacking cavalry were even more extreme than those
for attacking infantry. Indeed, during the Civil War, cavalry completely
lost its earlier role of charging infantry on the battlefield en masse, shat-
tering them with the "shock of cold steel." Instead, horse-mounted
troops were exploited primarily for their mobility. They could move
swiftly and were useful for reconnaissance and for disruption of enemy
communications. When they had to fight, however, they dismounted
and dug in.

The generals kept hoping their problems were only temporary, that
more experienced and trained troops would recover their effectiveness
in the attack, and they continued to order attacks involving frontal
assaults against infantry. When they did, the result tended to be carnage. At the Battle of Antietam in 1862, more than 25,000 casualties
occurred on "the bloodiest single day of the war."[11] At Gettysburg in
1863 the Confederates assaulted the Union center in an action that
would be immortalized as "Pickett's Charge":

> It was a magnificent mile-wide spectacle, a picture-book view of war that
> participants on both sides remembered with awe until their dying moment—
> which for many came within the next hour. . . . As the gray infantry poured
> across the gently undulating farmland with seemingly irresistible force,
> northern artillery suddenly erupted in a savage cascade, sending shot and
> shell among the southern regiments and changing to canister as they kept
> coming. . . . Yankee infantry behind stone walls opened up at 200 yards. . . .
> In half an hour it was all over. Of the 14,000 Confederates who had gone
> forward, scarcely half returned. Pickett's own division lost two-thirds of its
> men; his three brigadiers and all thirteen colonels were killed or wounded.[12]

The last stages of the war in the east were characterized by largely
static operations involving elaborate trench systems around the Confederate capital, Richmond, on the order of those which fifty years later
would dominate the western front in World War I. The war became a
huge, slow contest of mutual attrition, an exchange of casualties and
destruction, which ended only when the capacity of the South to support its military effort economically had collapsed.

The disparity in resources between North and South may seem to us
to have made the war's outcome inevitable. In manpower resources
available when the war began, the Union overmatched the Confederacy

by a ratio of about five to two. At the outset of the war Northern industries employed more than ten times the number of workers so employed in the South. The South manufactured only 3 percent of the firearms produced in the United States during 1860 and only 4 percent of the railroad locomotives. Southern railway mileage was less than half of the North's.[13]

Domestic and international political factors powerfully influenced the war, however, and could easily have allowed the South to survive. The huge military effort the North waged, and the huge casualty lists that resulted, produced intense domestic political opposition, including violent opposition in the form of urban riots against conscription. In the summer of 1864 it appeared probable to Lincoln that he would be defeated in the election that year, and replaced by an administration that would try to make a negotiated peace.[14] The Union capture of Atlanta in early September reversed the tide of popular opinion and led to Lincoln's electoral victory in November. Characteristically, military events were less important for themselves, than for their political and psychological effects, both at home and overseas. The Battle of Antietam had been, by any reasonable tactical standard, a bloody draw. But Lincoln labeled it a victory and employed it as a pretext to issue the Emancipation Proclamation, freeing the slaves in the states in rebellion. The effect of the proclamation was both to encourage Northern public opinion to continue with the war, by seemingly expanding the significance of the issues at stake, and, even more important, to ensure that the British and the French would not intervene in the war, when such action would have been seen as having the effect of rescuing so detestable an institution as slavery. European intervention would have rendered Union hopes for military victory futile. Encouragement of such intervention had been an important element of Confederate policy.[15]

It may even be argued that the South could have held out, had they not been so dominated by generals such as Lee who were mesmerized by the prospect of Napoleonic victories on the battlefield. To win the war by military means the Union had to invade and conquer Confederate territory. The South, on the other hand, had only to survive. In this it had the advantage of a relatively compact territory and could rely on the tactical superiority that lay with the defense. Lee and his colleagues instead squandered irreplaceable manpower and resources by repeatedly attacking and attempting to destroy Union armies. Had they tried to avoid battle and fought a more narrowly defensive campaign, it may be argued that the South could, at a minimum, have held out longer, allowing time for Northern passions to cool. Against this view is the contention that a defensive strategy still could not have prevented the Union from slowly dismembering the South and cutting the Confederacy off from the outside resources necessary to continue the war. Thus Lee's strategy of seeking battle was, in this view, well suited to the Confederacy's situation. Only the shock of dramatic defeat and great casualties could have created the political pressures that might have induced the North to have accepted a compromise peace.[16] Whichever side of this debate may have had the greater merit, the importance of the political context within which the war was waged was crucial.

In the end, the Union's ability to destroy the Confederacy's war-making resources derived to an important degree from the use of military power, not directly against the Southern armies, but against the civilian economic infrastructure behind the lines. The federal navy blockaded Confederate ports with increasing effectiveness. Military campaigns along major river and rail transportation networks had as their aim cutting up Southern territory and destroying the Confederacy's ability to transport troops and supplies from one region to another. The significance of such a campaign as Sherman's "march to the sea" after he had captured Atlanta did not lie in the armies he defeated on his way. Indeed, his main objective was to go behind the shield of the Southern armies and to destroy the civilian social and economic base that enabled the South to make war. It was the cumulative effect of campaigns such as these that produced the Southern collapse after four years of war.

PREDICTING THE FUTURE OF WAR: LESSONS LEARNED AND LESSONS FORGOTTEN

Among the many European observers of the Civil War were a number of acute analysts whose reports suggested the danger that wars in the future might become long drawn-out wars of attrition, decided in the end only by which side became exhausted first. Some emphasized the suicidal character of direct assaults by infantry against entrenched positions. For the most part, such reports were filed away and buried in European war ministries, overwhelmed by what European officers felt were the contrary lessons of their own wars. European officers cast doubt on the applicability of the American experience to the European future. American armies were overwhelmingly composed of poorly trained amateurs. Only untrained soldiers would dig in the ground the way the Americans had. Properly trained regular soldiers, European officers insisted, would stand and advance in the face of the firepower of the defenders. Ultimately the discipline that European military training instilled in their soldiers would enable them to advance successfully.

This was not necessarily a conscious effort at deception. Nor were those who took such views peculiarly obtuse. The European experience, or at least the European experience as the European military had come to interpret it, had a powerful attraction for the officer corps in Europe. These officers understood this experience to mean that military operations could make a difference in matters of value to the states employing them, and could do so at bearable cost. Furthermore, their interpretation of their experience provided arguments to support their budgetary requests and, in particular, the increases in those requests that flowed from an environment of constant qualitative improvement in military technology. Nor did those few contemporaries who were skeptical of these interpretations find it easy to say that the prevailing understanding was wrong. Only with hindsight can we say that it was, but from the perspective of the time, the evidence was ambiguous. It could, with some plausibility, support several contradictory conclusions.

Thus, the prevailing view that European militaries carried into the twentieth century, that they conveyed to their governments and that they spread throughout their societies, was that warfare, while demanding great sacrifice, while costly in blood and material resources, could still be an instrument of policy. There would still be circumstances where wars among the most technologically advanced states could bring governments external results that they could not otherwise obtain, and could do so at a cost and with a speed that would justify the effort.

ARMED FORCE IN PEACETIME

Few argued, however, that going to war would be as relatively trivial a decision as it had been during the eighteenth century. General mobilization of the immense numbers now enrolled in modern armies and their reserves would disrupt the entire economic life of a society. So in the last years of the nineteenth century the use of force and the means of force, short of actual warfare, grew in prominence as a way to achieve political objectives. International crises occurred with some frequency. An issue would arise, the powers would posture, threaten war in one way or another, mobilize partially or fully, and dispatch troops or warships to demonstrate resolve or willingness to contemplate war.[17] Usually this process of mutual threat led to some kind of negotiated settlement. These attempts to use not force itself, but the *threat* of force, to coerce or deter, became a part of diplomacy.

Arms races became a part of diplomatic activity also.[18] Since victory might go to the power with the best weaponry, competitions developed to acquire that weaponry, and in the largest quantities. Sometimes the arms races were primarily *qualitative* in character, such as the naval arms race waged between the British and the French for a good part of the middle years of the nineteenth century. This was an era in which major change was occurring simultaneously in most of the aspects of naval warfare.[19] Ship construction was changing from wood to iron. Propulsion by steam was replacing sail propulsion. More powerful armaments were pitted against more effective armor. The British and the French competed with one another to produce new types of warships. The changes that followed one another so closely were so radical that it was feared that each generation of warship would not only put its predecessors at a disadvantage, but make them irrelevant completely. A new type of armor, or a naval gun that had greater range, accuracy, or penetrating ability meant not merely that a new ship was worth three or four old ships if it came to a fight, but that the new ship might be able to sink any number of the old ships while remaining completely invulnerable itself.

At the end of the nineteenth century, the pace of technological change slackened. Great power armaments came increasingly to mirror one another's characteristics. Arms races on land and sea took an increasingly *quantitative* form. The Anglo-German naval race from the turn of the century until the eve of World War I was a competition to acquire greater numbers of weapons that were broadly similar on each side. The growing importance of technology and planning led to the belief that the outcome of war could be predicted with some precision on the basis of troop and weapons levels. The size of armies, and the numbers of troops by which they could be augmented within specified periods of time after mobilization, became crucial factors in these predictions. Powers consciously attempted to maintain certain levels of military personnel and equipment relative to one another, in order to achieve some political goal, whether it was to threaten a prospective opponent or to dissuade it from some undesired behavior.

Since Germany's victories seemed so tied to its ability to move fast and plan ahead, the great powers acquired general staffs, all producing elaborate plans for mobilizing and deploying their armies at the outset of war. To make the outcome of war more predictable, attempts were made to tie foreign powers into these war plans. Alliance agreements came more and more commonly to include talks between military staffs[20] and coordination of plans about the actions each ally would undertake militarily on the outbreak of war. The content of these agreements was of course kept strictly secret, but often the fact that military agreements of some kind existed might be made known—or hinted at— as part of the diplomatic game of influencing a potential opponent. Whereas the wars of the middle of the century had demonstrated anew the continuing importance of the political context during actual hostilities, the international crises of the latter part of the century showed that the instruments of force at the disposal of states conditioned their relations even while they remained ostensibly at peace.

The late nineteenth century and the early years of the twentieth were increasingly marked by attempts to manipulate the implicit or explicit threat of force during international crises, to achieve political objectives while remaining at peace. But all these measures were the same measures that would be taken in war. While military force was increasingly employed in conscious attempts to affect the behavior of others in time of peace, no distinction was made between the military requirements of coercion or deterrence in peacetime, and the requirements of military operations should fighting actually break out. These activities were all undertaken against the comforting and widely held belief that, if war did come again, it would repeat the lessons that Europeans felt the conflicts of midcentury had given them: that war under modern conditions could be a controllable, useful means for achieving political goals; that military victories through the clash of armies in battle were possible; that victorious battles would produce short wars and clear-cut political results; and that the advantages to be expected from going to war could well be worth war's risks and costs.

Military Surprise and Catastrophe: World War I

6

See that little stream—we could walk to it in two minutes. It took the British a month to walk to it—a whole empire walking very slowly, dying in front and pushing forward behind. And another empire walked very slowly backward a few inches a day, leaving the dead like a million bloody rugs.—F. Scott Fitzgerald, *Tender Is the Night*

World War I was a catastrophe so immense that we find ourselves compelled to believe that some cause equally great must have produced it. An entire generation of young men was destroyed all over Europe. Tens of millions of deaths resulted from the war, directly or indirectly.[1] It was a conflict without winners. None of the governments in those countries that began the war achieved what they had hoped to achieve by fighting the war. Indeed, many of those governments were destroyed by the war, and the states they had led were either destroyed with them or radically changed in a direction they could not have desired. All of Europe was enfeebled, the economic structure of "victor" as well as "vanquished" was shattered, and the seeds were laid of another great war that was to follow only twenty years later. World War I was to produce in Western consciousness images of colossal, senseless slaughter, and of incompetent leadership willfully blind to that slaughter, that would color our minds down to our own day.[2]

Surely such a monstrous result must have been produced by some equally monstrous pathology. Since rational statesmen could not have intended the results they produced, some of them must have been, if not insane, then afflicted by some grave malfunction in the psychological processes by which they perceived and understood the outside world. If the result cannot be attributed to psychological malfunction or insanity, then the outbreak of war must be attributed to some deterministic process that took all the choices out of the hands of those ostensibly making them. Governments and their leaders must have been caught up in the cogs of some huge inexorable machine that ground on irrespective of whatever they may have wished or expected.

What is difficult to accept is the proposition that the governments of Europe went to war in 1914 because they wanted to do so: that they were not stampeded into war by the ravings of a madman, or madmen; or propelled into it by impersonal forces beyond human control; that they were not surprised when the war started or when the war quickly grew to involve all the great powers of Europe. In August 1914 they each coolly came to the separate conclusion that their futures would be brighter if they went to war than if they did not.[3]

Wars in a curious way must be made by agreement. It takes at least two sides to make a war, and they must each come to the conclusion that they would be better off fighting than not fighting.[4] Absent such an agreement, no conflict can follow. Of course, in the nature of things at least one of those parties entering a war is bound to realize that it has erred in its calculations. As Clausewitz had put it, "the nature of war makes it a matter of assessing probabilities. . . . No other human activity is so continuously or universally bound up with chance. And through the element of chance, guesswork and luck come to play a great part in war."[5] Sometimes, as in this case, all sides discover that they have been mistaken. Although the governments of 1914 went to war with their eyes open and with deliberation, the sort of war they thought they were about to fight was not the sort that developed. In this they were surprised, and it was so great a surprise that, once into the war, they discovered that they did not know how to extricate themselves from it.

THE ORIGINS OF THE WAR

The use of force short of war as an instrument of diplomacy had grown in prominence in the decades before 1914. Although governments and military leaders were confident that future wars would be short and decisive, they did not think that future conflict would be completely cost-free. Armies now numbered in the millions. Removing such huge numbers of men from the factory and the farm and sending them into battle would mean that the normal economic life of belligerents would come to a halt for as long as the war lasted. Indeed the disruption of economic life was generally cited as another reason why wars would necessarily be short. A long war would simply cause the complex and interrelated industrial economies of Europe to collapse. Confident in their military plans, leaders now looked for ways to make their military forces achieve the results they expected from war without the inconveniences of actual bloodshed. The decades before 1914 were therefore characterized by international crises and arms races; by the conscious use of military demonstrations of resolve, including mobilization or the threat of mobilization; and by the coordination of military plans between allies through direct negotiations between their general staffs. But the growing role of force in peacetime did not itself produce World War I.

Although arms races in abundance preceded the war, it is difficult to maintain that they played a great part in causing it.[6] The beginnings and the development of arms races reflected the state of political relations between the parties to them. In the late nineteenth century a qualitative naval arms race between the French and the British took place during a period when each regarded the other as its major political competitor and security threat.[7] This naval race was more a product of a preexisting Franco-British hostility than a cause of it. With the turn of the century, as the two countries came increasingly to share a common concern with Germany, they drew closer together politically and the arms race between them was largely forgotten. Indeed, the Franco-British agreement in 1904 to settle colonial disputes between them, an agreement known as the "entente," led to naval staff talks in 1912 in which the two powers agreed to a division of responsibility in matters of naval defense. Under this agreement the French shifted the bulk of their navy to the Mediterranean, leaving the defense of their vital Channel and Atlantic ports to their hereditary British enemy.[8]

The Anglo-German naval race in the years before World War I was certainly a factor in producing hostility between the two countries in the public mind. In 1898 the Germans began a program to build a fleet of battleships,[9] ostensibly to defend their overseas trade and their communications with newly acquired colonies. Since the German battle fleet was incapable of mounting substantial operations outside the North Sea, however, the British were justified in perceiving it as an instrument that could only be aimed at bringing their own fleet to battle. The beginnings of British concern with Germany as a possible enemy ante-date the German building program, however. And it is often forgotten that the race was all but over in 1912. The Germans recognized that they could not afford an indefinite competition with the British in this area, especially as naval funds competed with those for army expansion. British entry into the war was precipitated by the German invasion of Belgium, not by a race with the German navy, which the British had already won.[10]

The Germans and the French, among other powers, competed directly in the decades before the war in weapons development and man-power levels. Decisions about the size of armies were affected by the size of a prospective enemy's army now, and its potential size in the future. Decisions to develop particular weapons were affected by under-standing of the other side's weapons program. Few observers would have denied that levels of manpower, speed of mobilization and deploy-ment, and technical superiority of weapons systems would all affect the outcome of wars. Thus, the powers made decisions on these matters in the light of their understanding of their prospective opponents' policies. The Franco-German arms race took place, however, in a specific politi-cal context. The French were keenly dissatisfied with the results of the Franco-Prussian War. The Germans knew the French were dissatisfied and both sides expected that there would be another round someday. These states armed because of their profound hostility to one another and their expectation that their arms would one day be put to good use, not merely because the other party acquired weapons.

By 1914 all the great powers of Europe had subscribed to agreements that attempted to foretell their position should war erupt among any of them. Bismarck had begun the process with his alliance with Austria-Hungary in 1879. His motive in concluding this agreement, was not to support Austrian aggressiveness, but the reverse. Austria had joined Turkey as Europe's "sick men." The Austrians were increasingly con-cerned about their ability to maintain control of their multinational empire and worried about the designs of outside powers on that empire. In particular, the Austrians were concerned about Russian attempts, directly and through the agency of the small independent Serbian state, to gain influence by supporting the separatist aspirations of groups of ethnic Slavs within the Austrian domains. For the new German empire, the prospect of conflict between Austria and Russia was dangerous, not for itself but because it might give the French an opening. Bismarck assumed correctly that the French hoped for an opportunity to gain European allies who might support them in a future war with Germany. Any conflict involving Russia and Austria presented the potential for such a French intrusion. Therefore, Bismarck attempted to find the means to prevent the conflicting ambitions of Austria and Russia in southeastern Europe from leading to war between them.

Bismarck's alliance with Austria enabled him to keep the Austrians on a short leash. He offered Austria protection against Russian attack, but on condition that Austria itself avoid provoking Russia. Bismarck's expectation was that, with the assurance of German support, Austrian security concerns in the Balkans would moderate and the prospect of a Russo-Austrian conflict would be lessened. Bismarck was even able to add an alliance with the Russians to this arrangement with Austria a few years later. Each of these empires wished the protection of the most powerful state on the continent. Thus Bismarck found himself allied with both Russia and Austria, and by being allied with both was able to keep them from each other's throat.

Bismarck's successors, arguing that to be allied with both parties to a potential conflict was illogical, dropped the relationship with the Russians.[11] Russia thus became a free agent, concerned about potential conflicts with the Austrians and their German protectors. Perhaps this situation would have come to pass eventually whatever policy Germany pursued, but certainly German actions accelerated the process. Shortly afterward, the French, as was to be expected, offered the Russians a military alliance, along with considerable financial support for Russian rearmament. Bismarck's hope to keep France isolated on the European diplomatic stage, and thus not capable of threatening German security, had been lost. Still later the British and French agreed on several of the colonial disputes that had been dividing them, and their military staffs began discussions on a possible British role in a European war, although the British never admitted that they were committed to any particular military operations should war come. The British later reached a similar accommodation with Russia over colonial disputes in central Asia.[12]

Thus, by 1914, all the great powers of Europe were tied into an alliance structure that made it highly likely that a war in Europe that involved any of them would involve all of them. It was on the basis of this structure that the military staffs made their plans. Wherever a war started, whatever the immediate object of dispute, whoever the initial combatants were, the German military expected that it would become involved in a two-front war against both the Russians and the French. To make plans on the basis that such a war could be confined to a campaign against the Russians was to run the grave risk that France would attack unprepared German forces anyway with disastrous results. Similarly, the French and the Russians assumed that they would fight together against the Germans. The Russians expected that they would have to fight the Germans, no matter how a war began. A war against only Austria, Russia's antagonist in the Balkans, might be preferable, but given Germany's relationship with Austria, German entry into such a war could not be ignored without grave risk. If Russia launched its forces against Austria only, Russia would be defenseless if Germany decided to attack.

Complicating and reinforcing the alliance structure were the technical assumptions on which military planning was made. The wars of the nineteenth century had suggested that great advantages would accrue to the belligerent who moved first and fastest. Preparations depended upon elaborate schedules for the use of the railways to mobilize troops and supplies and to bring them to the frontiers. Once these preparations had been set in motion, attempts to improvise could well lead to chaos.

The structure of mobilization plans, and the alliance structure on which those plans were based, introduced an expectation of certainty about European political arrangements. We must, however, not overestimate this. Italy found it easy to desert its alliance partners, Germany and Austria, when war began and even to go over to the other side. Thus, the alliance structures did not remove the power of decision from governments. These structures did ensure that local quarrels would swiftly become of interest to third parties. But concern for the implications of quarrels between others had been a feature of the politics of the eighteenth century also, although that century had not been distinguished by the standing alliance structures that characterized the years before 1914.

The crisis brought on by the assassination of the heir to the Austrian throne in July 1914 was only the latest in a series of problems involving Austrian decline, Austrian worries about growing Slavic nationalism in its empire, and Russian attempts to capitalize on its position as the great Slavic power to gain influence at Austria's expense in the region. Previous crises had been settled short of war between the great powers, after periods of posturing and threats. In previous crises, the Russians had seen fit to withdraw from many of their demands. In 1914 the Russians were determined not to repeat their previous behavior, which they feared had lost them influence in the region. The Austrians saw the crisis as a means to eliminate Serbia, whose independent position outside Austrian domains acted as a magnet for Slavic nationalists within the empire. The 1914 crisis differed from previous Balkan crises, not so much because of Austrian and Russian rigidity, but because of a different German attitude. In previous crises the Germans had used their alliance to restrain the Austrians, in the tradition of Bismarckian diplomacy. Now Berlin indicated to Vienna that it was prepared to support them in whatever policy toward Serbia Austria might pursue. This willingness became known as the "Blank Check."

Those making decisions in Berlin were not determined on going to war, but they believed that if war should come, 1914 would be a relatively favorable time for them to wage it. Because the Russians were increasing the number of troops that they could mobilize and making improvements to their railway network in the West, the Germans expected that in coming years the Russians would be able to mobilize against them at a considerably faster pace than previously. If there was to be war, it was preferable to fight now.

The existence of the alliance systems, and the military plans made on the basis of those systems, did not in any material way force the governments of the great powers to pursue policies that they would not otherwise have wished to pursue. The alliance systems simply reflected the structure of leaders' assumptions about the probable behavior of others toward the political conflicts that divided the European powers. Even if they had not been tied together by treaty, they probably would have adopted similar attitudes in 1914. The specific considerations on which governments decided for war in 1914, and which made those decisions differ from those which had not produced war in prior crises, were relatively unimportant. Had circumstances differed only marginally, a general war might well have come a few years earlier, or later. What was common to all these decisions, in 1914 and before, was that they were made in a context in which war was seen as a normal and controllable course of action that might periodically be resorted to without great risk. If they had not gone to war in previous Balkan crises, it was because they had not, for whatever reasons, agreed that circumstances were then propitious. Now they believed that they were. Each power felt it could see an advantage in appealing to arms now, rather than in accepting the situation that would result from the absence of war.

That the powers felt that they could see such advantages followed from the conception that they shared of the character a new European war would take. Such a war, they all expected, would be a repetition of the Franco-Prussian War: short, sharp, and decisive. Given this shared expectation, the decisions made in 1914 were quite plausible. Any attempt to explain them as products of stress-induced pathology or some other form of personality dysfunction on the part of the leaders becomes unnecessary. If governments had conceived that they were taking a decision in 1914 fraught with the disasters that in fact followed, it might be fruitful to search for such explanations. But they understood their decisions instead as part of the normal processes of international politics and expected the consequences of those decisions—win or lose—to be ordinary and manageable within the social and political structure of the world they knew. Results that we know in hindsight were extraordinary need not have had extraordinary causes.

FAILURE OF THE OFFENSIVE

That a European war would again be short, sharp, and decisive was the consensus of most military analysts but was not unanimous. A few commentators, such as the Polish banker Ivan Bloch, predicted quite another sort of war.[13] Bloch expected that the increased rates of firepower at the disposal of the defenders would make infantry attack suicidal, and that the war would quickly become a stalemate. Bloch was dismissed as an amateur, however. The military staffs of Europe were able to convey to their political masters the honestly held belief that, if war were to come in the summer of 1914, it could be fought to advantage. Furthermore, the risks that would be run should such a war be lost, would not be catastrophic. Each side could plausibly argue that now was the time to fight. For a variety of separate reasons, they each felt that, since time was on the side of their enemies, the sooner war came, the better.

Each of the military staffs was convinced that experience had shown that speed of movement was essential, and that offensive actions carried the best chance for victory. The result of this conviction was that most of the belligerents launched offensives shortly after the outbreak of war. The most famous of these was Germany's giant attack through Belgium into northern France. Known to us today as the Schlieffen Plan after the general staff chief who had first conceived it, this offensive would set the stage for four years of stalemate on the western front.[14] But the Germans were not alone in their offensive-mindedness. The war opened with an offensive by the French, who launched their right wing on an invasion of Germany, and by the Russians who attacked the Germans in East Prussia.

The calculations behind the Schlieffen Plan are well known. Because of the probability of a war on two fronts, the Germans reasoned that they dare not allow both of their enemies time to mobilize fully, since they would then be outnumbered. Germany's best hope, therefore, was to attack on one front while standing on the defensive on the other. Germany would attempt to achieve a quick victory through its offensive, and then would turn its attention to the second front. While its enemies might, if given the time, mobilize combined forces greater than those the Germans could put in the field, Germany had two advantages. It could count on mobilizing at a faster pace than either of its probable enemies, and its excellent railway network would enable German forces to shift quickly from one front to the other. After several years in which they had planned to strike Russia first, the German general staff decided to strike against the French at the outset, since they judged that the French would be capable of mobilizing faster than would the Russians.[15] The Germans hoped that they could attack and defeat the French, shifting their forces then to the Russian front before the slow-moving Russians would have had the opportunity to make any significant gains.

The solution adopted was a gigantic right wheel, whose most powerful armies would pass west of Paris. They would then turn east, cut the French armies off from their communications and pin them against the fortified Franco-German frontier. Surrounded, the French armies would be forced to capitulate, as had the French armies in the Franco-Prussian War.

In spite of the German general staff's pioneering expertise in the use of railways for military purposes, there was a glaring difficulty with this plan. While the Germans could employ their superior railways to mobilize faster than the French and to transport their armies to the frontiers, once they crossed those frontiers their soldiers had to march on foot through Belgium. The French railroad system had Paris as its hub. While this meant the French would be slower to get their forces to the frontiers than the Germans, the Germans overlooked that this Paris hub meant that, once placed on the defensive, the French could now use their railways to move their armies faster than the Germans. Yet the Germans persisted in a plan that required German troops to march on foot faster on the outside of the wheel than the French could move by rail on the inside.

In spite of these deficiencies in the German plan, the French almost made it succeed. By launching their own offensive, the French drew the bulk of their forces far away from the point at which the weight of the German attack would fall. Only after massive German forces had begun their march through Belgium did the French belatedly realize the danger they were facing on their left. By a prodigious effort General Joffre, the French commander, managed to shift enough of his forces from right to left through Paris to meet the German attack and bring it to a halt. The Germans may have contributed to their failure by shifting the extreme right of their attack to the east of Paris, in order to close some threatening gaps between units in their line. Whether the Germans might have succeeded had they kept to their original intentions is moot. Once the French did manage to mount their defense, a pattern that was to dominate the western front for the next four years emerged.

The armies attempted to outflank one another by extending their lines to the sea. Soon their entrenched positions stretched in a double line from Switzerland to the sea. The armies in effect besieged one another. Neither army could outflank the other. Each side periodically attempted to break through its opponent's positions by launching massive frontal infantry attacks, making pitifully small gains at horrible costs.[16] The firepower now available to entrenched defenders meant that infantry attacks upon such positions became essentially suicidal. Massive artillery bombardments were attempted in hopes of destroying the defenders before an attack. These bombardments proved ineffective against deeply entrenched defenders. Indeed, by churning up the ground and eliminating existing drainage patterns, the artillery may have impeded the attack more than it debilitated the defending forces. "The nineteen-day British bombardment at Third Ypres (1917) used 321 train loads of shells, a year's production for 55,000 war workers. The whole battle area reverted to a swamp in which the British army took 45 square miles in five months at a cost of 370,000 men, or 8,222 per square mile."[17] The hope that the belligerents had all shared at the outset—that they could achieve a quick, decisive result—was clearly mistaken. Bloch's worst predictions had been realized. Instead of producing a dramatic new Sadowa or Sedan, the war reproduced on a much larger scale the static trench lines around Richmond at the end of the American Civil War.

Although tactical details differed on other fronts, strategic results were similar. On the eastern front, the armies had much more space in which to maneuver. A war of movement remained possible here, and the Germans were able to gain some great battlefield victories over Russian armies. But the Germans could not convert these battlefield advantages into victory for three years, and then only in the wake of the Russian Revolution.[18] The quick, cheap victories that military leaders had convinced themselves were the lessons of the wars of the preceding decades were revealed to be illusions.

SEARCHING FOR AN END TO STALEMATE

The generals still thought of the war as one of "annihilation" of the enemy in the Napoleonic tradition and continued to search for the decisive battle.[19] The war had instead taken on the character of a contest in mutual exhaustion, a war of "attrition," whose outcome would in the end turn on the slow accumulation of comparative advantage, across a whole range of political, psychological, and economic factors, in which military results on the battlefield formed only one component.[20]

Unless the costs of war could be justified by its goals, Clausewitz had implied that there should properly follow a limitation of war aims or a search for a compromise peace. But that the war had indeed become a contest in mutual attrition was not recognized by a military leadership unable to rid itself of the professional presumptions of a lifetime, and efforts continued to achieve a decision on the battlefield: to discover a means to force the "breakthrough" that the generals thought was only eluding them momentarily. The most tragic effect of this was the simple belief that victory was just a matter of trying harder, of making more massive attacks, of finding some new tactical variation that would allow the offensive to carry the day. Both sides kept attacking, kept throwing tens and hundreds of thousands of men at the enemy. Another effect of the stalemate was the search for a solution through expansion of the war. Expansion occurred in three dimensions: means, geographic extent, and political goals.

One form of expansion of means was not novel. Each side mounted a naval blockade of the other's coasts, hoping to cut it off from the wherewithal to make and sustain its war effort. As it came increasingly to be understood that the ability to make war was a function of the entire industrial base of society, the two sides attempted to expand the scope of their blockades so as to cut each other off from *all* trade, not just from that sort of trade, such as traffic in weapons and ammunition, that in previous periods had been regarded as having an essentially belligerent character. Now the warring parties attempted to cut each other off from food supplies and the resources necessary to support their civil economies behind the lines. In the recently developed submarine, the Germans almost found their hoped for "breakthrough" device, which could enable them to use the old idea of blockade to destroy British commerce, and through that to destroy the British war effort.

The British were wedded to the notion that war at sea would be decided by the clash of great battle fleets. The submarine would be only a subsidiary weapon accompanying the battle fleets, serving as a scout and "sharpshooter," trying to pick off the other side's battleships. To achieve command of the sea, one maintained a quantitatively superior fleet of the most advanced warships. A superior naval power could defeat in battles at sea any fleets his opponent maintained. Indeed, to avoid certain defeat, the inferior naval power might never take to the sea at all. Thus, with command of the sea one could use the oceans for whatever purposes desired, while denying an opponent the opportunity to use the sea.

These notions of maintaining a dominant fleet had been publicized at the end of the nineteenth century by the American naval officer Alfred Thayer Mahan, using this phrase, "command of the sea."[21] Mahan, however, did not create this orientation among naval officers. In the Royal Navy, concentration upon the importance of the battle fleet and upon engagements between those fleets was an important legacy of the

Napoleonic Wars. Mahan's function was to make explicit these implicit notions and to give them a scholarly veneer by extensive reference to historical materials. In the Royal Navy and in other navies, Mahan's work was accepted because it supported their domestic political struggles for budgets sufficient to build and maintain large fleets of battleships.

The school of naval warfare epitomized by Mahan was not unchallenged. There were alternatives that cast doubt on the universal utility of the battle fleet. A power with an inferior battle fleet, for example, might attempt to avoid fleet battles and instead concentrate on destroying the commerce of its enemy. Such a power might not acquire first-line battleships at all, but might acquire instead smaller, faster warships, which could readily destroy civil commerce while evading destruction by the enemy battle fleet. Such a power might concentrate on new and unorthodox techniques that were relatively cheap, yet might put the big battleships of the superior power at considerable risk. The *Jeune École* in the late nineteenth-century French navy advocated such an alternative naval strategy.[22] These officers proposed to make maximum use of such newly developed devices as torpedoes, naval mines, and submarines. By such an approach, French partisans of the *Jeune École* claimed they could convert the huge British battle fleet from an advantage for its owners into a liability. The British would find themselves forced to devote an inordinate amount of time and effort simply to protect their fleet from these unconventional attacks.

The German navy began World War I with a Mahanian conception of its strategic role. In the preceding decades German admirals had concentrated on the construction of a large fleet of the most advanced and powerful battleships, whose purpose in war would be to engage the main British fleet in battle. If the British were to lose such a battle, or even if in winning it they suffered serious losses, they would lose that command of the sea on which their ability to reap the fruits of their naval supremacy rested. Submarines, in the orthodox German scheme of things, were vessels secondary to the battle fleet. Almost accidentally, however, the Germans were to discover that the submarine was a highly efficient vehicle for the destruction of surface ships of all sorts, most notably for the destruction of commercial vessels.

A civilian ship could easily be destroyed by gunfire or by a torpedo fired by a submarine. If the submarine attacked on the surface, however, it could be disabled even by small-arms fire; and the British promptly armed many of their commercial vessels. Vulnerability on the surface, and the submarines' small size, soon induced German submarine captains to ignore the gentlemanly conventions that had previously governed naval warfare at sea. Under these conventions, a warship had been obliged to warn enemy commercial vessels before firing, escort them to a port if possible, or at least provide safety for their crews. A submarine could do none of these things without endangering itself. The Germans eventually adopted the practice of firing without warning on any ships found in areas they had designated, and without making any provision for the safety of their civilian crews. Submarines were much less vulnerable to detection and counterattack than were surface warships operating as commerce raiders.

By this means the Germans came close to destroying the British economy and driving the British out of the war, but at the cost of growing hostility from neutral powers, the largest of whom was the United States. The German declaration of unrestricted submarine warfare was at least the immediate occasion for American entry into the war in 1917. British strategy inadvertently assisted the Germans in this new means of destroying commerce. Because the British could not at first comprehend the significance of the German submarine threat to their commerce, and because of their fixation on the importance of the battle fleet, they devoted considerable resources to the protection of their fleet, resources that might otherwise have been useful in antisubmarine warfare. In the one battle that actually occurred between the two main fleets, the Battle of Jutland (1916), the British were so concerned to protect their battleships against the threat of torpedoes and mines that they failed to press home their advantage and pursue the inferior German fleet, with the result that the battle was indecisive. The battle fleets never fought again and mostly spent the rest of the war warily watching out for one another.

The practice of employing warships to convoy groups of commercial vessels proved to be the most effective measure against the German submarine threat. Whereas submarines were difficult to locate and destroy in the open ocean, with a convoy the submarines obligingly came to the hunters. The British resisted the institution of convoys, however, largely because it was perceived as a defensive activity, unworthy of the Royal Navy's heroic offensive tradition. But once the British had been forced to accept the necessity of convoys, they were able to reduce the German submarine threat to acceptable proportions.

The stalemate produced a geographic expansion of the war, in the form of the establishment of new fronts. Since it was no longer possible for the belligerents to outflank each other's armies on the western front, the war expanded, as the belligerents tried to find areas elsewhere where their opponents might be vulnerable to a decisive blow. Such an attempt led to the disastrous British campaign against Germany's ally Turkey in the Gallipoli Peninsula at the eastern entrance to the Mediterranean, in which the British sacrificed the troops of their Australian and New Zealand allies. The British hoped in this campaign to knock the Turks out of the war and, by opening a new supply line to the Russians, to increase decisively military pressures on Germany and Austria. The British instead soon found themselves bogged down here in the same sort of bloody war of attrition against the Turks as that on the western front that they had hoped to evade.

Military stalemate drove expansion of war aims. Instead of responding to the bloody war of attrition in which they found themselves by attempting to reduce military costs, to moderate the goals that they hoped to accomplish through war or to lessen their opponent's will to continue the war, governments reacted by justifying the war in terms more and more grandiose and universal.[23] A horrible price was being paid. Therefore, the goods that were being bought for that horrible price must truly be goods of the greatest value.

From being a war for limited territorial gains and relative influence in the Balkans, the war's goals expanded on both sides until it became conceived as a contest between opposed philosophical principles or ways of life, a contest between civilization and barbarism, good and evil. Political leaders in most of the warring states were unable or unwilling to induce their militaries to pursue less costly approaches to military operations, to impose less grandiose policy goals, to look for opportunities for negotiated peace. Governments retreated from making policy, and in effect allowed policy to be dictated for them by their military leaderships' conceptions of the requirements of military victory.[24]

In Germany the military high command led by Field Marshal Hindenburg and General Ludendorff after a while became the de facto government, capable of forcing out any civilian officials who were less than completely enthusiastic about the military's views. Even so masterful a politician as British Prime Minister David Lloyd George was unable to do anything to resist the military's simple and incessant demand for more troops and more material to throw into the front. To some degree the French provided an exception to this tale of governmental impotence on the western front. After a disastrous offensive in 1916 and widespread mutinies in the French army, the French political leadership was able to force the military high command to place a greater emphasis on the defensive in hopes of reducing casualty levels. Because of the passions that the costs of the war had stirred up, most governments rightly felt it politically suicidal to preach policies of moderation. Thus, the inability of governments to modify their policies, when faced with military means incapable of achieving their goals, only forced an expansion of the war in an unlimited direction, more and more divorced from its original political context.

When geographic extension of the war, its expansion to civil trade on the oceans, and universalization of its political implications all failed, new means were explored to break the stalemate at its source. The belligerents searched for new techniques and technologies that might enable them to overcome the dominance of the defense and achieve a "breakthrough" on land. Germany introduced chemical weapons to the battlefield. These poison gases killed or incapacitated those who came into contact with them. In their initial use, these weapons achieved local successes. Surprised and unprotected troops panicked or were overwhelmed by poison gas attacks. The allies found they could easily produce such weapons in turn, and each side discovered quickly that ways could be found to protect troops against the effects of gas. Thus, chemical weapons merely added to the horrors of the battlefield, without giving advantage to anyone.

The aircraft became a weapon of war. It was first employed as a means for reconnaissance and artillery spotting. Then ground troops, realizing enemy aircraft were helping to kill them, began shooting at the planes. Aircraft began dropping explosives onto ground targets. Pilots of aircraft on opposing sides began shooting at one another. By the end of the war, airplanes had begun to be employed not only to assist armies on the ground but in a small way to attack the infrastructure, communications, and economy of the other side behind the lines. Almost simultaneously with the introduction of aircraft, grandiose claims began to be made for the utility of military air power, but its era of promise still lay in the future.

Air power in World War I added incrementally to the effectiveness of ground armies, acting in a subsidiary and subordinate role to those armies. But the aircraft was not yet the means for achieving the "breakthrough."

Another new technology was to provide at long last the ability to end the stalemate on land. Oddly enough, when the first of these new weapons was developed by the British, the work was sponsored by the navy rather than by the army. The problem to be solved was the vulnerability of attacking infantry to artillery fire, and to the fire of other weapons of the defending infantry. The navy had considerable experience in the development of armor to protect its ships. The solution proposed was to provide armored protection to a motorized platform that could move with, or ahead of, the attacking infantry. This platform could carry with it machine guns or artillery to destroy the weapons of the defenders. Mount the platform on tracks rather than wheels, and it could move readily over the broken terrain of the battlefield.

When the new armored, motorized vehicle, which would come to be known as the tank, was first employed on the battlefield, the long hoped-for "breakthrough" was at last accomplished. Tanks shattered the German infantry line, although the earliest tanks were so prone to breaking down or getting stuck in the mud that the allied advances tended to stop after a few miles. Thereafter the Allies produced tanks in quantity. The Germans, however, produced very few tanks, and very few antitank weapons. The result was a technological asymmetry between the belligerents in land warfare that allowed the Allies to make major advances on the western front of a sort that had not been seen since the war's earliest days. These advances, when added to the cumulative effect of four years of attrition on the German economy and its industrial base, and the fresh infusion of resources and men from the United States, produced the German collapse at the end of 1918. Even at the end, one must wonder about the extent to which the Germans themselves caused their own collapse, not only by their failure to respond in quantity to the new land-based armored weapons, but by their persistence in the hope of perfecting the old-style infantry offensive, throwing away some of the last of their best troops in futile new assaults in the spring of 1918.

As with their experience of the French revolutionary wars, European governments had been surprised by unanticipated change in the character of international conflict. In addition to the political and social transformations with which they had struggled more than a century before, they were now bedeviled by the problem of predicting the effects on warfare of technological change. Although technology was in reality making it more and more difficult to use war between major powers as a tool to achieve political objectives, leaders continued to believe that war could still produce quick victories. The quest for victory had led to stalemate and social collapse. Their inability to predict the effects of technological change correctly plunged European governments into an unanticipated and unintended cataclysm.

The experience of World War I was to produce several often contradictory lessons that would be carried into the coming decades. It had of course been an awful carnage. That it was difficult to find anything to justify the carnage would produce an enduring atmosphere of cynicism and revulsion, not only at warfare but at the ability of politics in general to produce results, much less progress; and an enduring image of military incompetence producing meaningless suffering. The belief became widespread that future wars must be like the one just past—or worse. It was widely recognized that the war had moved closer to totality, that it had been decided in the end by a contest between entire societies in their capacity to endure privation and disruption. While the blockade and the submarine attacks at sea represented the most clear-cut way in which the war had transcended traditional distinctions between combatants and noncombatants, between those it was legitimate to attack and those it was not, it was expected that these limits would be evaded even more extensively in the future. Horrific images abounded of the future use of air power and chemical weapons against civilians, making European publics extremely vulnerable to fears about the effects of future war.

At the same time, and paradoxically, the experience of the war would lead to an intense search for ways to fight new wars while evading or avoiding the horrible attrition that had characterized the war just past, a search for ways to return decisiveness, predictability, and low cost to warfare. These contradictory impulses, and the new grievances and insecurities that would emerge in a world in which "peace" had itself created new conflicts, provide the setting within which strategic developments unfolded in the years leading from the first to the second of the world wars of this century.

Fear and Hope: Military Power between the Wars

7

In the next war . . . any town which is within reach of an aerodrome can be bombed within the first five minutes of war from the air . . . and the question will be whose moral[e] will be shattered quickest by that preliminary bombing? I think it is well also for the man in the street to realise that there is no power on earth that can protect him from being bombed. Whatever people may tell him, the bomber will always get through. . . . The only defence is in offence, which means that you have to kill more women and children more quickly than the enemy if you want to save yourselves.—Stanley Baldwin, House of Commons, November 10, 1932

When the United States entered World War I, it was, in Woodrow Wilson's words, to fight the "war to end wars," to fight for a "peace without victory." Wilson proclaimed that the American purpose was to fashion a peace settlement that would remove the grievances that had led to the war, that would last, and, above all, that would not create new grievances. The settlement was to be based on the principle of national self-determination. If the national grievances that had led to the war were satisfied by the peace, the causes of future wars would be removed. Unfortunately the settlement that was actually made at Versailles in 1919 created new problems in the name of solving old ones, engendering in the losers a deep-seated resentment, while at the same time failing to provide effective mechanisms for the winners to protect the peace settlement against the desire of the dissatisfied to change the territorial status quo by force or the threat of force. As conflict over the settlement grew, fears of renewal of the horrors just witnessed competed with speculation that wars of the future could be fought in a manner that would not repeat the disasters of the past. The traumas of World War I stimulated both the hope of preventing war altogether, and the hope that renewed change in military technology could return cost-effectiveness to international conflict.

THE PEACE SETTLEMENT AND THE FAILURE OF COLLECTIVE SECURITY

The makers of the settlement proclaimed that it was violation of the principle of national self-determination, which led to the tensions that produced war in 1914.[1] The case of Slavs forced to live under Austrian rule was only one example of this. The restiveness of Slavic peoples forced to endure alien rule had set off the conflict. The solution? Redraw the map of Europe, so that no national group would again be forced to live under the domination of an unwelcome government. Boundaries should be changed to reflect the ethnic and linguistic divisions of the inhabitants. Where necessary, the people of an area should simply be asked to vote under what government they wished to live. If peoples were no longer forced to live under undesired governments, no group would any longer have an incentive to use force to get rid of a government perceived as alien.

The problems posed by the "sick men of Europe," the multinational Austro-Hungarian and Turkish empires (both of whom had, of course, been among the losers), were solved to the satisfaction of the peacemakers by dismemberment. Out of the former Austrian territories were formed several new states (among which were Czechoslovakia, Hungary, and Yugoslavia) based on ethnic principles. Turkey was stripped of vast territories where ethnic Turks were not predominant. An independent Polish state was created out of territories formerly held by Austria, Germany, and Russia. Germany was stripped of territories in the east on the ground that these were not populated by Germans. Russia found herself at the end of the war stripped of territory in the Baltic and eastern Europe that had formerly belonged to the tsar. (Although Russia had begun the war as an ally of the western powers, it had been militarily crushed by the Germans and revolutionized by the Bolsheviks, who accepted a punitive peace settlement at the hands of the Germans rather than continue the war. This had drawn upon Russia the hostility of the western powers and Japan, who had then tried without success to overthrow the Bolshevik regime by force.)

Problems soon became evident in this attempt to remake the map of Europe according to the principle of national self-determination. It proved impossible to settle all border issues to the satisfaction of all interested groups. In many regions members of different ethnic, religious, and linguistic groups lived side-by-side with one another in a crazy-quilt pattern. No boundary could be drawn without leaving a dissatisfied minority somewhere. Demographic patterns in central and eastern Europe were not similar to those in western Europe where, by and large, peoples of different groups were clumped together in large contiguous areas, clearly divided from one another by major geographic features.

If borders could nevertheless be drawn to allow self-determination to national groups, such borders might create new problems on other grounds. Such borders might split up areas that had previously formed parts of large economic or trading units. They might cut off agricultural or manufacturing areas from their markets, or from their ports or transportation routes. "Ethnically pure" borders, if they could be drawn at all, might be difficult or impossible to defend militarily. A state constructed on national principles alone might find its territory divided into separated parts. It might find itself without important mountain passes or river boundaries on which it could base a viable defense of its territory, or without the ability to secure assistance from allies elsewhere.

These difficulties were recognized by the makers of the Versailles settlement. Several exceptions were made to the application of the principle of national self-determination, exceptions whose intent was to make some of the new states more economically or militarily viable, but at the cost of giving them territories containing hostile minorities. Not surprisingly, such exceptions were generally made at the expense of those who had lost the war. It was usually German-speaking minorities, therefore, who found themselves living in states in which non-Germans were the majority. Thus, a Czechoslovak state whose boundaries conformed precisely to ethnic principles would be without crucial mountain passes on three sides; without the possession of these mountain passes military defense of its remaining territory would be an absurdity. Czechoslovakia was therefore given these mountainous areas, which were, however, populated by German-speakers, before the war subjects of the Austrian emperor. Similarly a Polish state with strict ethnic boundaries would have no access to a seaport. The Poles were therefore given a corridor of territory through German-speaking areas to the port of Danzig on the Baltic. Poland now had access to the sea, but in order to provide this access German territory had to be split up and ethnic Germans placed under Polish jurisdiction.

These were among the most dramatic problems that had been produced by the Versailles settlement. All over central and eastern Europe, there were dissatisfied minorities, governments with aspirations to territory given to someone else, or borders that were so vulnerable as almost to invite the militarily adventurous to cross them. While before the war a multinational empire such as the Austrian had indeed dominated many unwilling subject national groups, it had also formed a single large economic unit, with a single market without tariffs or other barriers to trade. Many of the newly independent states that emerged from the demise of the empire now found themselves cut off from their traditional suppliers, markets, or sources of capital. For many of these states the period between the wars was one long period of economic privation, during which they never were able to regain their prewar living standards. This was complicated further by the worldwide economic depression that took hold in the early 1930s. Versailles had put to rest some grievances that had preceded the war, but only by creating many new ones. Many national groups and governments felt disadvantaged by the way in which the wartime disputes had been resolved.

The Versailles settlement had fallen between two stools. It was not a peace without victors: the losers felt very much like losers. But it was not a thoroughgoing vindictive peace either. The Germans were stripped of territory, made to suffer humiliating military occupations for a while, and required to pay huge sums as reparations. They were subject to a variety of stringent legal limits on the quantity, type, and location of the military forces that they were allowed to retain. But Germany was not dismembered. It retained an autonomous central political system governing the bulk of its prewar population and industrial resources. It remained potentially the most powerful state in Europe. Versailles had not rendered Germany physically incapable of some day mounting a military threat to the Versailles settlement.

Under the circumstances, the victors could deal with the Germans in one of two ways.[2] They could conciliate them, and try to accommodate their grievances peaceably. Or they could physically restrain them by mounting an overwhelming military superiority which would permanently prevent the Germans from overturning the settlement by force. Unfortunately, the Allies never really chose a consistent course of action. They neither conciliated the Germans nor effectively threatened them. They oscillated periodically between these two policies and, in the end, pursued neither.

Outside of Europe the attempt to apply the principle of national self-determination had not even been made. The victorious powers were left with their empires. German colonial holdings were carved up and assigned to the victorious powers without reference to any concerns of the indigenous populations. In East Asia China was rebuffed in its attempt to recapture full control of its territory. European great powers, Japan, and America were left with territorial holdings or legal rights on Chinese territory to the exclusion of Chinese governmental authority. Japan took advantage of the departure of the Germans, the diminution of Russian influence in the region after the Revolution of 1917, and the weakness of Chinese central governments to make increasing demands on China, and to seize vast areas of Chinese territory by force when the Chinese resisted. To these Japanese moves the European powers and the Americans responded with a mixture of attempts at conciliation and pronouncements of moral disapproval not unlike the inconsistent and contradictory policies that they had followed in Europe.

These failures to pursue consistent policies are often attributed to the American failure to join the League of Nations, the international organization that the Treaty of Versailles had created. The league was to be the vehicle through which international disputes could be accommodated peacefully. If peaceful accommodation failed, the league would be the vehicle by which attempts at forcible territorial change would be put down. The British and the French were prominent members of the league, yet their membership did not suffice to enable them to defend the Versailles settlement effectively. The principles of collective security underlying the league rested ultimately on the willingness of its most powerful members jointly to oppose violent attempts to change the status quo. It rested on their willingness to do so, no matter who the offender might be, and no matter what attitude members of the league might have about the merits of the dispute. The most powerful members of the league consistently refused to make their opposition to offenders effective, however, if to do so risked war with a powerful opponent, as in the case of Japanese aggression against China, or risked alienating a desired ally, as in the case of the Italian invasion of Ethiopia.[3]

We may doubt whether mere American membership in the league would have significantly changed matters, unless the United States had been prepared to pursue policies carrying major risks of involvement overseas. This was a period of great domestic opposition in the United States to external adventures, and it is hardly likely, therefore, that American domestic politics would have allowed an activist policy, member of the league or not.[4]

STRATEGIC STALEMATE AND MILITARY INNOVATION

Left to their own devices, an enduring difference of attitude between the French and the British arose over the most effective manner of dealing with the Germans.[5] For the British, after the immediate postwar anti-German xenophobia had subsided, policy was dominated by the determination never again to fight such a ground war on the continent as had been fought between 1914 and 1918. This led to a persistent search for diplomatic accommodation of German grievances. It led also to a search for means to fight the next war in a manner that would not involve repetition of the trench warfare of the last one. It was a search that engaged innovative military analysts in all the major powers.

The French had consistently held much less hope than the British for a diplomatic accommodation with Germany. The French instead placed primary emphasis upon the attempt to make it physically impossible for the Germans to overturn the settlement and again threaten France. The French hoped to do this by maintaining a military capability sufficient to overawe the Germans while preventing German rearmament, and by maintaining an alliance system that would perpetually threaten Germany with a multifront war. The French were able to sustain this approach for a few years, and indeed occupied Germany's industrial heartland, the Ruhr, in 1923, in hopes of forcing the Germans to keep up with the reparations payments they owed to the Allies under the Treaty of Versailles. But the French faced limits to their capabilities. The gap between their population and industrial capacity and those of the Germans was growing steadily. And the French could not maintain such military pressure indefinitely without the help of allies. With the United States out of European affairs, the French were dependent on British willingness to cooperate with them. Increasingly, French policy became limited to actions in which the British could be induced to join.

The French were thrown back also upon their smaller allies in central and eastern Europe, for the restraint of Germany. Unfortunately, it would become more and more apparent that the military capabilities and plans that the French had developed were incompatible with the alliance structure on which their policy was based. The French, like the British, tried to find the means to fight the next war in such a fashion as to avoid the horrible costs of the last one. The most important lesson of World War I to be drawn by the French military was that the defense had a permanent advantage. Large-scale infantry assaults would, in the future, remain far too costly to contemplate against an opponent whose society remained intact.

The solution the French adopted was to accept as inevitable that the next war would be another war of attrition, and to make such a conflict work to French advantage. The French proposed a return to reliance on fortification. In the event of an attack, the French would meet it from behind prepared fortified lines, whether these were permanent fortifications constructed long in advance, such as the famous Maginot line of massive fortifications on the Franco-German border, or field entrenchments. Behind these lines they could keep their losses minimal, while the long process of economic blockade would weaken the attacker. Unfortunately, this strategy gave them no means to support allies in central and eastern Europe, such as Poland and Czechoslovakia, in waging war against Germany on other fronts. To support their allies, the French would require an offensive capability and plans to carry the attack into German territory. This, the French believed, was, if not impossible, far too costly to contemplate. The French desired by their alliance system to threaten the Germans with another multifront war, but denied themselves the military capability to actually prosecute such a war.

For British military planners, the experience of World War I was initially understood to mean that the massive commitment of British ground forces to the Continent had been a colossal mistake. If diplomatic accommodation should be insufficient to defuse the threat of German revisionism in the future, means must be found to wage war without again committing large forces to a land war on the continent of Europe. Some of these means lay to hand in the traditional British strategy of naval blockade. Britain would simply stand off and starve out the Germans. The British gradually came to realize, however, that a strategy based on blockade alone would not be sufficient. It would not work fast enough to prevent irreversible German military victories on the ground. In the 1930s, British military planners reluctantly accepted the necessity of once again putting a major land force into northern France. In reaching this decision the British shared the French view that land warfare would remain attrition warfare, in which the advantage would lie with the defense. The British simply expected to add to the French capacity to mount such a defense and hoped that, if foolhardy temptations to mount offensives could be resisted, the Allies could simply keep their casualties minimal during the extended period it would take to wear the Germans down through blockade.

Where the British went beyond their traditional views was in their hope that the new technology of the airplane could bring the attack home to the Germans and produce a German collapse far sooner than might be anticipated as an effect of the naval blockade alone. The British were not alone in this. The military possibilities of air power had intrigued groups of military analysts in many countries since the war.[6] During the war, small German raids by gas-filled air ships called Zeppelins had managed to reach British population centers on a few occasions, dropping small amounts of explosives. Extrapolating from the death, damage, and panic these raids had caused, air power advocates claimed that mass air raids in the future could completely disrupt the rear areas of a major power and produce a collapse of its will to continue the war, well before any decision could come out of the clash of armies on the ground.

Writers such as the Italian officer Giulio Douhet were among those who announced that the aircraft would completely change the shape of war. These advocates generally shared a number of assumptions. They argued that there was no defense against aerial attacks. Aircraft would get through. Any attempt at intercepting attacking airplanes with other aircraft, or at shooting the attackers down by ground fire, would be of such marginal significance as not to have any appreciable effect on the air offensive. The air war would be decisive in character. It would constitute a return to a war of annihilation, an escape from the battles of attrition that had so characterized the years 1914–18.

The prophets of air power also had high expectations of the destructive capabilities of attacking aircraft. The attacker could destroy anything he desired, at will and with irreversible consequences. The effects of air power would be as much psychological as physical. Air power would achieve its goals by destroying the capacity of the opposing society to wage war. This meant the obliteration of the distinction between the front lines and the rear, between military and civilian, between legitimate and illegitimate objects of attack. Aerial bombing attacks, overwhelming in their character, and the sense of being powerless against them would produce panic and terror in the civil population at large. This panic would make it impossible for the opposing government to continue the war. The effects of terror would be as important, if not more so, as the direct physical consequences of the bombardment.

Douhet argued that the war of the future would open with mutual air bombing strikes against industry and population. The bomber would be the principal air weapon. The only function remaining for ground armies would be to hold off the enemy's army long enough for the air offensive to take effect. Douhet did not ignore the usefulness of measures to reduce an enemy's ability to launch air strikes. But he felt that one could not significantly reduce an enemy air offensive merely by defending oneself against it. A power defeated an air attack against itself by in turn attacking enemy planes on the ground, by destroying enemy air bases, and by destroying the technical and industrial structure supporting the enemy air force. Douhet expected that in future wars, marked by an exchange of air strikes, the advantage would go to the side able to achieve the greater destruction and disruption.

Interwar prophets of air power were not unanimous in their views of the aims that would make the air attack most effective, or of the capabilities that military aircraft should have. Some felt that air bombardment should be directed against industrial targets to affect the enemy's ability to wage war. Others thought that direct attack on the population itself, designed to create terror and pressure on the enemy government to capitulate, should be the object of the air campaign. All, however, believed that decisiveness could be returned to warfare by the use of the offensive in the new military medium; and that speed and mass would carry the day. Victory would go to the side that attacked first and in the greatest strength.

Predictions about the effects of air attacks were not confined to military analysts. Many of the assumptions that underlay their arguments were widely believed by the public, especially in Britain and France. Vivid images of catastrophic civil destruction through bombing from the air became widespread and commonplace. Indeed, in Britain, air power advocates capitalized on these popular assumptions to win independent status for the Royal Air Force as a separate armed service, and then to gain a major place in national military strategy for the RAF in the years between the wars. The interests of the RAF coincided with political forces who were attracted to air power for budgetary reasons.[7] A military strategy that revolved around the effects of strategic bombing of the other side's homeland promised to deliver victory far more cheaply and far more quickly than strategies relying on more traditional means of waging war.

The RAF proposed to place central emphasis on the strategic air offensive, with the German homeland, its population and industrial centers, as the target. This was presented, not only as the principal means to gain victory should war occur, but also as the essential military means by which war might be avoided altogether. The threat to initiate such an offensive would dissuade the Germans from taking aggressive actions that might lead to war. The RAF's Bomber Command had begun to justify its mission, at least in part, by what we would later come to call a doctrine of "deterrence." The threat to inflict massive pain and punishment behind the lines in Germany was presented as the most effective means to keep the Germans from acting in ways that the British wished to discourage.[8]

The British soon found, however, that encouraging such a popular belief in the efficacy of strategic bombing cut both ways. Emphasis on the horrible rain of destruction from the air, which the RAF would visit upon German cities in the next war, caused the British population to feel that they too would be terribly vulnerable in the event of war. When Stanley Baldwin spoke the words quoted at the beginning of this chapter, his purpose was to resist demands for budgetary expenditures on defense against an air attack on the British isles, by arguing that attempts at such a defense would be useless. But such statements reflected, and reinforced, popular fears of the effects on Britain itself of bombing in the next war.

These fears were to be manipulated by German policy in the years after Hitler came to power in 1933. The Germans encouraged and took advantage of these British—and French—popular fears of bombing by suggesting that the new German air force that Hitler had created, the Luftwaffe, was to be a force designed primarily for strategic bombing, when in fact it had been designed for quite different tasks. What the Germans actually could do to enemy civil populations was less important in creating fear in other countries than the image of ruthlessness that the Germans cultivated. The manipulation of popular fears of the horrors of a war against civilians was used to great effect by Hitler and the Nazi leadership to reduce popular support in Britain and France for any act of opposition to Hitler's prewar demands that might conceivably lead to war. While the British may have first conceived the notion of using strategic bombing as a deterrent against the Germans, the Germans realized its utility to deter the deterrers. Air forces were thus manipulated with varying degrees of effectiveness by both sides to achieve political results in peacetime, short of their actual use.

Nor was air power the only new technology whose use in warfare was the subject of intense analysis by military prophets in Britain and on the Continent in the years between the wars. The use of armored forces had of course played a central role in allowing the final Allied offensives in World War I to succeed, and it was widely expected that armor would play a major role in all future war on land. There were, however, crucial differences of opinion about the role that armor could and should play. The dominant view in most armies was that armor would be an important but not decisive addition to the infantry's striking power. Armor would be added to infantry formations and would move along with them. It would add to the foot soldier's firepower and protect him from the weapons of the defending infantry. Since it was assumed that the defender would have added armor to his own infantry formations, however, it was not at all obvious that it was likely to make a fundamental change in the character of land warfare. Indeed, the prevailing view in the French army was that armor would add to the ability of French defending forces to hold out against German attacks in a future war.

A minority of those who speculated on the role of armor in future warfare took a different and fundamentally more revolutionary view. The difference was not over buying tanks. Everyone agreed that tanks should be acquired and deployed in large quantities. All agreed that the tank would be an important part of any future land war. Where the two schools of thought differed was in how the tanks should be organized and employed in combat. Officers and analysts such as de Gaulle in France, Fuller and Liddell Hart in Britain, and Guderian in Germany[9] argued in various ways that the tank could make far more radical changes in land warfare than was admitted by more orthodox military authorities.

Partisans of a new mobility in land warfare did not oppose the distribution of armor to infantry units. But they argued also for the creation of new types of formations, composed primarily of large numbers of tanks. These formations would be accompanied by artillery and infantry, with all units motorized so they could keep up with the tanks. These armored formations could be used to recapture the initiative on the battlefield. They could punch through defense lines and rampage at will in the rear areas behind those lines. They could destroy the defender's ability to maintain and supply his forces and to control his forces in a coordinated, coherent manner. Because it would not be necessary to attack and destroy an enemy's most powerful combat units directly, attacks need not become a contest in mutual attrition; they could instead be directed at the opposing command's ability to organize and support his forces. In a way, the vision of these analysts was of a new means by which to do what William Tecumseh Sherman had done in campaigns like his "march to the sea" in the American Civil War: to achieve the destruction of the enemy's ability to wage war, without frontal attack upon its strongest points.

The use of military air power was an element in these new notions of armored warfare, but the air arm was to be used in a fundamentally different fashion than had been advocated by enthusiasts for strategic bombing. The airplane in armored warfare would be employed to assist the progress of armies on the ground—for reconnaissance, for attack on enemy forces, and for interruption of the movement of enemy forces and supplies to the battlefield. The airplane had an important role, similar to that which had been played in the past by artillery or cavalry, but it was a role to be played at or close to the battlefield itself.

As with the prophets of strategic bombing, some advocates of armored warfare claimed that they saw a way to leap over the attritional warfare at the front and, by disrupting the rear areas, to return quickness and decisiveness to warfare. Where the armored warfare advocates differed from the strategic bombing enthusiasts, of course, is that the former felt that this renewed decisiveness could be achieved by a form of warfare in which combat between armed forces would remain central. Armored columns might maneuver around and behind the principal fighting forces themselves; they might direct their attacks tactically against weak portions of the opposing line; but they would still direct those attacks against troops, supplies, and communications, all of which were identifiable components of the enemy's military structure. The partisans of strategic bombing, on the other hand, did not expect victory to be achieved as a result of combat between armed forces. The bomber's real target was not the enemy's air force. The air campaign would achieve its results by inflicting terror on the civil population and by disrupting the civil economy, whether or not it was consciously intended to make the civilian populations themselves the direct objects of attack. On the eve of war, strategic bombing dominated the outlook of at least one major power armed service: the Royal Air Force. The advocates of massed armored attack, however, remained very much in the minority everywhere, regarded with much skepticism by those in charge of planning for land warfare.

ATTEMPTS TO LIMIT ARMS

With such stark prospects as renewal of the horrors of the trenches, or the even greater horrors that might be inflicted by air power, confronting people and politicians in the major states, it is not surprising that the period between the wars offered the first modern experiments in the limitation and control of warfare. In addition to the attempt to establish international collective security through the League of Nations, a noble but quixotic attempt was made to abolish war by treaty in the Kellogg-Briand Pact of 1928. Although over sixty governments would sign this treaty, under which they renounced war as an instrument of national policy, the treaty provided no mechanism to enforce its obligations, and it had no effect on the actual behavior of states. The only experiments in the control of warfare to achieve any success were some notable attempts to limit armaments through multilateral agreement.[10] Even here, success was to prove only partial and temporary. The problems and issues raised during these attempts between the wars at limitation of armaments, however, would reappear when similar attempts were made many decades later.

Extended negotiations were conducted, and international conferences held, to produce multilateral disarmament treaties, covering both land weapons and naval weapons. The only successes these efforts produced, however, came with respect to naval armaments.[11] On land, disarmament efforts foundered on the problem of definition. Agreement could be reached easily enough on the general notion that weapons categorized as offensive should be limited, while those which were defensive could remain. This agreement collapsed, however, when discussion turned to the detailed assignment of particular weapons to these respective categories. No agreement could be reached on the question whether a given weapon was inherently defensive or offensive. Nor could all agree on a standard of comparison for the effectiveness of weapons in the field.

Was a tank, an artillery piece, an infantry formation, or an aircraft a defensive or an offensive weapon? A conclusive answer to this question depended not on some inherent quality of the weapon itself, but on the manner in which it might be employed in war. Each power chose to interpret the weapons on which it depended as inherently defensive, whereas those on which a prospective enemy depended were depicted as inherently offensive. This technical problem, the difficulty in finding some objective criteria by which weapons could be characterized as either offensive or defensive, was never resolved. Complicating this, the same weapon in one place might be more effective than in another place. A tank in open country, for example, might be more effective against infantry than the same tank in mountainous or wooded terrain. Thus, it was difficult if not impossible to agree on a standard of comparison among weapons systems.

Even if the technical problems of defining weapons as defensive or offensive and agreeing on a standard of comparison could have been settled, however, it is doubtful if general agreement could have been reached to limit land weapons. Underlying the technical issues were fundamental political disagreements about the purpose of the arms talks. For the Germans, the purpose of the talks was to achieve equality in armaments, a situation in which they claimed that neither side would be in a position militarily to threaten the other, but which the French feared would allow a new German attack. For the French, the objective was to ensure a situation in which permanent French superiority over the Germans could be maintained. This fundamental political disagreement doubtless would have prevented a successful conclusion to land disarmament talks, even had the technical problem of definition not stood in the way. When Hitler came to power in 1933, land disarmament negotiations collapsed. He made no secret of his distaste for the whole idea.[12]

In the area of naval armaments, by contrast, both the technical issues and the political context conspired for a time to produce an environment in which unprecedented agreements became possible. The principal naval powers after World War I all desired budgetary relief from the pressures of competitive naval building. Surprisingly enough, the major naval arms race in the immediate post–World War I environment was that between the British and the Americans. While the United States Navy now aspired to a fleet second to none, the Royal Navy felt equally strongly that it could not sacrifice its naval primacy, no matter who its competitor might be. At the governmental level, however, neither power felt that continued naval competition served any political purpose. Except for one disturbing scenario, neither side saw any likelihood that they might one day be enemies. The British and the Japanese remained allies under a treaty originally signed in 1902. In the postwar environment this treaty might conceivably force the British into support of Japan should a conflict arise with the United States. The British and the Americans had some motivation therefore to find a way to put an end to this alliance, but in a manner that would not encourage the Japanese to threaten the interests of either in East Asia and the western Pacific. Similar budgetary pressures and lack of a sense of immediate political requirements operated also for the smaller European naval powers—the French and the Italians—as well as for the Japanese, who saw an opportunity to put limits on the naval capabilities that others could mount against them in the Pacific. The political environment was favorable, therefore, to the achievement of an arms limitation agreement that might also enable everyone to save money.

Unlike land warfare, the character of warfare at sea was such as to make technical problems of definition easier. The ocean was a uniform medium. Differences in terrain would not make a weapon more effective in one place than another at sea. A naval weapon would be used in essentially the same fashion by all navies, whatever their larger purposes in a war. Furthermore, an objective standard of comparison seemed to exist, by which the effectiveness of one warship could be compared with that of another. A battleship of a certain weight with a certain armor and armament would be the equal of another with the same characteristics. And it would have a measurable relative effectiveness against other ships larger or smaller than it. Furthermore, it would have been difficult to evade the major provisions of disarmament agreements. Large warships were not easy to hide; their dimensions, weight, and armament could be calculated by observers with considerable accuracy. Governments could be confident, therefore, that if an agreement could be reached it would be observed, at least in its major aspects.

With the technical environment favorable to agreements, the naval powers were able to translate their common desire to save money, and their mutual assessment that political arguments for expanding navies were not compelling, into the Washington and London naval disarmament treaties of 1922 and 1930, respectively. These treaties specified ratios between the naval powers for various types of large capital ships. They even resulted in the scrapping of some ships that had already been deployed or which were under construction. While the naval treaties did help various powers to save some money, however, it is questionable whether over the longer term they had any effect in the more ambitious goal of making war less likely. Just as the naval disarmament treaties could be created only in a period in which the interests of the great powers coalesced, the rise of tensions among the powers at the beginning of the 1930s prevented further agreement or even the extension of existing treaties. A new naval disarmament conference was held in London in 1935 and 1936 in a political environment now dominated by growing antagonism over Japanese military advances against China and attempts by Japan to restrict Western influence in the Asia-Pacific region. This conference collapsed over Japanese demands for naval parity with Britain and America.[13] After this, little was left of the structure of agreed limitations on naval armaments, and the powers were legally free to build warships as they wished. Even in a situation where technical matters seemed to facilitate arms limitation agreements, therefore, it was the state of political relationships that determined the degree to which such agreements were possible. Arms limitation could not survive the revival of great power hostility.

Neither national self-determination nor collective security offered believable insurance against a repetition of World War I. In the years between the wars, therefore, fear and uncertainty about the character of the next war was rampant. Would it be another war of attrition, or could the arguments of those visionaries who claimed to have found the means to give war again a decisive character be trusted? A new war of attrition held the prospect of renewal of the endless bloodletting that had destroyed a generation. If the new technologies offered the hope of a return to decisiveness that might avoid that bloodletting, however, they also offered the prospect of new and greater horrors. Attempts to avoid answering these questions through the creation of new international institutions, or by agreed restrictions on the tools of war, fell victim to divergent attitudes toward the political and territorial status quo represented by the Versailles settlement. As political tensions rose in the 1930s and the reality of forcible territorial change reappeared, the fears remained and the questions were still unanswered. These uncertainties about the course a new world war would take allowed a fertile field for the manipulation of military instruments to achieve political advantage short of actual warfare. Those most adept at this manipulation, however, would prove to be those most intent upon overturning the state of affairs established by the Versailles settlement in Europe and Asia, and prepared to use whatever means were necessary to achieve their goals.

Return to Attrition: World War II

8

The enemy did not reckon with my great strength of purpose. Our enemies are small fry. I saw them in Munich. . . . I shall give a propagandist reason for starting the war, no matter whether it is plausible or not. The victor will not be asked afterwards whether he told the truth or not. When starting and waging war it is not right that matters, but victory.—Adolf Hitler, August 22, 1939

During the period between the wars, new methods of waging war appeared to offer novel but contradictory hopes: either to prevent future wars or to bring them to decisive conclusions once they had begun. In the event, neither hope proved justified. Attempts to manipulate the new military technologies to achieve results short of war did not prevent the outbreak of World War II. Indeed these attempts may have brought on the very result they sought to avert. The initial phases of the war did seem to offer a dramatic vindication of the claims of partisans of the new military technologies—armor and air power—that means had at last been found to return warfare to its long-departed Napoleonic decisiveness. But the war would go to even greater lengths, and would carry even greater human and material costs, than did its predecessor. The attempt to avoid a repetition of World War I resulted in a conflict that shared the first war's costliness and its bloody intractability.

THE THREAT OF FORCE TO PREVENT WAR

It would be wrong to maintain that the primary intent of those who developed the new approaches to warfare was the prevention of the next war. The attraction of these approaches was precisely the possibility of fighting the next war while avoiding the worst consequences of the last. However, a subsidiary rationale for the new military technology—especially for the airplane—was that the societal pain and terror that would result from its employment must make those inclined to take warlike actions shrink from the attempt. Both the British and the Germans attempted to manipulate the threat of bombing raids on the other's cities as a means to keep the other side from actions that would lead to war.[1] Once at war they each attempted to manipulate this threat to keep the other side from bombing its cities. Insofar as these attempts were made, however, they obviously failed. Why?

In the Nazi regime the Western powers were not faced with a cautious, conservative regime concerned with the defense of its status quo but one dedicated to territorial expansion—not only to reversing the Versailles settlement but, as we now know, to making huge new conquests in Europe and to the mass physical extermination of millions of Jews, homosexuals, Gypsies, handicapped people, and others whom it considered members of "enemy" groups. It was a regime that would make this program of mass murder a prime element in its national policy, to which it would subordinate even the military requirements of waging war. It was a regime prepared to take considerable risks to achieve its ends. Its rise to political dominance in Germany had been due in large part to the message that it conveyed to the Germans, demoralized by their loss of the first war and now struggling in the depths of the Great Depression, that German difficulties were the fault of others and that violence to rectify these difficulties was not only justified but was commendable.

It was a regime of thugs and sadists, led by a psychotic, a paranoid, who unfortunately combined that paranoia with brilliant oratorical and manipulative skills.[2] Nor should we forget the role of democratic processes in bringing this regime to power. The Nazis had received the largest number of seats of any party in elections to the German parliament in 1932 and Hitler, as the leader of the party, was offered the opportunity to become head of the government in January 1933, according to normal and legitimate constitutional practice.[3] Once in office, Hitler would quickly eliminate those groups still openly opposed to him by means of violent repression. But that such a monstrously evil regime could have initially come into being through the electoral process should cast grave doubt on the claim that democratic forces are inherently pacific.

The manifestly evil qualities of Hitler's regime often so mesmerize us, however, that we overlook the extent to which the Allies, by the inept way in which they met his growing challenge, contributed to his successes. We can never know the extent to which a less aggressive regime might have been dissuaded from the expansionist actions that led to the war. We can observe, however, that the Allies, insofar as they attempted to restrain Hitler, produced policies that were incoherent and stifled what little inclination there was in German ruling circles to oppose Hitler's expansionist moves. As discussed in the previous chapter, the French and the British together could threaten the Germans with another multifront war, the British alone with the pain and punishment of strategic bombing. Yet the Western powers' willingness and ability to employ these threats were severely limited. Because the threat of strategic bombing only accentuated the Western publics' sense of vulnerability to a German response, it was rarely made explicit. The French had formed alliances that might have made the threat of another multifront war believable to the Germans, but they did not support this policy with a military strategy that would have enabled them to assist their allies in eastern Europe in a multifront war. To these limitations the Western powers added other decisions in the years before the war that reduced further any concern that Hitler might still have had that the Allies would impose serious costs on his regime if he pursued continued expansionist activities.

By the time Hitler came to power, public opinion in western Europe was horrified by the potential of the next war. Actions by governments that seemed to make such a war more likely were highly unpopular. Hitler understood very well the domestic constraints under which Western governments operated. Although he had written as early as 1925, in *Mein Kampf*,[4] of the full scope of his ambitions for conquest in eastern Europe, he was careful when he came to power to frame each demand as an issue in itself, an issue not connected to any larger scheme. Consequently, his policies were interpreted to have ends no greater than reversal of the injustices of Versailles. Few in the West wished to believe that they were faced with an inherently expansionist regime. He played on Western fears of war and framed his demands in such a manner that, taken one by one, each demand was eminently justifiable in terms of unassailable Western liberal principles of national self-determination. Why should Germany be singled out for restrictions on the size, character, and location of its armed forces, restrictions that others did not have to accept? Why should the German government be prevented from stationing its military forces on its own territory in the Rhineland, when other governments were subject to no such restrictions? Why should the German-speaking people of Austria not be allowed to unite with Germany?

Hitler successively ignored provisions of the Versailles treaty restricting German armaments, prohibiting remilitarization of the Rhineland, and forbidding unification of Germany and Austria.[5] His actions raised only verbal protests from the Western powers, despite the overwhelming military superiority that the Allies—especially the French—still maintained over Germany. Thus, if the Allies had decided to use force against his military occupation of the Rhineland in 1936, the Germans would not have been able to resist, nor would Germany have been able to inflict any material punishment upon Allied homelands. When the German army marched into the Rhineland, its orders were to withdraw if it should encounter the French. Indeed, in many of the early crises caused by German moves, the most significant resistance to Hitler's plans came from the professional officers on the German general staff. Fully aware of the state of the military balance, they were horrified at the prospect of entering a war they knew they would lose if challenged, so they argued strenuously against Hitler's schemes. Hitler's keen sense of Western politics and psychology convinced him, however, that the Western governments would not use force to resist him.

Each time the Western powers did not forcibly resist a German expansionist move, they contributed to the erosion of any lingering German concern that the West might use armed force against some new German move in the future. The Germans were also growing militarily stronger relative to the Allies, as the German rearmament program continued. In the outcome of the Munich crisis of 1938,[6] however, Germans were justified in seeing something more than another in a series of incremental Western acts of acquiescence in the German program to reverse the Versailles settlement.

In this crisis Hitler outwardly appeared to have an argument similar to those he had successfully employed in his previous actions. Ethnic Germans in the Sudetenland had been assigned by the Versailles settlement to the newly created Czechoslovak state. Germany demanded only that the Sudeten Germans be allowed the freedom that had been given to others, to unite with their ethnic fellows across the border in Germany proper. What gave the Czech situation a character different from the otherwise similar crises that had preceded it was the role that Czechoslovakia played in the French alliance system, and the peculiar demographic geography of the Czech state. Czechoslovakia was a fairly impressive military power, with a modern army of sizable dimensions. Not only was it allied with the French but it was the linchpin of the French alliance system on Germany's eastern frontier. Without Czechoslovakia, France had no hope of believably threatening the Germans with the possibility of a war on two fronts.

The Sudeten Germans were concentrated in the mountainous regions on the border between the Czech lands and Germany. Stationed in these regions, the Czech army could mount a powerful defense. If these regions, and the passes through the mountains they controlled, should pass to Germany in the name of self-determination for their inhabitants, the Czechoslovak capacity to defend against a German attack would largely disappear and the remainder of Czechoslovakia would find itself gravely threatened by German armies that could now invade without obstacles from three directions.

At Munich the Western powers abandoned their most viable ally and military position in central Europe, agreeing that the Sudeten lands would go to Germany, in return for German guarantees of the integrity of the rest of Czechoslovakia. When the Germans a few months later tore up their guarantees and disposed of the rest of Czechoslovakia, the Allies belatedly realized that they were dealing with a power bent upon expansion, with whom they could no longer deal solely on the basis of the particular rights and wrongs of specific disputes. Hitler moved on shortly to threaten the Poles, focusing on the territorial arrangements that had given Poland access to the sea through territory dominated by German speakers. The Allied response was an unconditional guarantee of Polish territory. If Poland were attacked, the allies would go to war in its defense. Unlike their previous guarantees to Czechoslovakia, the Allies were ready to honor their commitment to Poland.

Unfortunately, the Allies now intended to honor a commitment that, from the German perspective, was no longer believable. The Poles were much less capable militarily than the Czechs. Polish territory did not present the formidable natural defensive barriers that pre-Munich Czechoslovakia had presented. The French and British had no way to support the Poles militarily. The Soviet Union could support Poland in a war against Germany, but to do so the Red Army would need to cross Polish territory. This the Poles, as concerned with Soviet threats as with German, refused to allow. The Western powers, regarding the Communist regime in Soviet Russia as anathema, were reluctant to deal with it or to encourage the Poles to cooperate with it. There was thus no way the Allies could design a strategy to fight a war that would stop a German invasion of Poland, or credibly threaten to drive the Germans out of Poland at some future date. Having seen the Western powers abandon a much more powerful position in Czechoslovakia, few Germans could now believe that the British and French were serious in their threat to go to war for the Poles, whom they could not in any way materially assist. The Allies must be bluffing; or perhaps they intended to declare war pro forma to enable them to claim that they had honored the letter of their commitments, and then negotiate a peace settlement after the inevitable demise of Poland. Germany need anticipate nothing other than a short victorious campaign in the East. The Germans did not believe that the Allies intended to embark on a new world war.

There was yet another element to this situation that justified German skepticism about Western intentions to fulfill a commitment to Poland. Before the Munich conference in 1938 the Soviet government had offered to discuss with France and Britain joint military action against Germany. The Western powers never took up this Soviet proposal. In the summer of 1939, having determined to resist further German expansion, the Western powers began hesitantly to talk to the Russians. But Western reluctance was obvious to all concerned, including the Russians, who had long suspected that the Western powers wished to divert German aggression to the east at Soviet expense, and who deduced from the Western collapse at Munich that the British and French were not serious in opposing the Germans. Stalin opted instead for a nonaggression pact with Germany, assuring the Germans that Russia would not interfere with his plans for Poland. In return Germany agreed to a Russo-German partition of Polish territory, and to allow the Soviet government a free hand in various countries bordering on its territories in eastern Europe and the Baltics.

With the Russians thus neutralized and no apparent obstacles remaining, Hitler invaded Poland. The British and the French responded by declaring war on Germany. Poland was duly conquered and partitioned in short order. In the months following, however, Britain and France surprised Hitler by not seeking to end hostilities once the fate of Poland had been sealed, acting instead as if they were serious about waging a major and protracted conflict.

Perhaps Hitler's Germany was a regime so dedicated to forcible expansion that it could not have been restrained short of actual war. If so, it is easy enough in hindsight to suggest that such action would have been better undertaken earlier in Hitler's tenure, when his regime could more easily have been destroyed. But the intentions of his regime in practice, as opposed to the rhetoric employed before its coming to power, could only be proved by events.

If we take the years 1933–39 in Europe as a test of the utility of threats of force to dissuade an aggressive power, then the results of that test must be inconclusive. Insofar as the Western powers attempted to deter Hitler from using force to overturn the Versailles settlement, they went about it in an inept fashion, demonstrating their reluctance to carry through their threats at every turn, and backing away from actions that could have been effective because of their relatively low cost. They succeeded neither in dramatically conveying a threat to inflict pain on the aggressor nor in inducing him to believe that he faced a long war that he could not win, should he not desist from his expansionist activities.

Two years later, the outbreak of war in the Pacific followed a similarly inept attempt to manipulate the threat of military force short of war to produce a change in behavior by an expansionist power.[7] Japan had been pursuing a policy of forcible territorial expansion at the expense of China since the outbreak of fighting over Manchuria in 1931. For the remainder of the decade the response of Western powers, including the United States, had been limited to strongly expressed verbal condemnation. Even after Japanese forces invaded southern China in 1937 and began interfering with Western economic interests in those regions, Western policy remained confined to stern moral and verbal outrage. Japanese expansionism was propelled by military factions that dominated the Japanese government and equated Japanese dominance of China with Japan's survival as an independent power. Western governments felt that any attempt at forcible restraint of Japan would likely provoke direct Japanese assault on their positions in the region and would, in any case, require huge military forces that could not be diverted from the growing problems in Europe.

No shift in Western or American policy was evident until the outbreak of war in Europe, when Japanese attention became increasingly directed toward the acquisition of economic resources in European colonial possessions in the Pacific, taking advantage of European concerns with events closer to home. In May 1940 the American Pacific Fleet, which had been at a temporary base in Hawaii for maneuvers, was ordered to remain there indefinitely, rather than return to its permanent base on the American west coast. Following the fall of France, the Japanese pressured the now powerless French government to accept a Japanese military presence in the northern part of its colonial possession of Indochina. The American response to these events was a series of expanding restrictions on the sale of metal and petroleum products to Japan. When Japan extended its military occupation to southern Indochina in July 1941, the American response, in which Washington was joined by London, was to freeze Japanese assets in the United States and to cut off exports of oil and gas to Japan. These expanding economic measures coincided with plans to reinforce the American military position in the Philippines, plans that were to include the stationing of a major force of strategic bombers in those islands.

American military measures in late 1941 were still, however, at an early stage of preparation. Only thirty-five heavy bombers had been shipped to the Philippines by December. Before 1941 American military analysts had not believed that the Philippines could be held if the Japanese attacked. There was now greater optimism that they could be held, but the military capabilities that might justify that optimism existed as yet only as plans. The admiral commanding the Pacific Fleet had been sacked at the end of 1940 for repeatedly protesting the continued retention of the fleet in Hawaii. He had argued that in its temporary advanced base the fleet was less prepared for hostilities than it would be if it fell back to its permanent bases in California.

American military deployments, economic actions, and diplomatic positions had been undertaken without serious understanding of the effect of these measures upon the Japanese appreciation of the situation. Japan was dependent upon foreign oil supplies, of which most came from the United States or European colonial territories in Southeast Asia. Without such supplies, not only would its economy collapse, but Japan would be unable to conduct military operations. At the time the embargo was imposed the Japanese estimated that they had approximately three years of supplies remaining at peacetime levels of operations, or eighteen months at a wartime pace. Once the American embargo had been imposed, it was understood in Japan that, unless the American government could be induced to lift it, Japan would within a short time be required either to secure supplies by force or to forfeit its capacity for independent action. Negotiations were undertaken between the two governments, and the Japanese discovered that the Americans now demanded a greater price for ending the embargo than had conditioned American imposition of the embargo in the first place.[8] The embargo had been imposed in response to Japanese moves into Indochina, especially southern Indochina. To lift the embargo, the Americans now sought Japanese withdrawal from China. To the Japanese, however, retention of their position in China was essential to their ability to play an independent role in world affairs. In any case the Americans and other Western powers had tolerated the Japanese presence in China for years, without more than verbal protest. The apparent expansion of American demands in the negotiating process gave added weight to those in Japan who argued for a military solution to the impasse.

Once the Japanese began to consider hostile action, they determined that American and European military capabilities in the region could not prevent Japan from making swift initial gains, which Japanese military planners calculated could then be defended successfully for an indefinite period. German successes in the war in Europe would make it difficult for the British, or the Americans, to divert resources to defend against Japanese moves in the Pacific.[9] Direct attack on American interests was not strictly required for Japan to occupy those regions from which it could secure the needed resources. Ample oil supplies would be available, for example, in the Indonesian islands, then Dutch colonial territory. Indeed, a grave concern in Washington in late 1941 was that Japan might strike at British and Dutch possessions alone, while leaving American interests untouched. In such an event the American administration might well be unable to force a declaration of war through Congress. From the Japanese perspective, however, American nonintervention could not be assumed. Once the Japanese had launched themselves on an attack to the south, the Americans could attack their flanks with devastating consequences. To avert this threat, the Japanese decided to attack the United States directly at the beginning of hostilities. By occupying the Philippines and dealing a major blow to the American fleet at Pearl Harbor, Japan would render the United States unable to interfere militarily in the western Pacific for some time.

As in Europe, military measures short of war did not restrain an expanding power. Indeed, these measures in Asia may well have provoked the very actions they had been designed to prevent. As a further irony, the American government in late 1941 was primarily concerned with the European theater, and had every interest in avoiding an involvement in Asia that threatened to draw American efforts away from Europe.[10] In both Europe and Asia, failure followed gross lack of coordination between military measures and other aspects of policy. In Europe the Western powers possessed ample military capabilities during the early phases of their confrontation with Hitler, but political constraints prevented them from pursuing policies that exploited these capabilities. In Asia Western negotiating demands were allowed to expand out of proportion to the military capabilities available to support them. Although the attempt to employ force short of war as a means to influence the behavior of Germany and Japan had been an important component of Western policy, the outbreak of war showed that this attempt had borne little fruit.

RETURN TO ATTRITION

With the outbreak of war the Western powers prepared for what they expected would be another war of attrition on the western front in Europe, this time fought behind the relative comfort of the Maginot line.[11] The Franco-British strategic calculus was to avoid the offensive and to defend behind lines of fortifications along the French border with Germany and behind prepared entrenched lines backed by tanks and artillery in Belgium. By exploiting the advantages that the defense offered, they would avoid the horrendous losses of the previous war, keeping the Germans at bay for the lengthy period it would take a naval blockade of Germany to work its debilitating effect on the German economy and war machine.

The Allies were determined that they would not again be surprised by another German attack like that proposed in the Schlieffen Plan. To ensure that the German right wing would not again come smashing down to threaten the Allied left, the French and the British planned to make their own left very powerful. At the first indication of an impending German advance, the Allies would swing their left wing up into Belgium to meet the German right, thus forming a short, easily defended front.

Once Hitler realized that the British and the French would not come to a settlement after the occupation of Poland, he determined that an attack in the West would indeed be necessary before he could return to his long-term goal, the conquest of the vast territories and resources of the East. The initial plans presented to him by the German general staff for an attack in the West would indeed have been repetitions of the Schlieffen Plan, precisely the sort of attack against which Western military plans were designed to defend.[12] These plans accidentally fell into Allied hands, however, and had to be changed.

What the Germans hit upon instead was to put the weight of their attack not on the right wing but in the center. It was not the location of the attack that the Germans would launch in May 1940 that was crucial, however, but the character of the attack. Nor was the mere use of tanks in the German attack crucial. Indeed, the French used as many, or more, tanks in their defense as the Germans employed in their attack. The German attack was led, however, by massed armored formations. The Germans had concentrated large numbers of tanks in their armored panzer divisions, with motorized infantry and artillery units that could keep up with the tanks. The Germans supported these armored formations with their air force. The French, on the other hand, had mostly spread their tanks out in small packets accompanying their infantry divisions.

These panzer divisions struck at the center of the Allied line, breaking through near Sedan (where ironically the French had lost an army and an emperor in 1870) and then raced for the sea. In the process they cut the supply lines to the cream of the British and French armies, which the Allies had moved up into Belgium where they anticipated that the weight of the German attack would fall. These armies in Belgium were cut off and faced with the predicament that, to regain contact with the rest of their forces, they had to attack south against the Germans. Since the Allied armies were largely World War I–style infantry armies, they did not possess the offensive power of the German panzer divisions. Thus, the Germans were able to rely on the advantages of the defense to beat back the Allies' attempt to regain their communications.

The British barely managed to get the bulk of their now almost surrounded army across the Channel. Most of the French forces trapped in Belgium were forced to surrender. The Germans then attacked the remaining French armies in northern France and quickly broke through. Paris was captured and the French government decided to capitulate.[13] Germany occupied northern France while allowing a satellite French government to continue to govern the remainder of the country from a capital at Vichy. The campaign of 1940 had thus apparently demonstrated, in the most dramatic fashion, that decisiveness had returned to land warfare. The use of massed armor, in conjunction with close support by air, could give back to the offensive that advantage which the machine gun and trench warfare had taken away from it in World War I. The prophets of armored war seemed vindicated. Swift armored thrusts had destroyed the coherence of Allied infantry forces, rendering them so many disorganized crowds of men incapable of effective military actions. Yet German victories in 1940 did not end the war, which was to continue until 1945 and would produce destruction and death in quantities even greater than the war that had preceded it.

In the Pacific, the war began with Japan's exploitation of naval air power to cripple the American battle fleet at Pearl Harbor.[14] In the great naval battles that followed, such as Midway and the Coral Sea, the fleets clashed in the best traditions of Alfred Thayer Mahan, although the aircraft carrier and the airplanes it carried had clearly supplanted the battleship with its guns as the principal element of naval power. Air power now dominated war at sea. But these great fleet battles, while yielding tactical victories, did not end the war any more than did the smashing German exploitation of armored warfare in 1940. "The Pacific War was in many respects a war of attrition."[15] The war in this theater became a long series of small advances, island landings against fierce opposition and with great casualties—landings that, with excruciating slowness, brought American and Allied forces closer to the Japanese home islands. Clearly, the new techniques of warfare had not produced, in either theater, the return to a short Napoleonic war of "annihilation" that partisans of those new techniques had hoped for.

In 1940 there had been a gross asymmetry of operational approach between the Allies and the Germans. The Germans had employed armor in mass, whereas the Allies had fought in the manner of World War I, with their armor used as support for their infantry. This asymmetry had allowed the Germans to overwhelm their opponents quickly and with little cost. It would be a while before the new approach could be assimilated and mastered by the other belligerents, but when all parties employed massed armor and close air support in the fashion of the German panzers, it was not at all obvious that the new techniques of armored warfare had shown the way to easy victories. When Germany turned upon the Soviet Union in 1941, Hitler initially made huge advances against a surprised and disorganized foe. The Russians gradually were able to exploit their huge territory to foster their growing powers of resistance and finally to force the Germans back. The great clashes of armored forces on the eastern front became a contest between German and Russian forces in their relative ability to endure losses. The Russians were eventually to prevail in this contest because, with Western aid, they could dispose of greater human and material resources. Similarly, when the Allies returned to Europe in 1943 and 1944, it was to campaigns in which resistance could only be beaten down slowly and with great cost.

Of course, the war could not have continued had the British not remained in it after the fall of France. With Britain remaining an active belligerent, eventual Allied support for Russia would become possible, as would a base from which the Americans, when they entered the war in 1941, could support a return to the Continent. The factors that allowed the British to survive and continue fighting provide additional support for the view that the new military technologies had not after all returned warfare to a condition of decisiveness.[16]

If the Germans had been able to put as few as two or three armored divisions across the Channel in the summer of 1940, it would undoubtedly have been all over for Britain. The British had managed to save most of their army in Belgium, but had to leave behind most of its heavy equipment. After the fall of France, the British chiefs of staff advised the government that, if the Germans did succeed in making a lodgment on the English coast, the British did not possess the force to drive them out. But the Germans did not come, because the Luftwaffe never succeeded in destroying British air defenses to gain that control of the air over the Channel that would be necessary to protect a landing force.[17]

Under domestic political pressure to defend the island against the German air threat, the British leadership in the 1930s had invested in interceptor aircraft.[18] These planes were designed to do what the prophets of air power had argued it would be a dangerous heresy to attempt: to destroy attacking aircraft in the air. In Fighter Command the RAF had formed an organization whose purpose was to provide such a defense. Providentially, Fighter Command just before the war had been given a powerful advantage with the development of the first forms of radar, an electronic means to detect and locate attacking aircraft. The British thus did not have to wait for observers on the ground to inform them there were German planes overhead. They were not reduced to launching their fighters in hopes that they might serendipitously come upon attacking aircraft whose movements they could not predict. Radar gave the defenders an indication of the strength and direction of enemy aircraft well before they were over British territory.

What became apparent in the Battle of Britain, which followed in the summer and fall of 1940 as the Germans attempted to establish air supremacy over the Channel, was that air battles need not have the character assumed by Douhet and the apostles of air power. Aerial conflict need not consist of decisive encounters decided irrevocably by the side that launched the first massive attack. War in the air became as much a battle of attrition as ground conflict had become. The Germans lost aircraft and aircraft crews at a faster rate than did the British. When the Germans decided that they could not maintain their attack on the RAF and shifted their effort away from British air bases and the British radar system to attacks upon British urban industrial areas, they gave up the attempt to support an invasion and, in effect, lost the Battle of Britain.

Nor was the air bombardment of urban industrial areas the panacea that prewar partisans of air power had hoped for. Fear of the effects of urban bombing had at first led each side to refrain from such raids in hopes that the other would accept comparable restraint. A German raid on London, perhaps in error, gave the British an excuse to launch a reprisal raid on Berlin to which the Germans replied.[19] The Germans and British soon began to exchange bombing raids on each other's cities. It became apparent early on that any hope for targeting precision in strategic bombing was not justified. The Germans and the British quickly realized that daylight raids subjected the bombing aircraft to unacceptable levels of losses, from defending antiaircraft fire and from interceptors. They each, therefore, shifted the weight of their strategic bombing raids to the night. Nighttime raids were highly inaccurate. The British came merely to aim for the center of a German urban conglomeration. And they often missed even that.

Contrary to expectations before the war, defense against bombers had a militarily significant effect. Strategic bombing raids did not produce their results all at once. The prophets of air power had grossly overestimated the destructive effect of the explosives that aircraft could then deliver. To affect the ability of an opponent to support his war effort, air raids must be repeated many times. If the defense could consistently destroy as little as 5 to 10 percent of the bombers on a single raid, that level of loss would make it difficult or impossible for the attacker to keep up the campaign. Strategic bombing became a contest between offense and defense. Nor did bombing of populated areas produce any significant popular pressure on governments to end the war, as Douhet had anticipated.[20] If anything, the reverse of this occurred. Among both German and British civilians subjected to bombing, the effect seems rather to have been to *increase* their support for their government's war effort.

In the last months of the war in Europe, Allied strategic bombing of Germany shifted toward attacks directed at particular production "bottlenecks" related to the support of the German war effort, targets in such areas as petroleum refining and transportation. Improved accuracy in bomb targeting and the collapse of German air defenses made such campaigns possible. Rather than attempting to destroy German industrial production directly, these attacks concentrated upon certain especially vulnerable networks through which crucial supplies must pass. These attacks did succeed in producing steep declines in petroleum production and in the production of certain weapons systems. Arguably, had these attacks continued for a short time longer, Germany might have been rendered physically incapable of carrying on the war, solely through the use of air power and before its territory had physically been occupied by Allied land armies. But the German armies collapsed before this possibility could be conclusively demonstrated.

In the Pacific, the combination of strategic bombing and naval blockade had, by the summer of 1945, severely constricted Japan's warmaking capabilities. Massive strategic bombing raids were being carried out against a defense that had become practically nonexistent. The use of incendiary bombs had been adopted to intensify destruction of the urban residential areas that were commonly found near Japanese industrial centers. It was still widely expected among those making military plans in America and its allies that these measures alone would not prove sufficient, and that a ground invasion of the Japanese home islands would be necessary to bring the war to an end. As in Germany, however, other events intervened and this expectation could not be put to the test.

Air power had its most unquestioned effect on warfare, however, in an area not anticipated by the great air power theorists. It was in the tactical sphere that air power revolutionized warfare. The use of aircraft in support of land and naval forces became essential. Aircraft took on the function previously performed by artillery, but with vastly greater range. Armies or navies that could not employ aircraft to assist them, or which could not protect themselves against air attack by the other side, were at a great disadvantage. This was the lesson of the Blitzkrieg, and of Pearl Harbor. By the end of the war, however, the central claim of the prophets of air power—that the aircraft would directly exercise an independent and decisive effect on the outcome of war—had yet to be demonstrated.

Generalizations about this war, as about all such conflicts, must be contingent. If the British had been forced out of the war in 1940, the extent to which warfare remained a contest in endurance might well have been disguised indefinitely, as it had been by the European wars of the mid-nineteenth century. If Germany had not declared war on the United States three days after Pearl Harbor, American entry into the European war might have been delayed, or even prevented. The great American industrial machine might never have had the opportunity to come into play to produce the huge quantities of war material that eventually supplied the Allied victory there. Neither of these possibilities occurred. The British survived, and American economic and industrial strength was given the opportunity to bring its weight to bear. Both on land and in the air, new approaches to waging war, which, it had been hoped before the war, would bring back decisiveness to warfare, became instead new forms of attrition conflict. Although the static trench lines that were so horrible a feature of World War I were much less prominent a feature of World War II, it still would become a slow, grinding struggle, producing tens of millions of casualties, with victory going finally to the combatants who were able, because of some mixture of superior manpower and industrial resources, to outlast their enemies.

COALITION POLITICS AND UNLIMITED WAR

In addition to the sheer reality that it had become a war of attrition, World War II shared other features with its predecessor. The distinction between the front and the rear, between military and civilian, a distinction substantially eroded by World War I, was largely obliterated. The second war, like the first, was a war of coalitions.[21] On the Allied side, the hopes of the British, the Americans, and the Russians that the conflict could be brought to a favorable conclusion depended above all on keeping the alliance together. The Western states feared the possibility that the Russians might try to make a separate peace. The Russians feared that those in the West might be tempted by an opportunity to do the same. Neither's fears were wholly unjustified.

Mutual agreement to forswear the search for a negotiated or compromise peace was the only common denominator on which the alliance could remain united. To raise the question of a negotiated peace would be to raise the question of who would gain more by such a peace, and thus would tend to pit the Allies against one another. For this reason the only war aim on which the Allies could agree was "unconditional surrender." Elimination of the evil enemy governments themselves—not some settlement that might leave those governments in place—was the only goal to which all the Allies could subscribe. Unlimited war aims were necessary not only to bind the coalition together, but to ensure that the populace of each of the combatants remained committed to bearing the sacrifices of the war. Insistence on "unconditional surrender" was a means to avoid substantive questions about the nature of the peace that would follow the war.

It is reasonable to ask whether a greater Allied willingness to contemplate a negotiated peace might have shortened the war and reduced the level of devastation that the war produced. Perhaps the opposition to Hitler among the German military might have moved earlier to depose Hitler if its officers had been assured that an independent Germany might be allowed to remain after the war. Perhaps an early explicit willingness by the Allies to leave the Japanese imperial dynasty in place might have produced a compromise peace in the Pacific.[22] It can be argued that the Allied reluctance to begin dealing explicitly, while the war still raged, with the shape of the settlement that would follow contributed heavily to the new problems and conflicts that emerged after 1945. But "unconditional surrender," or words like it, may well have been the unavoidable formula if the coalition were not to fracture, and if domestic publics—especially the American public—were not to falter in their support for the war. As with World War I, a war of attrition had the effect of rendering any significant limitation in the goals of the belligerents politically impossible. The goals to be gained expanded to meet the costs borne.

Before World War II began, many had hoped that the horrendous character war could be expected to take in the future would allow the threat of force to supplant the use of force itself as an instrument of policy. Others held out the hope that new means of waging war would eliminate the stalemate of 1914–18 and allow a return to the decisive character that they supposed war had taken in the distant past. Neither expectation would be justified by the events of 1939–45.

The attempt to manipulate the fear of war to dissuade an aggressive state from expansionist behavior did not achieve its goals, in Europe in 1939 or in the Pacific in 1941. Whether this failure was due to the inherent aggressiveness of the expansionists, to their inability to see an unwanted external reality correctly, or to the ineptness of those who attempted to dissuade them must remain uncertain. That the threat of war had failed to deter war was certain.

In spite of their dramatic early tactical successes, the new military technologies—armored warfare and air power—had not justified either the equally ardent hopes of their proponents, that they could be the means to avoid a new war of attrition or that they could serve as the vehicles for a return to decisive success in war. World War II remained, like its predecessor two decades before, a war of attrition.

Insofar as these conflicting hopes were to be vindicated at all by the manner in which World War II was at last brought to an end, it was only through the appearance of new means of destruction undreamed of by military prophets in the years between the wars.

The Emergence of Nuclear Weapons

9

We waited until the blast had passed, walked out of the shelter and then it was extremely solemn. We knew the world would not be the same. A few people laughed, a few people cried. Most people were silent. I remembered the line from the Hindu scripture, the Bagavad-Gita; Vishnu is trying to persuade the Prince that he should do his duty and to impress him he takes on his multi-armed form and says, "Now I am become death, destroyer of worlds."—J. Robert Oppenheimer, July 16, 1945

The lessons that we might have derived from World War II were made irrelevant by a development that appeared at the very end of that war. The nuclear weapon seemed at last to justify the claims of the air power advocates—claims that were not justified by the record of strategic bombing before Hiroshima. And nuclear weapons provided this ex post facto justification, by a means of which visionaries such as Douhet could not have had the slightest conception. Nuclear weapons would come to dominate plans to fight wars and to prevent them. But their limitations in either of these roles would become increasingly apparent, as had the limitations of the revolutionary transforming weapons that had preceded them. Nuclear weapons, like air power, or armor, or the crossbow, or gunpowder, would come to be constrained by the political environment within which they were required to operate by men and governments. The "nuclearization" of the strategic relationship between the Soviet Union and the United States was the consequence, not the cause, of the cold war. Nuclear weapons stockpiles would grow to immense quantities, but certainty in using them, either to prevent wars or to fight those wars to advantage, would prove elusive.

While the nineteenth and twentieth centuries have seen steady growth in the interconnections between the realm of science and technology and that of weapons, the scale of the Manhattan Project, the secret scientific and industrial program mounted in the United States during the war to produce the first nuclear weapons, was unprecedented. By the end of the 1930s, physicists had begun to realize that certain otherwise inexplicable laboratory findings might be explained by assuming that the nuclei of uranium atoms had split, or "fissioned," into atoms of lighter elements, under bombardment by neutrons. Although the transmutation of elements had been a goal of scientists since the age of their predecessors, the medieval alchemists, nuclear fission carried with it an even more dramatic possibility. When fission occurred, it released an immense amount of energy and more neutrons, which might go on to induce fission in still other nuclei. If each fission liberated more neutrons than had been required to produce it, the result might be a self-sustaining "chain reaction." Even before the war, physicists worldwide had begun to consider the theoretical possibility that the energy release from nuclear fission could be made to produce a militarily usable explosive if some way could be found to keep the fissioning mass from flying apart from its own heat before a sufficient amount of energy had been released. If this could be done, and no one could yet identify a practical route to this goal, it was recognized that the resulting weapon would be orders of magnitude more powerful than existing explosives.

Speculation about the possibility of a nuclear weapon was thus no secret among the international scientific community before the war. Germany had many of the most prominent scientists and most advanced laboratories in nuclear physics, and important experimental discoveries had been made in Germany before the war. Once the war began, it was reasonable for British and American scientists—along with the large numbers of émigrés who had fled from Hitler-occupied Europe—to conclude that, if a bomb could be produced, the Germans were well situated to be the first to produce it.

Paradoxically—but this would only be discovered after the Allies had returned to Europe in 1944—the Germans had never mounted an intense effort to produce a nuclear weapon.[1] Why they did not do so remains uncertain. Doubtless an important consideration was that the leadership was interested only in weapons that could be produced quickly enough to be employed in what they felt would be a short war. Even optimists about the likelihood that a nuclear weapon could be constructed measured the time to do so in years. Because the concepts of quantum physics that lay behind nuclear fission were not familiar notions to the Nazi leaders, they seem to have regarded the possibility of nuclear weapons as too vague, too theoretical, to be worth making a major investment in their development. Some German scientists also claimed that they deliberately minimized the possibility of nuclear weapons,[2] hoping that their government would not become interested. Many of these claims, however, are questionable and self-serving. Many of these scientists had few qualms about advancing the Nazi war effort in other ways. More likely the German scientists were genuinely in error about the quantities of fissionable materials that would be necessary for weapons, and the time it would take to produce these materials. Reliable conclusions about such matters could only be produced by a great deal of experimental work with fissionable materials. Such work was, in turn, only possible if major efforts were mounted to produce enough of the materials for experiments to be performed to determine their precise characteristics. Such efforts were never mounted in Germany. The result was that German scientists believed that the "critical mass," the amount of fissionable material that must be brought together to produce a self-sustaining fission reaction, was far greater than in fact the British and the Americans discovered it to be.

There was no way, however, that the German government's lack of interest in nuclear weapons could have been known or believed in the West. To knowledgeable observers aware of German scientific and industrial capabilities, there was every reason to believe that Germany would remain at the forefront of nuclear weapons research. When conveyed to the British and American governments, this assessment was accepted, and it was decided that an effort to produce nuclear weapons—or to prove conclusively that they could not be produced—should be mounted. Those engaged in this effort felt an overwhelming sense that they were racing against time, a fear that the barbarous regime in power in Germany might well be the first to acquire this new weapon.

The British had performed much valuable experimental work early in the war, but they were in no position financially to mount by themselves the massive scientific effort that would be necessary. Because British territory was subject to German bombing, the large industrial facilities that would be required to produce fissionable material in quantity would be vulnerable. The British therefore handed over their knowledge, and a considerable cadre of their knowledgeable personnel, to the American effort when it was mounted. (After the war the Americans would respond to this British openness by denying the British access to knowledge about nuclear weapons production, knowledge that the British had been instrumental in producing.)

The Los Alamos laboratory in New Mexico, charged with the theoretical design and production of the first weapons, was set up in early 1943. At its head was the eminent theoretical physicist, J. Robert Oppenheimer.[3] Its staff grew to include many of the most eminent scientists in the world: Americans, Britons, and European refugees from Hitler. After a series of scientific breakthroughs and extensive detailed experimental investigation,[4] they concluded that a nuclear weapon was both possible and feasible, and produced two designs for an operational weapon.[5] In vast production plants elsewhere, enough fissionable materials for the weapons were produced.

On July 16, 1945, one of these designs was tested in southern New Mexico at a site named Trinity, in a stark and barren desert region known in Spanish as the Jornada del Muerto, the "Journey of Death." It produced an explosion equivalent to twenty thousand tons of TNT. At the time of the Trinity test, there were only two other nuclear weapons in existence. One of them was aboard a ship about to set sail from San Francisco. This weapon was of a design that had not been tested. It was a uranium "gun" in which two subcritical pieces of highly enriched uranium were blasted together to form an explosive mass inside an artillery gun barrel closed at both ends.[6] This weapon was dropped on the city of Hiroshima in Japan on August 6, 1945. Another weapon existed at the time of the "Trinity" test, only as disassembled pieces at Los Alamos. This weapon was of the design that had been tested at Trinity. A subcritical sphere of the new element plutonium was squeezed by simultaneous conventional explosions around the edge of the sphere until it achieved explosive density.[7] This "implosion" weapon was dropped on August 9 on the Japanese city of Nagasaki. On the same day the Soviet Union had entered the war against Japan. Japan surrendered on August 14.[8]

Each explosion destroyed the city center and killed about one hundred thousand people.[9] They were not, however, the most destructive strategic bombing raids the American air force had made on Japan. Earlier in 1945, the Americans had made mass raids on Tokyo, involving hundreds of bombers, which dropped conventional incendiary bombs designed to start fires in the largely wooden structures below.[10] These raids had probably killed more people than the atomic bomb raids. But the destruction at Hiroshima and Nagasaki was caused, of course, in each case by a single bomb dropped from a single plane.

The destruction of Hiroshima and Nagasaki revealed the presence of a new weapon of unprecedented destructive power. In retrospect these raids are now seen as marking the opening of a new chapter in world politics, a qualitative shift in the strategic relationships among nations. Because of these events, it should not surprise us that the decision to employ the only two nuclear weapons thus far detonated in war has been subject to considerable ex post facto analysis and criticism.

It has often been argued that use of nuclear weapons against Japan was unnecessary, and even racist in motivation. This is to ignore that the German surrender, in May 1945, came before the first nuclear weapons had been completed or tested. Before the surrender, Germany had been subjected to mass conventional bombing raids that produced firestorms and other destruction similar to that produced by the first nuclear weapons.[11] Since the American motive to embark on the atomic bomb project was fear of the Germans, it is difficult not to believe that if the nuclear weapon had been ready before the German surrender, its capabilities would eagerly have been added to the destruction then being visited upon Germany.

The war against Japan, however, was still being waged in August 1945. From the perspective of decision makers in Washington, early cessation of the war did not seem a likely prospect. While the naval blockade and the strategic bombing campaign had done overwhelming damage to Japanese war-making potential, the belief remained widespread that the war could not be brought to an end other than by land invasion of the Japanese home islands. The number of casualties sustained in the assaults upon such island strongpoints as Iwo Jima and Okinawa suggested that the costs of such an invasion would be horrendous, for the invaders as well as the defenders.[12] The new weapon was now complete. To use every conceivable means to avoid the necessity for an invasion struck the political leadership as the only reasonable course of action. It should be understood, furthermore, that the revolutionary character of the nuclear weapon was not recognized at the time. Rather, use of the new weapon must be placed in the context of contemporary ideas. In the summer of 1945, the nuclear weapon was seen only as a more powerful means to carry out what had become a conventional military operation: strategic bombing directed against urban centers.

Why did those in authority not first order a demonstration of the bomb's power, perhaps on some uninhabited island? This was indeed suggested at the time. Recall, however, there were only three of the devices in existence at the time. What might follow if an announced demonstration of a dramatic new weapon was a failure? How could the Japanese be convinced that a large conventional explosive, or some other ruse, had not been prepared to fool them? If a demonstration had been tried and had failed, this would risk making the Japanese more inflexible, and thus lengthening, rather than shortening, the war. For these reasons Oppenheimer and other senior scientific advisers argued against a demonstration beforehand.

It has been argued in retrospect that naval blockade and strategic bombing would shortly have induced Japanese surrender unaided, or that the Soviet entry into the war, when added to these other inducements, would have been sufficient to do so.[13] Against these arguments must be placed evidence that powerful sections of the Japanese military leadership hoped that losses sustained in an invasion campaign against a determined defense would be so great that the Americans would at last accept terms significantly less than unconditional surrender; and that the Japanese were in fact engaged in the preparation of such a defense. Even after the destruction of Nagasaki and the Soviet declaration of war, a military coup was attempted, to keep the imperial decision to surrender from being publicly disseminated.[14] Even if the proposition that the Japanese would soon have surrendered without the nuclear bombings was in fact valid, and there can be no way of showing this conclusively, the leadership in Washington had no way of knowing at the time that the Japanese were so inclined.

NUCLEAR WEAPONS AND THE COLD WAR

Against the backdrop of the almost four decades of the Soviet-American cold war that would follow, it is often argued that American motivations in using the new weapon must not have been primarily related to the Japanese at all. The American decision to drop the bomb was instead, it is claimed, motivated primarily by a desire to intimidate the Soviet Union. Against this claim, however, we should note that, at the time of the Allied Potsdam summit conference during which the Trinity test occurred, securing Russian entry into the war remained one of the American government's principal objectives.[15] The new Truman administration had little expectation that the war would soon be over. On the contrary, every assistance was sought from the Russians. Until the Trinity test no certainty existed about the levels of destruction of which the new weapons might be capable. Even after Trinity, there could be little confidence that the weapons in the tiny stockpile then in existence could be detonated reliably under combat conditions.

Just as it is questionable, therefore, to claim that intimidation of the Soviets was the American motivation for using the new weapons against Japan, it is equally questionable to argue that nuclear intimidation was at the core of American policy in the first months and years after the Japanese surrender, and that this policy caused the cold war that would follow.[16] If the American administration did attempt such a policy of intimidation, it was notably unsuccessful in achieving the desired results; with few exceptions the Soviet Union remained dominant in all those areas reached by the Red Army in the course of World War II. If a threat was mounted, it was not a very effective threat.

At the center of power in Washington in the first months and years after the war ended, there was little confidence in the efficacy of nuclear weapons as a means to affect the behavior of other powers through the manipulation of threats. The destructive power of the first generation of nuclear weapons did not go beyond that which conventional weapons had wreaked upon the Germans and the Japanese in the war (albeit in mass raids), without decisive effect. The Russians had themselves suffered extreme losses of population, territory, and industrial resources in the war against the Germans and had still carried on. Indeed, it was assumed that, because of the Soviet Union's great size and population, bombing the Russians into submission would be a task even more difficult than it had been when undertaken against the Germans and the Japanese. Beyond this the American government had little confidence in the potential of nuclear threats in the first years after the war because it had hardly any bombs at its disposal. The weapons were literally handmade. The processes available to produce the quantities of fissionable material necessary for weapons were extremely laborious. The number of bombs in the immediate years after the war was extremely small. Indeed, the American bombing pause after the Nagasaki raid had not been a function of deliberate restraint. The United States simply had no more atomic weapons available in the theater.

How few weapons resided in the American nuclear stockpile at the end of World War II was perhaps that government's most closely held secret.[17] If there were any inclination at senior levels in Washington to employ nuclear weapons for intimidation, that knowledge of nuclear scarcity alone would have effectively squelched the inclination. Ironically, the size of the American stockpile, while carefully held from public view, was doubtless well known to the Russians, in general terms if not in specific figures. The Soviet nuclear program had not been a response to Hiroshima. Astute Russian physicists before the war would certainly have known as much about the possibilities of nuclear explosives as American, British, or German scientists. Small Russian research efforts were begun before the German attack, although a major effort could not be mounted as long as German armies were fighting on Russian soil.[18] Russian scientists knew the Allies were embarked on an effort to produce a nuclear weapon shortly after that effort had begun. That an effort to produce nuclear weapons had begun was apparent to technically knowledgeable observers at the time from the sudden disappearance from scientific journals of papers in the burgeoning field of nuclear physics, and of articles by many previously prolific scientists, now secretly employed in the laboratories of the Manhattan Project.

Most crucially—although this did not become known until many years later—it is now known that the Soviets had placed at least two espionage agents, Klaus Fuchs and David Greenglass, at Los Alamos during the war, able to provide significant information about the American atomic weapons program. The most important of the Soviet agents at Los Alamos, Fuchs was a theoretical physicist. A refugee from Germany who had fled to Britain, he had then gone on to Los Alamos as part of the British scientific contingent. Because of the manner in which Los Alamos was organized during the war—it had sensibly been decided that the work would go faster if there could be free discussion of all aspects of the project among the scientists—Fuchs would have been in a position to give the Russians a good picture of the feasibility of various methods of producing nuclear explosions, and the rate at which the American project could accumulate fissionable materials. A veteran of the Soviet nuclear program has even indicated recently that "We regarded our first bomb as an American copy." Espionage information "narrowed and focused our efforts," enabling the Soviets to avoid unproductive lines of effort and to produce a nuclear weapon some years earlier than they might have done otherwise.[19] Soviet observers would have known from that information the limits of the American ability to do them damage.[20]

The period of what might be called "nuclear scarcity" would end by 1947–48, but by then the cold war had begun. The origins of the cold war lie not in the development or early use of nuclear weapons, but in a clash of concepts of security, between the Americans (with their allies in western Europe) and the Soviets. For the Soviet Union, security from future attack demanded a belt of friendly states to its west. Stalin may have examined the idea of achieving this through the creation of a belt of states autonomous in domestic affairs but obliged to coordinate foreign and defense policy with the Soviet Union. He quickly came to the conclusion, however, that the easiest and surest way to achieve the desired result would be to impose on the eastern European states, as those states were freed from the German yoke, domestic governmental and economic systems in the Soviet image. Throughout eastern Europe, the Soviets set up governments led by local communists, forcing other political groups out of power. The Red Army was massively present in most of these areas as it drove the Germans westward, and the process was carried out under coercion from the Red Army, or under the thinly veiled threat of coercion.

Even if the Russians had no more in mind by these measures than protection of their own security, a proposition in itself not at all obvious, the measures they took seemed threatening when viewed from the West. The Soviet Union retained large military forces in the center of Europe after the defeat of Germany. Whether or not Stalin intended to push his sphere of influence further west, this presence was worrying—especially so when it was considered in combination with the chaotic state of post-war western European economies and the social unrest that this chaos engendered.

The American and Western response took the form of a policy of "containment" of the Soviets inside what had become their sphere of control in eastern and central Europe.[21] Some in the American government argued that the principal danger that followed from the social and economic chaos in western Europe was the threat of direct external Soviet military invasion. Others felt that military invasion was a lesser danger than was internal collapse in western Europe, supported, and perhaps assisted, by outside forces exploiting economic conditions. American policy to meet these dangers included the Marshall Plan and other forms of economic assistance to reconstruct the economies of western Europe, as well as rearmament. Later, in 1949, the North Atlantic alliance was created. At first this was to be simply a treaty of guarantee, in which the Americans merely pledged to come to the assistance of their European allies if the latter were attacked. Only later, after the coup that overthrew an elected government in Czechoslovakia in 1948, after repeated crises over the status of Berlin, and after the Korean War had begun in 1950, was the alliance supplemented by the North Atlantic Treaty Organization (NATO) institutional structure with its integrated military command, headed by an American general.[22]

The nature of Soviet intentions in the earliest years of the cold war has been the object of a great deal of controversy. Were the Soviets on the point of further military moves to the west? Some have argued that they were, and others that they had already acquired as much as they could manage. Still others have argued that, although there might not have been an active intent in Moscow to make further military advances to the west, this could quickly have changed if such advances had appeared to the Soviets as easy or cost-free. Did the West overreact to the threat and place more emphasis than should have been the case on military means to resist the Soviets? Many critics, including George Kennan the original author of the containment doctrine, have argued that the West emphasized the military aspects of containment too much and too soon, while ignoring its political and economic dimensions.[23] Whether or not Soviet intentions were correctly characterized, however, the widespread belief in the West that an external danger existed was genuine. From the American perspective, the Soviet Union seemed to be posing a danger similar to that posed by Germany and other powers in the past: that a single great power might come to dominate the European continent. That the Soviets combined this apparent external geopolitical danger with a ruthless domestic totalitarianism led by a dictator who had murdered millions of his own citizens, and with an economic structure widely regarded in the United States with distaste, only added to the intensity of American feelings of hostility toward the Soviet Union.

During this growing pattern of conflict between East and West, as the 1940s came to a close, the period of "nuclear scarcity" ended. The succeeding period of "nuclear plenty" was to come about for several reasons. Motivated by international tensions, the United States vastly increased its capacity to produce fissionable materials, developed techniques that could make nuclear weapons much more powerful, and facilitated the achievement of a given explosive effect with a much smaller amount of fissionable material. These techniques to enhance the power and efficiency of the existing type of nuclear weapons were developed and put into effect before the development of the "hydrogen" bomb.

In 1949, American aircraft collected air samples containing radioactive residues that showed that the Soviet Union had detonated an atomic explosive. The reaction in Washington to this revelation was largely one of panic. Most of the political leadership had convinced themselves that the nuclear weapon was a product of a "secret" known only in America, and of a fundamental American technological superiority to the Russians. It was assumed among the American leadership that any foreign acquisition of nuclear weapons was many years, if not decades, away. This confidence was not shared by most of the scientists knowledgeable about nuclear weapons development, who realized there was no such "secret" that could be divined only in the United States, and who were much less optimistic than the political leadership about the likelihood that the United States could retain its nuclear weapons monopoly for any lengthy period. The immediate result of this panic on the political level was to create great domestic pressure for a "crash" effort to produce the hydrogen bomb. Such a weapon would depend in an important way on the energy derived from the fusion of the nuclei of lighter elements. Thermonuclear fusion would be triggered by the great temperatures and pressures created by the explosion of an atomic bomb. The energy derived from thermonuclear fusion would be orders of magnitude greater than the energy produced by nuclear fission in the first atomic bombs, as the first atomic bombs had produced energy releases that were orders of magnitude greater than conventional explosives.

The hydrogen bomb was the object of great controversy among the weapons scientists. The theoretical possibility that such a device could be triggered had been known for some time, the question having first been examined in some of the earliest theoretical calculations performed at Los Alamos. Theoretically, there was no upper limit to the destructive power of a thermonuclear device. The larger the mass of hydrogen that could be made to undergo fusion, the larger the resulting explosion. No one, however, could explain convincingly how to ignite this mass in such a way that the growing heat of the fusion reaction would not immediately cause the mass to expand and the reaction to stop. All schemes concocted to produce a thermonuclear explosion seemed to require an apparatus larger than a house, and many scientists doubted that any such schemes could be made to work at all. Combined with considerable moral opposition to making weapons of such appalling potential was considerable technical opposition in the scientific community, on the grounds that the device simply could not be produced, and that the attempt to do so would constitute a vast diversion of effort and resources better directed to making larger numbers of more powerful and more efficient fission weapons.

In the end the fear that the Russians would get there first produced a political decision to do both: to go ahead with the hydrogen bomb *and* to continue development of fission-based explosives. This political decision itself would not have produced a successful hydrogen bomb. No way to produce a thermonuclear weapon was yet known. In 1951, a new method that pointed the way to a practical thermonuclear device was proposed by the physicist Edward Teller and the mathematician Stanislaw Ulam, and the American scientists at last saw a technically feasible way to proceed. Technical opposition to the development of the hydrogen bomb collapsed. The Americans field-tested the Teller-Ulam proposal in 1952; the first American test of a practical thermonuclear weapon occurred in 1954. The first Soviet test of such a weapon probably took place shortly afterward, in 1955.[24] The period of overwhelming American technological superiority in nuclear weapons had proved to be very short-lived.

The advent of thermonuclear weapons would open the prospect of horrendously powerful weapons. Weapons yielding explosions equivalent to tens of millions of tons of TNT could be constructed. The largest device known to have ever been detonated was a Soviet monster with the explosive force of near sixty million tons of TNT.[25] The efficiency of thermonuclear weapons also meant that weapons could be produced that were many times more powerful than the Hiroshima or Nagasaki weapons, but only a small fraction of the size and weight of those weapons. These new thermonuclear weapons no longer needed the world's largest aircraft to lift each one of them, as had been the case with the first generation of nuclear weapons. As these weapons were developed further, they were made small and light enough that strategic bombers could carry dozens of them. Weapons could be mounted on smaller aircraft, on artillery pieces, on rockets. The advent of thermonuclear weapons, with advances in fission weapons and in the quantity production of fissionable materials, meant that nuclear weapons need no longer be regarded as extremely scarce curiosities. With the end of the era of nuclear scarcity, serious thought about the role of nuclear weapons as military instruments began.

Until then, nuclear weapons had merely been fitted into a preexisting set of notions about strategic bombing and its role in warfare. Nuclear weapons would add a degree of destructive potential to the accomplishment of military missions that air forces had attempted throughout World War II: strikes at the urban-industrial centers of an opponent, as part of a larger military effort. Although nuclear weapons were individually immensely more powerful than previous explosives, they would not produce strategic results qualitatively different from the mass conventional bombing raids of World War II. Bombing strikes would still have to be understood as part of a larger process, in which these strikes assisted land and naval campaigns in a war that was bound to be a long and bloody war of attrition. Thus, the first reaction to the appearance of nuclear weapons was to insist that they did not fundamentally change the character of warfare.

Insofar as it might be desired to deter, to prevent an opponent from performing some undesirable activity by making a threat of punishment, one threatened the pain of a renewed war of attrition. Insofar as the West believed that it must deter a Soviet military attempt to overrun western Europe, the threat was simply to fight World War II over again. The means by which one would attempt to deter were no different from the means by which one would attempt to fight a war. This was the era of belief in the notion of "broken backed" warfare.[26] A war might open with an exchange of strategic bombing raids against cities and industry. These raids might gravely wound the contenders, but the war would in the end be decided by the maneuvers and engagements of armies and fleets against one another on the surface.

With the emergence of nuclear plenty, the idea that nuclear weapons are fundamentally different from previous explosives became increasingly important in strategic thought. In the words of Bernard Brodie, one of the first of those to think seriously about the implications of nuclear weapons: "Thus far the chief purpose of a military establishment has been to win wars. From now on its chief purpose must be to avert them. It can have no other useful purpose."[27] While the manipulation of military means short of war to change the behavior of others had by no means been absent, as we have seen, in previous decades, it was now made the central role of military force. And in nuclear weapons the means necessary to prevent war became fundamentally different from those which might be used to fight one.

All the developments that have taken place since the dawn of the era of nuclear plenty, developments in strategic thought, in nuclear weapons technology and in the military structures to control those weapons, have been concerned above all with Brodie's definition of purpose: how best can nuclear weapons be used to avert, and deter, war? Yet paradoxically these developments have also been driven by a persisting hope that the distinctiveness of nuclear weapons could somehow be cast aside, that nuclear weapons could somehow be restored to a useful role in waging war. In Clausewitzian terms, the hope has persisted that nuclear weapons could somehow be used in war to achieve some political object worth the cost and risk. These are conflicting desires: to prevent war and, at the same time, to develop the means to fight wars for meaningful goals. Whether strategists have found a way in the succeeding forty-five years to fulfill either desire with any assurance remains an open question.

Until well after the emergence of nuclear weapons, these devices, for all their horror, were of subsidiary importance in shaping the international political and strategic environment. They had not revolutionized warfare when they were introduced in World War II; at best they had added an additional increment to Japanese motivations to surrender. They were not the cause of the beginning of the cold war; although the cold war did spark an intensification in their development and production. The advent of nuclear bipolarity and nuclear plenty, however, seemed to carry revolutionary implications.

The most dramatic effect of nuclear plenty was how it apparently validated, after the fact, the claims of Douhet and the classical air power theorists twenty-five years previously. Such destruction could now be wreaked upon an enemy that attack from the air, by itself, could win a war. The destruction would be swift and complete. It would be carried out above all by the offensive; the side that could mount such an attack would win the war. Nothing else is necessary. The mere threat to inflict such overwhelming destruction and pain would be sufficient to prevent a potential aggressor from making a move.

Americans thus came to rely for deterrence on their ability to mount catastrophic attacks against the Soviet Union. As the implications of the first Soviet fission tests grew, however, followed by Soviet development of thermonuclear weapons, other considerations became more and more apparent. As the Soviet stockpile increased, Americans came to understand that others could do to them what they threatened to do to others. The importance of surprise, of getting in the first blow, was crucial. Pearl Harbor, for Americans, had been a great national trauma. The overwhelming fear was that the United States could be faced with a new Pearl Harbor on a cosmic scale, a surprise attack that could be successful in a way Pearl Harbor had not been. The great nightmare was that such an attack at the beginning of a war could end it too; that if an attacker could destroy the most important American military striking forces at the beginning of a war, the defenders would then be at the aggressor's mercy. As nuclear weapons were developed, and as the potential for war between nuclear-armed states arose, the awful possibility dawned that the conditions for Clausewitz's theoretical concept, "absolute war," might have turned into realities: "If war consisted of one decisive act, or of a set of simultaneous decisions, preparations would tend toward totality, for no omission could ever be rectified."[28] America would never have the opportunity to bring into play the great industrial machine that had ultimately enabled it to prevail in World War II.

To make the American threat to inflict punishment upon an opponent believable, it was thought necessary to make certain that American forces could not be surprised, disarmed, or otherwise rendered incapable of carrying out such a threat. It was necessary also to face the question of the manner and amount of destruction that would be required to keep an expansionist Soviet Union from engaging in behavior that the United States might desire to prevent. The calculus of deterrence demanded that the United States have the size and kind of nuclear forces that could visit upon the Soviets sufficient damage to deter them from undesirable behavior; it was necessary also to be certain that the United States would retain forces capable of doing this even after the other side had done its worst against the American homeland. Increasingly elaborate rules were developed to specify the practical requirements of this calculus. But the calculus would not yield the firm and reliable conclusions demanded of it. The practical requirements of nuclear deterrence and defense would remain ambiguous, and this ambiguity would fuel a huge expansion in nuclear arsenals on both sides.

Nuclear Weapons: Uses and Uselessness

10

What in the name of God is strategic superiority? What is the significance of it, politically, militarily, operationally, at these levels of numbers? What do you do with it?—Henry A. Kissinger, July 3, 1974

The development of nuclear strategy represented an attempt at a Jominian solution to a problem that was essentially Clausewitzian in nature. Rules were propounded, and calculations elaborated, designed to ensure with certainty the successful accomplishment of a wide range of national goals through the deployment, threat, or even use of nuclear weapons. Rules and calculations for nuclear weapons attempted to ensure the deterrence of undesired actions by prospective enemies, as well as to ensure success in warfare. Nuclear arsenals grew in size and complexity in hopes of finding ways to ensure that these weapons could serve as useful and reliable instruments of national policy. But the outcome of the conflicts and crises that were played out under the shadow of nuclear weapons turned far more on the attitudes, expectations, perceptions, and behavior of the antagonists, than they did on sophisticated calculations about the results of the hypothetical clashes of armed forces in battle. It would gradually come to be realized that, in any attempt to use nuclear weapons to prevent undesirable actions, or to bring about desired behavior, the intangibles of politics and history would likely overwhelm the purported certainties of what were proclaimed to be the rules of the nuclear game. In the end it would be understood that the area in which nuclear weapons could reliably produce desired political effects was far narrower than partisans of the new weapons had hoped, at the outset of the period of nuclear plenty.

The military objective of nuclear strategy in the United States was most commonly defined, in Brodie's terms, as "deterrence." The political premise that underlay American military programs from the late 1940s was that the United States again faced an expansionist power that might employ its military capabilities to do grave damage to American interests. The American objective was to use nuclear weapons to deter behavior by others—and, in particular, by the Soviet Union—that might lead to war. The assumption was made that the threat to inflict sufficient pain upon an opposing state would suffice to prevent it from carrying out undesirable actions. Given a successful use of military force in this deterrent role, strategies to achieve political objectives by the engagement of armed forces in direct conflict against the forces of an opponent would be irrelevant.[1] Behind this straightforward statement of objective, however, lay several problems that introduced ambiguity into the calculus.

How much damage and pain were sufficient to guarantee deterrence? How should that pain and damage be measured? Drawing upon the experience of strategic bombing in World War II, the assumption was made that successful deterrence could be equated with an ability to destroy a given percentage of an opponent's industry, its urban centers, or its population. In the case of an opponent with strategic offensive forces of its own, however, deterrence should be measured also by the American ability to destroy its means to attack the United States. Perhaps, however, a fanatical government might accept the destruction of cities, population, and industry in order to destroy a political and economic system it held to represent the utmost in evil. When dealing with such an opponent, some argued that the criteria for successful deterrence must be measured ultimately in the threat to destroy those things that a potential enemy's leaders held most dear. Thus deterrence could be measured in an ability to destroy the leadership directly, or to destroy its ability to continue to exercise control over society.

Further complicating this search to codify the requirements of successful deterrence was the great range of actions that the threat of nuclear weapons might counteract. What might be required to deter one action might not be sufficient for another. Presumably the advantages an attacker hoped to acquire by engaging in undesirable activities would determine the level of pain that it would regard as acceptable to acquire those advantages. Deterrence was therefore assured if the defender could inflict pain above that threshold. The specific context in which a deterrent threat might be made also would be of great importance in determining the level and type of pain that would suffice to make the threat effective. Thus, an attack in cold blood might be successfully deterred with the threat of less pain than would be required to dissuade an attacker moved by the emotional passions of a crisis.

If the only undesirable activity that the United States wished to deter was a major military assault on North America, it seemed that the requirements of successful deterrence were straightforward and easy to assure. The designers of military strategy in the age of nuclear plenty were asked to develop military mechanisms to achieve much more than this, however. The cold war had begun in Europe over the mutually incompatible security requirements of East and West. From the outset of the nuclear era, therefore, it was desired that nuclear weapons be put to use in preventing the Soviet Union from attempting further advances in Europe, and perhaps in remoter geographical areas, such as northeast Asia. The deterrent role of nuclear weapons was to be expanded to cover threats to the physical security of American allies and of other places deemed of special importance to American security.

Undoubtedly American capabilities to inflict pain and destruction upon the Soviet Union were immense, once thermonuclear weapons were introduced into the stockpile in quantity during the 1950s. To those designing nuclear strategy, however, deterrence remained uncertain. After the Soviet Union itself acquired a supply of thermonuclear weapons, the difficulty was understood to lie not in making the threat, but in convincing the prospective opponent that the threat would be carried out. The side that had been threatened would not, of course, remain passive but would threaten reciprocal damage. American strategy came to center upon the problem of convincing an opponent that Washington intended to carry through on a threat, knowing that it would bring down upon American heads destruction and pain beyond historical experience.

One way to enhance the believability of a threat to employ nuclear weapons is to find ways to use these weapons in a manner that would make some apparent sense in terms of policy, that would bring gains outweighing the destruction that would result from their use.[2] If a nuclear power's only threat was to take actions that would hurt the threatener as much or more than the threatened, it would not carry believability. Paradoxically, the search for a believable threat to employ nuclear weapons would lead strategists away from purely deterrent roles for nuclear weapons and toward the exploration of methods of employing nuclear weapons in the fashion in which weapons had historically been most commonly employed: as a means of combat against opposing armed forces.[3] The attempt was thus made to find types of nuclear weapons, and means of employing those weapons, that a power might rationally and believably employ against an opponent's military forces, in the expectation of gaining advantage through their use. Those who made this attempt were guided by a denial of Brodie's distinction between deterrent weapons and those which offered success in combat. They believed that deterrence was enhanced insofar as one could demonstrate a capability to prevail in war, or at least to frustrate an opponent's ability to prevail. If I could discover a means by which employing nuclear weapons could offer me an advantage, could leave me better off than not employing them, my threat to employ them would gain plausibility.

Several levels of "nonstrategic" nuclear weapons were designed and introduced into the forces. These weapons were generally, but not always, less powerful than the "strategic" weapons designed for use against the Soviet homeland. They were mounted on vehicles designed for strikes at less than intercontinental distances: on aircraft, rockets, warships—even artillery pieces. If a conventional war should begin in Europe, such weapons might be employed against the armies attacking from the east. They might attack targets in eastern Europe directly related to the Soviet ability to mount an attack to the west. Such targets could include troop and armor concentrations, road and railway junctions, and airfields. These weapons might assist the defenders in repulsing the attackers. Use of these weapons would demonstrate resolve and commitment, thus making the threat of more extreme action, such as strategic nuclear strikes against the Soviet Union itself, more believable. Yet because these nonstrategic nuclear strikes had not emanated from American territory and would not impact upon Soviet territory, they would not automatically provoke a massive Soviet attack on North America. If nonstrategic nuclear use stopped a Soviet attack in Europe, and yet did not produce Soviet strikes on the American homeland, such nuclear use might thus, it was hoped, gain advantages worth the risks of employment.

Various arguments were made to justify this approach. Weapons based in Europe, or close to it, would be more vulnerable to being overrun by Soviet forces. The threat to "use" the weapons gained plausibility, if the alternative was to "lose" them. If these weapons were distinct from American strategic forces, their use would not be mistaken for a general attack on the Soviet homeland. For such reasons it was argued that an American threat to use nonstrategic nuclear weapons might be believed in circumstances, such as an attack against Europe in which American territory was not directly threatened, where a threat to employ strategic forces would not be believed. A war might involve the exchange of nuclear strikes, yet remain in some important sense limited.

But these limitations would depend on Soviet willingness to cooperate, and to draw the same distinctions as the Americans. If the Soviets felt, however, that they were disadvantaged by a situation in which nuclear exchanges occurred but remained limited in ways defined by their opponents, and if they felt they might gain by raising the stakes, what incentive would they have to allow those limits to remain?

Furthermore, a conflict that remained limited from the American perspective might, from the perspective of America's allies, be indistinguishable from the ultimate catastrophe. Europe might be destroyed in what was for the Americans a "limited nuclear war." Western European governments allied to the United States saw little advantage for themselves in a military strategy that sought to exploit a limited nuclear exchange. In the event of a Soviet attack short of a direct strike upon the American homeland, the allies pressed the United States to rely on the very threat of immediate and massive strategic nuclear attack that the Americans had feared would be unbelievable to the Soviets. To the Europeans such a massive threat meant, instead, that no conflict at all could start, however limited it might be.

In the first years of nuclear plenty some hoped that nuclear weapons might be a panacea, that they might allow the United States to prevail in conflicts of any size or degree of intensity, in any geographic location, with any opponent.[4] Military planning came to be increasingly based upon the assumption that nuclear weapons would be used early in any conflict and as an integral part of battlefield operations. Considerations such as those we have just mentioned, however, made the wisdom of such approaches questionable. Once nuclear weapons had been used, it became doubtful that a nuclear-armed opponent would respect limitations on their use that might run to its disadvantage. And those allies who might be offered protection by an American ability to start a limited nuclear war saw the cure as far worse than the disease. Thus, the utility of nuclear weapons for deriving advantage in situations other than those involving the most massive of threats to the interests of the nuclear powers came to be doubted.

In the early 1950s, the United States based its strategic nuclear forces on a large fleet of heavy bombers stationed on North American and overseas airfields. This force could wreak great destruction on Soviet urban-industrial targets. As Soviet nuclear forces grew, however, American strategists concluded that American forces had to grow also. The target list, those things whose destruction provided the criteria for successful deterrence, grew as the Soviet nuclear forces grew. The Americans concluded that successful deterrence required that they possess the means to attack and destroy Soviet nuclear forces before those forces could be employed against the United States. Furthermore, the Americans came to realize that their bomber fleet, powerful as it was, was still vulnerable to attack if the other side struck first.

The Americans were thus driven to increase the numbers and accuracy of their forces, because they now defined deterrence as requiring the destruction of a host of new targets. Most of these targets, such as nuclear missiles, were more difficult to locate and destroy than were cities and industrial complexes, and thus had to be struck with greater precision. The more weapons one side possessed, the more the other side felt it needed.

Both sides diversified the vehicles that carried their nuclear forces. They were each driven away from bombers and toward ballistic missiles because the latter were considered less vulnerable to attack than were bombers on the ground. To destroy a missile buried in a reinforced silo in the ground would require a much more accurately aimed strike than would be needed to eliminate a bomber. Each side began to mount a portion of its ballistic missile forces on submarines, because the location of submarines could be hidden more effectively than that of ground-based missiles. It would thus be even more difficult to attack submerged submarines in the open oceans.

Each thermonuclear superpower also explored the possibility of defending its territory and its military forces against attack.[5] World War II had suggested that defenses against bombing were important, contrary to the assumptions of Douhet and the early prophets of air power. At various times in the war, the Allies and the Germans were each able to mount defenses against incoming bombers that were effective in stopping the attacker. If the defense could degrade the attacker by 5 to 10 percent on each raid, it would soon make it impossible for the attacker to continue. Such defenses were mounted using interceptor aircraft and antiaircraft artillery. But the immensely greater magnitude of the new explosives in the age of nuclear plenty complicated any attempt at such a defense. Attrition rates like those achieved against bombing raids in World War II would no longer be sufficient. On the other hand, developments in electronics and in rocketry meant that incoming attackers could be located and defending interceptors guided to their targets far more precisely than previously. This led to the hope that the defense could be made far more effective than even the most successful defense in the previous war.

The United States first attempted to mount defenses against Soviet strategic bombers in the 1950s, employing a combination of interceptor aircraft and antiaircraft missiles. As ballistic missiles replaced the heavy bomber as the principal vehicle for the delivery of strategic nuclear weapons, American authorities increasingly turned their attention to the development of means to intercept these missiles. Throughout this time the Soviets pursued a parallel effort, involving probably the commitment of even greater resources, in developing defenses against attack. Both powers began to deploy defenses against missile attack at the end of the 1960s. These deployments were capped by the Anti–Ballistic Missile (ABM) Treaty concluded in 1972, and by a protocol to that treaty concluded in 1974, which further restricted permissible deployments. The Americans deactivated the single ABM installation that they were allowed in 1976. The Soviets, and now the Russian government that succeeded the Soviet Union, retain an operational ABM system for the defense of Moscow.

President Ronald Reagan initiated a new research effort, termed the Strategic Defense Initiative (SDI), in 1983, to develop defenses against ballistic missiles that would rely on new means to destroy incoming missiles and that might include elements based not on the ground but in space. The avowed purpose of this new program was initially to create an effective defense for the entire American homeland, although this would later be scaled back to a defense of American retaliatory weapons. No weapons systems developed under the aegis of SDI, however, have so far been deployed, more than a decade after the program was inaugurated. On taking office in 1993, the Clinton administration sharply cut back the program and further narrowed its scope.

By the late 1950s the United States had a defense against bombers that, by the standards of World War II, would have been regarded as phenomenally successful. Had an attack against North America then been launched, the defenders might have been able to destroy perhaps half of the incoming bombers. Even if the remaining bombers had been directed to military targets far removed from population centers, however, the resulting death and destruction would have been beyond all historical precedent in the American experience. If more than a few of the remaining weapons had been aimed at urban areas, the very structure of American society could not but have been threatened. In any case, as the Soviets increasingly shifted the weight of their offensive forces to ballistic missiles, defenses against bombers became more and more irrelevant.

The defenses that the superpowers have thus far deployed against intercontinental ballistic missile attack consist of ground-based radar detection and tracking systems that would guide ground-based nuclear-tipped interceptor missiles to the vicinity of incoming targets. Against small numbers of attackers, this method might work with a high degree of effectiveness. But if the attack were a large one, and the attacker deliberately set out to confuse, swamp, or blind the defenders, the attack would get through. The defense would possess only a limited ability to distinguish a real nuclear warhead from a harmless decoy. The attacker could "blind" the defense radar with a high-altitude nuclear explosion just before the main attack. Missiles directed against targets on the ground immediately after this "precursor" explosion might remain undetected until too late. While methods were devised to increase the adequacy of the defense against such attempts, improved methods of attack swiftly restored the primacy of the offense. It would be wrong to argue that the problem of defense against ballistic missile attack was an insoluble problem. Indeed, quite robust defensive systems were devised. All attempts at defense against missiles, however, ran up against the difficulty that it was cheaper for the attacker to add an increment to the offense than it was for the defender to add an increment to the defense.

Any useful defense required an attacker of limited resources unable to swamp the defense, or an attacker who would agree to limit his own offensive arsenal. To mount a defense that might meaningfully reduce the potential damage to the defender's society required the cooperation of the attacker. Defenses might be devised that would reduce an attacker's ability to destroy a defender's strategic forces, buried deep in concrete, or difficult to locate; but it would remain easy for an attacker to wreak catastrophic damage to cities and the civil population, because cities and populations were "soft," vulnerable targets, easy to destroy.

The SDI program of the Reagan and Bush administrations followed the plot lines of earlier attempts at strategic defense. The SDI program emphasized new methods for destroying incoming warheads by means other than nuclear explosions. Intercept vehicles might be guided to their targets by means that allowed accuracies unimagined in previous decades. Conventional explosives, subatomic particle or electromagnetic beams, or even direct collision could all be used to destroy the attackers. Vehicles orbiting in space would remedy the deficiencies earlier attempts at strategic defense encountered in identifying, tracking, and destroying incoming warheads.

The SDI program was begun largely as a response to wide erosion of confidence, on both the Right and the Left, with the threat to inflict death and destruction beyond measure that lay at the root of continued reliance on deterrence.[6] The program aspired initially to mount an effective defense of the cities and people of North America. It was soon realized, however, that SDI had not surmounted the problem that had bedeviled earlier attempts at strategic defense. It remained cheaper to increase the size of the attack than to add to the capabilities of the defense. Before its demise, backers of the SDI program had been driven to justify it as adding to the defense of weapons, not people, and to the survivability of the offensive retaliatory forces. SDI had come to embrace and enhance the very notions of deterrence that its advocates had originally hoped to surmount.

During the years in which the cold war dominated international politics, the nuclear forces of the superpowers increased. The weapons and delivery systems making up these forces became more diversified and complex. The doctrines and operational procedures governing the deployment and use of these forces grew more elaborate and sophisticated. All these changes were motivated by the belief that deterrence required something other than the sheer ability to inflict vast damage on the other's society. If both sides possessed such a capability, it was feared that a threat to unleash it would not be believed, because of the damage that each feared he would suffer in return.

In hopes of restoring believability to nuclear threats, a variety of tactics were developed. Thus plans were laid to limit strategic nuclear strikes in various ways. Such strikes might be limited in number, in geographical extent, in the category of targets struck. Attacks might be limited to military forces, while sparing urban and industrial concentrations. Attacks might be directed narrowly against the opponent's ability to control its military forces, or against its political leadership's continued ability to dominate its society. The ability to mount limited strikes required not only new plans but often specially designed weapons and new vehicles to carry those weapons. The threat of limited attacks such as these would, it was argued, be more believable than the threat to launch an all-out nuclear attack, with the inevitable all-out response. In all such cases it was reasoned that the opponent might prefer to yield politically rather than risk the greater destruction that would occur if it ignored the limits in its response.

If one side could demonstrate an ability to come out ahead in such an exchange, perhaps the ability to "win" this sort of war would make the threat to start it more believable. Even this would depend, however, on the losing side continuing dutifully to play their hand by the rules that their opponents had laid down for them. There could be no guarantee that a disadvantaged government would not reject these rules and resort desperately to greater levels of destruction. Even if there was an inclination to observe the rules of a limited conflict, moreover, how could there be any assurance, in the destruction, chaos, and confusion of a nuclear exchange, that what had been intended as a limited nuclear attack would be understood and perceived as such? No refinement of nuclear strategy could exorcise the fear that, once such an exchange had begun, Clausewitz's "friction" would cause it to get out of hand and escalate to more and more catastrophic levels of destruction. The quest for absolute certainty for the deterrent threat eluded its seekers. It was this quest, however, that drove continual expansion in nuclear forces and constant experimentation in force structure and doctrine.

Much as nuclear strategy did not show the way to victory in the event of war, it failed also to show how desired outcomes in political bargaining short of war could be achieved. Building forces that could "win" some hypothetical nuclear exchange was driven by the belief that these capabilities would affect the actions of states in peacetime, and would especially influence how crises were resolved. In a conflict between a nuclear-armed state and one without such arms, the former could clearly dictate terms at will to the latter. In a dispute between nuclear-armed states, the advantage would go the party best able to climb the "escalation ladder." The parties to a crisis would continually calculate their positions relative to one another as they expected them to be after a hypothetical nuclear clash. If a party felt it would be disadvantaged by a limited exchange, but stood to gain by removing the limits and initiating a more extensive exchange of nuclear blows, it would be tempted to do so. If a party feared that it would lose by allowing escalation to proceed to the next level, it would give way to the demands of its opponent. Nuclear crises would be like cosmic hands of poker. Each side would compete with the other in a competition to raise the stakes. The side that could be more certain of coming out ahead, if the stakes were raised, would possess "escalation dominance."[7] It would be more aggressive and assertive in its behavior and, in the end, the "dominant" side would prevail.

Thus, according to this view, the details of nuclear weapons balances mattered. Numbers of nuclear weapons counted, as had numbers of prenuclear weapons. The advantage would go to the power with the larger nuclear arsenal, as the advantage had gone to the power with the bigger battalions in prenuclear times—a power gained politically by maintaining larger forces. Who was ahead in the nuclear arms race cast a shadow on all sorts of relationships among states—especially relationships among the great powers—short of actual violence.

The years of the cold war did not, thankfully, provide occasion for empirically testing theories about the course of a nuclear war. They did, however, provide numerous occasions for testing notions of the influence of nuclear weapons on state behavior in conflict situations short of nuclear war. Even in situations of conflict between nuclear-armed states and nonnuclear states, nuclear weapons have been far from an invariably effective coercive tool. As early as the Korean War, before the notion that nuclear weapons were peculiarly illegitimate weapons had become general currency, the United States was not able to dominate the behavior of its nonnuclear North Korean and Chinese opponents. Although it might be argued that the Soviet Union implicitly offered nuclear protection to its communist allies, the Soviet stockpile in those years could not have been other than rudimentary. Nor can it be conclusively demonstrated that an American nuclear threat was instrumental in bringing China and North Korea to agreement on ending the war in 1953.[8] In other early cold war crises, supposed American nuclear threats were either not unambiguously delivered or, if delivered, were without notable effect.[9] The possession of nuclear weapons, even when the fear of nuclear retaliation was absent, did not have the political utility that the theory of "escalation dominance" implied.

Nor did nuclear weapons balances have a straightforward influence on the outcome of conflicts between nuclear-armed states. Evidence about this influence is ambiguous.[10] The greatest of the Soviet-American encounters, and the one where the powers came closest to war, was the Cuban missile crisis of 1962.[11] This crisis occurred in the context of a considerable American superiority in nuclear strategic forces. Perhaps one of the Soviet motives in putting shorter-range missiles into Cuba was that these missiles, once operational, would reduce the imbalance between the superpowers in nuclear weapons with which each could target the other's territory.[12] Once the attempt had been discovered, the Russians' awareness of strategic inferiority may have been part of the reason for their withdrawal. But accounts by most of the American participants in the crisis, however, do not suggest that the Americans took any great comfort from their own nuclear superiority, or even that they took this superiority as such into account. More important to American leaders, as they later recounted their views, was the realization that the United States had a military superiority in conventional armaments in the region. Moreover, in recent years it has been revealed that the Cuban missile crisis was less the clear-cut victory for the United States than it had seemed to be at the time. In spite of an overwhelming American nuclear superiority, a secret bargain was nevertheless struck, linking American removal of short-range missiles from Turkey with the Russian removal of missiles from Cuba. In the greatest crisis of the nuclear age, the power possessing an overwhelming nuclear superiority did not feel comfortable in relying on that superiority to gain a great political advantage in the crisis, even though the inferior nuclear power may have been somewhat constrained by its knowledge of that inferiority.

In crises over Berlin in 1958–59 and 1961, on the other hand, local superiority in conventional military forces was in the hands of the Soviet Union. The Soviets also possessed a quantitative superiority in nuclear weapons in Europe. The Soviet Union thus probably would have "won" a nuclear exchange in Europe, had one taken place. In the end the Soviets refrained from pressing their advantage, however, perhaps because of their recognition that the Americans took the issue extremely seriously, however unwise such an attitude might be for the Americans, from the perspective of the nuclear weapons calculus. Whatever those who calculated might conclude, there remained a residual risk that nuclear exchanges might begin and, once begun, go beyond the original locale of the conflict. No one knew what might happen then, how far the destruction might reach. There developed a mutual fear of stepping close to this unknown, no matter how the elaborate technical calculations about nuclear exchanges might actually turn out.

On those occasions where relations between the superpowers became tense, it was difficult to see a clear relationship between the state of the nuclear balance and political behavior. In 1973, the United States successfully employed a change in the readiness status of its nuclear forces, a change that the Soviets would know had occurred, as a means to underline the seriousness with which it viewed the threat of direct Soviet intervention in the Arab-Israeli war of that year. By this time, however, the United States had clearly lost the overwhelming nuclear superiority it had possessed during the Cuban missile crisis a decade before. So Soviet behavior in 1973 cannot be explained by the nuclear balance.

Although fears grew in the United States at the end of the 1970s that the Soviets had attained nuclear superiority, or intended to attain it, the Soviets never exploited this supposed advantage in matters at the center of their relationship with the United States. Insofar as the Soviets expanded their influence during this period, it was only in areas at the periphery of that relationship—in the Third World, where there was an enlargement of the Soviet conventional military presence. At most points in the cold war, the relations between the superpowers could be understood far better on the basis of the history and stakes of the specific disputes at issue, the domestic politics of the superpowers, and their relative degree of commitment, than they could on the basis of the nuclear weapons balance between the United States and the Soviet Union.

THE SOVIET NUCLEAR EXPERIENCE

Soviet thinking about nuclear weapons broadly paralleled the movement of American thought, arriving after a while at similar conclusions, although by a different route.[13] The Soviets cast their analysis in terminology that differed from that of the Americans. Soviet strategic analysts never formally embraced "deterrence" as an objective, in the sense it had been embraced by the American strategic community, or the notion, as a final goal, of relying for protection on inducing an opponent's reluctance to attack. Soviet thought was more oriented to the notion that ultimate reliance should be placed on one's ability to *prevent* an opponent from carrying out undesirable action, no matter what his state of mind might be. Soviet strategic thinking on nuclear weapons was more Clausewitzian than American thought. The Soviets never ceased to look upon nuclear weapons as means to achieve political objectives. They consistently felt that nuclear balances mattered and attempted to find ways to use nuclear weapons to achieve political results in warfare. But, still, the Soviets found that devising ways of achieving those aspirations in practice was as elusive for them as it was for the Americans.

In the immediate postwar period, a time of American nuclear monopoly and overwhelming superiority, the official Soviet view was that nuclear weapons were not as important or as revolutionary as had been claimed in the West. Nuclear weapons only scared those who had weak nerves. The decisive factors in warfare remained what Stalin called "the permanently operating factors," which had led the Red Army to victory over Germany in World War II. One cannot, of course, judge the extent to which these public statements were actually believed by policy makers. In any case, it was to the Soviets' advantage to deny the importance of a weapon in which their opponent was so obviously superior.

As the Soviets developed their own nuclear forces, capable of threatening, first, the western Europeans and then the Americans, Soviet writers came to analogize nuclear weapons to a giant artillery barrage that would be fired at the beginning of a war. Much as the artillery traditionally had been used to "soften up" the other side before a ground attack, massive salvos of nuclear weapons would begin the next war, destroying the enemy's forces, infrastructure, and communications, as prelude and assistance to the occupation of territory by the advancing Red Army. The analogy with artillery provided the rationale for military demands for large numbers of weapons. The size and power of the nuclear force necessary to achieve the desired level of destruction in the barrage were largely a function of the number and character of the enemy targets that must be destroyed.

As the Americans toyed with a variety of doctrines attempting to limit nuclear war, the Soviets loudly denied that a nuclear war, once begun, could be limited, except by attacks against an enemy's forces, attacks that would render the latter incapable of further response. The Soviet presumption was that, once a nuclear war had begun, each side would attempt to do its worst, not necessarily by attacking the other's cities directly, but by launching the most powerful attacks possible against all military means that enabled their enemy to wage war. Although horrendous destruction would result, Soviet military analysts insisted there would still be a winner. The forces of socialism would survive to build the new world. Again, we cannot know the extent to which this was believed, but it was clearly in the Soviet interest to deny to the Americans any advantage from adopting sophisticated limited nuclear attack strategies. The Americans during this period may have possessed a greater capacity to launch discriminating, selective limited nuclear attacks. The Soviet response was that the attempt at discrimination would be to no avail. Once a war had begun, the Soviet Union would ignore all attempts at limitation and respond with all the force of which it was capable. During the 1970s and 1980s, as the Soviets acquired quantitative parity or even superiority in nuclear weapons, they began to hint that limited nuclear exchanges were indeed possible. Now, of course, they asserted that they could prevail in any such exchange, and they wished to convey to the Americans the pointlessness of attempting one.

While the Soviet military was exploring the possibilities of limited nuclear exchanges, doubts came to be openly expressed, at the level of the political leadership, that there could indeed be a winner in such a conflict. By the late 1980s, these doubts were even being expressed in military literature. In fact, a group of senior Soviet officers emerged who argued that quantitative advantages in nuclear weapons could not be used to bring about useful political results. These officers were arguing for a reorientation of Soviet military doctrine and resources, away from huge numbers of nuclear weapons and toward new conventional military technologies, when the Soviet Union collapsed in 1991.

On both sides of the Soviet-American relationship, there was a feeling that nuclear weapons were tremendously important in influencing behavior, but neither side was sure it could reliably predict how. There was little dispute that the sheer levels of destruction of which these weapons were capable would be likely to preclude major direct nuclear attacks in cold blood against a nuclear power. But what was a major attack? And what was a direct attack? What of an attack on one's neighbors? And how much was enough to deter? When these questions were raised, the level of certainty was further depressed. And the usefulness of nuclear threats against nonnuclear attacks was subject to even greater doubts. This is not to maintain that anyone could be certain, either, that nuclear weapons were completely useless in any of these contingencies. The difficulty was that deterrence was ultimately a speculation about psychology, about human behavior in situations without historical precedent. In spite of elaborate attempts to do so, there was no way to achieve certainty about such speculations. That nuclear weapons were powerful deterrents and coercive tools was certain. But what the content and limits of that deterrence or coercion might be could only be the object of guesswork.

Whether a nuclear war could remain limited, whether the details of nuclear balances had a predictable impact on state behavior in peacetime, were questions that could not be answered. All that could be said with certainty was that any situation that implied the remotest possibility of nuclear weapons use produced the utmost caution in all the participants. After decades of thought and effort, no one knew for certain either how to design the perfect deterrent or how to make nuclear weapons serve the ends of policy.

Just as armor and air power had failed previously to transform war, so nuclear weapons now failed in turn. For all of their terrible destructive potential, and indeed because of that very potential, nuclear weapons were unable to produce either a return to decisiveness in warfare or a new certainty in achieving the goals of policy short of war. Revolutionary change in the means of violence had once again failed to revolutionize international politics itself. Paradoxically the growing realization of the inadequacy of nuclear weapons as a tool for achieving policy goals would lead to the reemergence of interest in the use of conventional warfare to gain what nuclear weapons could not achieve.

The Revival of "Conventional War"

11

Therefore, the only rational course is to develop a strategy capable of limiting warfare and fighting limited wars successfully.—Robert E. Osgood, *Limited War*

Nuclear weapons remain the most dramatic and ominous military feature of the world since 1945. Since Nagasaki, however, no nuclear weapon has been fired in anger. There has been no direct armed conflict between the great powers. Until the outbreak of fighting among the successor states to Yugoslavia in 1991, there had been no interstate wars in Europe, where the cold war began. This is not to suggest, however, that the world as a whole has enjoyed an especially pacific international environment since World War II. In spite of the overhanging presence of nuclear weapons, many wars have been fought, often involving powers possessing such weapons. The frustrations introduced by nuclear weapons and the difficulties nuclear weapons states have faced in finding ways to make these weapons serve the ends of policy have not resulted in the disappearance of force from international politics.

That wars can be fought by nuclear powers, yet without nuclear weapons use, illustrates the ease with which wars historically have been limited. That weapons have been available but not used, that levels of destruction that are possible have not been reached, are commonplace occurrences in the history of international conflict. Thus, the wars of the eighteenth century were more limited in goals and effects than the wars of the seventeenth. In this case, the reasons were probably to be found in the politics and sociology of the states of Europe. Poison gas was not used as a weapon of war in World War II, though it had been used extensively in World War I. Neither gas nor biological warfare was used against coalition forces in the recent war in the Persian Gulf, though the Iraqi government had previously used gas, against both Iran and its own Kurdish citizens, and apparently had large amounts of such weapons still on hand. It would therefore be wrong to maintain that the existence of a weapons capability mandates the inevitability of its use. The likelihood of specific limits depends rather upon whether decision makers anticipate that use of a given weapon or technique in warfare will give them an advantage. If they believe it will, they will be tempted to use it. If they believe that the consequences of its use cannot be predicted, however, or if they feel there is a good chance its use will leave them worse off, then they will be reluctant to use it.

In the nuclear age limited wars have been the norm. Not only have many violent encounters taken place in which the most destructive weapons have never been employed, but wars have been limited in other ways also, at least from the perspective of the great powers fighting them. There have been geographical limits, in which the parties accepted that conflict should not extend beyond certain areas. There have been limits on weapons used, on targets attacked, and on the goals for which wars were fought.

The variety and extent of these limits bear some relationship to those of the European eighteenth century, another era notable for the degree to which political groups carried on violent conflict with one another, yet without engaging all the military means of which they were physically capable. Yet insofar as similar results were reached in each of these eras, they were produced by different conditions. Indeed, many of the conditions that prevailed in the period since 1945 should, if viewed though eighteenth-century lenses, have had effects opposite from those actually produced; these conditions should have driven wars away from limits rather than toward them.

A fierce ideological hostility between its two camps characterized the cold war. During the periods in which mutually abusive rhetoric was at its height, attitudes came close to those of the religious wars of the seventeenth century. Each side proclaimed the other the embodiment of evil. Each side argued that it was contending for principles of transcendent importance, for the realization of which any sacrifice was justified. In such a struggle no neutral position was morally acceptable. The cold war was dominated by a conflict between two great power blocs. In this it was unlike the eighteenth century, characterized by fluid relationships among many powers. In the eighteenth century, today's enemy might be tomorrow's friend; during the cold war, the belief prevailed that today's enemy would remain tomorrow's enemy. These features of the cold war, ideological hostility and bipolarity, should arguably have exacerbated conflict, not produced an environment in which wars were limited. Nevertheless, the "hot" wars of the cold war era were limited wars.

No doubt the presence of nuclear weapons at least partially explains the limited character of warfare in the period since 1945. A degree of caution and circumspection was present whenever one nuclear power contemplated a conflict with another nuclear power or its client. In the first such encounter, the Korean War, it was not at all obvious from the outset that nuclear weapons would not be used.[1] That they were not was due to the combination of a lack of lucrative military targets for their use and the small size of the American nuclear arsenal. There was fear in Washington that Korea was merely a diversion, an attempt to draw American attention and assets away from the European theater where the main attack would surely take place. Concern that the United States not "waste" any of its limited supplies of nuclear weapons in a secondary theater of operations, rather than concern at the damage that the tiny new Soviet nuclear arsenal might be able to inflict in response, accounts for the American failure to use its nuclear arsenal in Korea.

Whatever the initial reasons for nonuse, Korea established a precedent and expectation of nonuse, an expectation that the growing reality of a Soviet nuclear arsenal only reinforced in the ensuing years. That nuclear weapons use was not compatible with limited war was not universally or immediately accepted, however. In American strategic thinking much consideration was given to employing nuclear weapons in conflicts that would nevertheless remain limited in other dimensions, such as in geographic extent. This approach foundered on doubt that nuclear weapons use of any sort could remain compatible with other limits.[2]

While relying on the nuclear deterrent in their mutual relations, the Americans, the Soviets, and later the other nuclear powers also wished to prevent additional governments from acquiring nuclear weapons. This discouraged the acknowledged nuclear powers from openly or directly employing nuclear threats when not directly engaged against other nuclear powers. When threats were made, they were hinted at, rather than openly and directly delivered.

An environment was thus established in which it was expected that wars could be waged without running serious risk that nuclear weapons would become involved. This meant that those engaged in strategic thinking had to return to many earlier questions about the role of war. Would such conflicts allow victors to gain decisive advantage? Or would they merely become wars of attrition again, without clear-cut results? Under the new conditions of the cold war, could nonnuclear warfare still be a useful instrument of national policy? The American experience of conventional warfare since 1945 suggested that, even for the United States with its unparalleled resources, the attempt to employ military power remained fraught with frustration.

KOREA: THE FRUSTRATIONS OF LIMITS

The Korean War established the possibility that superpower involvement in conflict would not necessarily involve nuclear war, or general worldwide war.[3] Operationally and tactically, the Korean War was similar in many respects to World War II. Politically, it was very different. The division of Korea was a legacy of the manner in which World War II had ended. What began as an administrative convenience designed to facilitate the surrender of Japanese armies on the peninsula (the Russians accepting Japanese surrender north of the thirty-eighth parallel of latitude, and the Americans south of it) soon hardened into a political division, even though all sides proclaimed their loyalty to the principle that Korea should be unified. The war began when the North Koreans moved south in June 1950, with the aim of forcibly unifying the peninsula, perhaps deluded into believing that the Americans would not resist such an attempt.

Korea was a war between large armies, fought in open terrain, not unlike that in Europe. It was a war that had "fronts." Usually, fighting occurred along particular lines where the armies met. One could measure the progress of the war by following the movement of these lines on the map. The Americans could exploit their superior resources in firepower, mobility, and the use of air power in support of land operations, the very characteristics that had distinguished their military operations in World War II. Furthermore, the South Korean regime, to whose assistance the Americans came, had wide support in its own territory as the embodiment of Korean national sentiment.

Where the Korean War was unlike World War II, however, was in the political constraints placed on military operations. Throughout the war, the political leadership in Washington was concerned about the possibility that the war might spread—that the Chinese or the Soviets might come into the war, or that the Soviets might use Korea as a diversion to draw off American forces preparatory to a major Soviet attack in Europe. For these reasons, the Americans wished to avoid a major effort in Korea; they feared that the Korean conflict might escalate into a general war on the Asian mainland, leaving the United States without the resources to deal with a war in Europe.

In World War II, American war aims had been effectively unlimited and simple: the elimination of enemy governments in Germany and Japan, and the occupation of their territory. In Korea, American aims were more limited. These aims expanded and contracted during the war, but they never could take on the simplicity of the war aims of World War II. After that experience, the notion of limited war aims was a distasteful novelty for most Americans.

The initial American aim (for which, through a fortuitous turn of events, the sanction of the United Nations Security Council had been obtained) was to use military forces to drive the North Koreans back to the thirty-eighth parallel, the demarcation line that had previously existed between North and South. The defense against the North Korean attack was not wholly a unilateral American military effort. Although the United States dominated, and an American officer had overall military command, the South Koreans were able to mount a progressively more effective defense, and contributions from a variety of other states were included in the effort. The Americans and their allies fought in the name of the United Nations.

In the early days of American involvement, the situation was desperate. American and South Korean forces were forced back to a small bridgehead around the southern port of Pusan. This bridgehead was successfully defended, however, and the Americans were soon able to outflank the North Koreans by a surprise amphibious landing on the west coast at Inchon. United Nations forces then proceeded to advance north rapidly, in the process destroying the now largely surrounded North Korean forces.

Until this point, the military objective of the coalition led by the United States was simply to destroy the other side's military forces, and its political objective was limited to ejecting North Korea from the South, restoring the situation that had prevailed before the initial attack from the north. With military success, however, came the temptation to expand this political objective. With the North Korean army largely destroyed, the Americans decided to cross the thirty-eighth parallel and march north to the Chinese border. Effectively, what this meant was that the coalition had expanded its war aims, from merely defending the government in the South by ejecting the invaders to destroying the government that had launched the invasion, thus unifying Korea politically by force of arms.

As allied forces approached the Yalu River, which formed the major part of the Korea-China border, the newly established Communist regime in Beijing grew concerned. While the Chinese Communists may not have been involved in the original decision by the North to invade the South, they were not keen on the notion of an American army approaching the major industrial regions of China in Manchuria, just across the Yalu. Furthermore, having just come to power themselves, they were not happy with the precedent that might be set by the Americans destroying a nearby Communist regime. The Chinese government began sending signals through diplomatic channels that they would not stand idly by while the North Korean regime was destroyed.

The American leadership either did not see these signals or, if they did see them, did not believe them. The new Chinese regime had not recovered from the great costs and efforts of the civil war that had brought it to power. The American assessment was that the Chinese hints at intervention must therefore only be bluffs. To this political assessment was added the military appreciation of the commander on the scene, General Douglas MacArthur, who believed himself to be one of the greatest military geniuses of all time and assiduously encouraged others in that belief. MacArthur and his staff asserted there was no sign of the Chinese in Korea, and no indication that they would intervene. Complete victory for his command, MacArthur believed, was at hand.

While MacArthur was making these statements, Chinese armies were entering Korea in great force. When the Chinese attacked, they threw the U.N. forces into headlong retreat. The allies withdrew below the thirty-eighth parallel, recovered, advanced, and were able, after great effort, to reestablish a line slightly to the north of the parallel. China was not capable of the technological sophistication that the Americans had at their disposal, but Chinese commanders could throw large numbers of troops seasoned in the Chinese civil war into combat. For the remainder of the war, each side limited itself to small-scale actions that produced minor movements in the front lines, but there were no further major advances.

The war remained, throughout its course, limited in its military means and its geographic scope. Allied forces used air power to attack targets throughout Korea but not beyond Korean territory. The Americans and their allies did not attack troop columns or supplies in Chinese Manchuria or in the Soviet Union. Neither the Americans nor the Soviets employed nuclear weapons. The Soviet Union, while supplying its communist allies, did not openly send military forces into hostilities. The Chinese and North Koreans, for their part, made no attempt to attack the sources of U.N. air attacks: American aircraft carriers at sea, and American air bases in Japan.

Considerable pressure emanated from MacArthur, and from many domestic political quarters in the United States, to eliminate these military limits. MacArthur urged the bombardment of Chinese bases and industrial concentrations in Manchuria. These pressures were resisted by the American government and allied governments, often with considerable difficulty. After U.N. forces managed to stabilize the front against the Chinese, the allied governments reverted to their earlier policy goal: simply to defend the South. Lengthy negotiations to end the war were begun.

MacArthur's demands, and those of his supporters, were of course not only to eliminate the restraints on permissible military means. They also constituted demands that coalition policy goals revert to elimination of the North Korean regime, and unification of the peninsula under the government in the South. MacArthur asserted that, "In war there is no substitute for victory."[4] The only legitimate goal in warfare is the destruction of the enemy's forces. While he may have thereby shown his ignorance of a good deal of military history, he struck a chord with the American public. After the experience of the two world wars, this was the popular image in the United States of the normal course of warfare. If a war was worth fighting, it was worth fighting by all means necessary. If it was worth fighting, this could only imply that the opponent was absolutely evil and should be completely destroyed. If these conditions were not met, the sacrifices that waging the war must require could not be justified.

MacArthur supported his demands by declaring that, if the Americans and their allies threatened to bomb Chinese territory, the Chinese would desist from their intervention. Even if they did not, there was no risk that the Russians might enter hostilities actively. The American administration saw no reason to run the risks that these assertions might be wrong. The administration did not again allow itself to be diverted from the limited political objective of restoring the status quo in Korea before the initial North Korean attack. It did not again allow the military effort to expand beyond what was necessary to accomplish that political objective.

The armistice negotiations were lengthy. Because no cease-fire was observed, considerable casualties occurred while negotiations continued and the fighting remained stalemated. Public distaste for fighting a war that did not have as its objective a clear-cut victory was an important reason the Democrats were swept out of power by the election of Dwight Eisenhower in 1952. Eisenhower made vague threats to widen the war—there is some claim that he threatened use of nuclear weapons, although this has not really been shown to have been the case[5]—and, after further negotiations, an armistice was finally reached in 1953. Perhaps the Chinese and the North Koreans came at length to the conclusion that the Americans were not prepared to abandon the regime in the South, in spite of the casualties the Americans continued to take. The settlement left American forces stationed in Korea but effectively stopped the fighting, except for occasional small incidents. It left the two Korean governments in place.

In its wake the Korean War left great dissatisfaction in the United States. Fighting a limited war that ended not in victory, or even a demonstrable gain, but in a negotiated settlement that left things as they had been before the war began was frustrating, but at least the Korean War did end. Once the armistice was signed, Americans no longer suffered combat casualties. Because of the nature of the war, with its conventional armies and its identifiable fronts, no means existed for the other side to resume military pressure, except by renewing conventional hostilities, with all the costs that would entail. Behind the armistice

lines, a stable, if not idyllically democratic, political structure developed
in the South.

VIETNAM: THE LIMITS OF FORCE

A decade and a half after the Korean War ended, the United States
became actively involved in the Vietnam War.[6] Inevitably, the Korean
conflict provided for American strategists a model to be followed in
Indochina. For all that the Korean War had produced only a compromise peace, it had at least come to a clear-cut, and lasting, conclusion.
In prosecuting the Vietnam War, however, the Americans ignored the
differences that existed between Korea and Vietnam. Korea and Vietnam differed in the stakes of the conflict, in the character of the battlefield, and in the political context within which the war was fought, most
notably in the domestic political position of the regimes the Americans
found themselves defending.

Although the American government may not have fully realized this
before hostilities began, the fate of Korea had been of considerable
geopolitical importance. This importance derived from its proximity to
Japan, the foundation on which the United States government intended
to erect its postwar alliance structure in Asia. Had the Americans not
chosen to defend the South Korean regime, this would have been
highly unsettling to the Japanese (who have historically regarded Korea
as essential to their own security). Japanese enthusiasm for the alliance
with the Americans would have declined if the Americans had thus
chosen to leave them vulnerable. Furthermore, the nature of such an
American geopolitical stake in Korea was easily understandable to the
Chinese and to the Soviets.

In Vietnam, on the contrary, the American leadership could never
quite decide precisely what the nature of the U.S. stake was. Few seriously argued that Vietnam was intrinsically important for its own stake.
At first, it was argued that the United States was engaged in stopping
Chinese expansionism, and that the Chinese were merely the instruments of the Soviets. This argument wore thin, however, as evidence of
the Sino-Soviet split mounted in the 1960s. As it became increasingly
obvious that great hostility bordering upon open warfare existed between China and the Soviet Union, the notion that the Chinese were

functioning as clients of the Soviet Union became increasingly fanciful. Indeed under the Nixon administration the Americans actively exploited the Sino-Soviet split diplomatically to put pressure on the North Vietnamese. Supporters of the war effort ended by making the argument more and more abstract. America was committed because it was committed, not because of any intrinsic importance that Vietnam had for American interests. Having engaged themselves in this place, the American leaders convinced themselves that they would suffer loss of credibility everywhere else if they did not hold on.

> They were frequently vague as to what they were containing; sometimes they stressed China, other times Communism, and still other times wars of liberation in general. In any case, they believed that to withdraw from Vietnam would encourage disorder throughout the world and drastically weaken American influence. Men of action and achievement, leaders of a nation with an unbroken record of success, they were unwilling to face the prospect of failure.[7]

For the North Vietnamese, the stakes were understood to be much higher. They conceived that their national existence itself was at stake. The North Vietnamese made the fundamental political judgment, which was to be borne out by events, that, because of the disparity between themselves and the Americans in what was felt to be at stake, they would be able to outlast the Americans. They realized that they could never drive the United States out militarily. Almost always, whenever it came to a direct clash between military forces, the North Vietnamese suffered tactical defeats. But they judged that American domestic opinion provided a weak point on which they could play. They could make the Americans tire of the conflict.

It has often been argued that the American administration could have remedied this situation if the president had prevailed upon Congress to declare war, or to provide the functional equivalent of such a declaration, unequivocally tying American representative institutions to the prosecution of the war and thus presumably ensuring enduring domestic support.[8] However, major dissent has been present in most of America's wars, including wars formally declared by Congress.[9] For example, New England was on the point of secession during the War of 1812. Widespread opposition prevailed in the northern states to the Mexican War, which was perceived in the North as an instrument of the slaveholding southern states for the purpose of expanding their territory. If the Spanish-American and Mexican wars had not produced decisive, swift, and dramatic victories at minimal cost, if they had resulted in stalemates, domestic opposition would have eroded the American willingness to continue fighting. If the United States had declared war in Vietnam, and the war had then taken the same course that it in fact did, there is little reason to believe that domestic opposition would have been any less than it was. The North Vietnamese calculated that, because of their greater stake in the war, time would give Hanoi more advantages than it would give Washington. And they were proved correct.

The differing character of the battlefields in Korea and Vietnam flowed from their respective geographical features. Korea is a peninsula with riverine boundaries on the north. Supply routes for North Korean and Chinese forces were restricted to a few highly vulnerable bottlenecks. The Americans, with their command of the sea and the air, could be highly effective in isolating Korea from the mainland of Asia. Vietnam, on the other hand, is not a peninsula or an island. It is geographically an intimate part of the mainland. America's opponents could be supplied across an arc of almost 240 degrees: from the north, the west, or the south. The North Vietnamese were never restricted to a few bottlenecks, as the North Koreans and Chinese had been.

The terrain in the two wars differed substantially in its military implications. The terrain in Korea did not provide much cover for the movements of military forces. It also restricted the type of military operations in which the combatants could engage. While there were some unconventional or guerrilla operations in Korea—small bands of men behind the lines trying to make life miserable for the enemy's soldiers—this sort of operation was relatively unimportant. The North Koreans and the Chinese were essentially restricted to conventional military operations, carried out with large units.

In Vietnam, no such restriction existed. Because of the terrain, which provided much greater opportunity for cover, and because of the political situation of the regime that the Americans were supporting, the other side was able to change its tactics up and down the spectrum of violence at will, ranging from guerrilla tactics to conventional operations. Consequently, the North Vietnamese and their allies in the South were normally able to retain the initiative. If American or allied forces were tactically successful at some level, this could not readily be exploited, because opponents were able to respond by shifting the level of their operations. If the Americans were successful in conventional operations, their enemies were free to dissolve their large units and revert to guerrilla operations. Unlike Korea, America's enemies in Vietnam had an effective alternative to waging conventional operations.

The northern forces in Vietnam may never have been able to achieve more than momentary and localized tactical success by this ability to keep shifting their operations. What they did achieve was negative and political in character. The Americans could never effectively deprive their opponents of the means to keep hurting allied forces and the regime those forces were protecting.

The political context within which the Vietnam War was fought differed in important ways from the context of the Korean War. The French had ruled Indochina since the 1880s, interrupted only by Japanese occupation during World War II, departing in 1954 in the wake of military defeat. The South Vietnamese regime was the successor to institutions that were the creation of this French colonial occupying power. The regime in the South was never able to shed the burden of its origins. The government in the North, on the other hand, grew out of a movement that was the principal focus of the nationalist opposition against France.

Korea had been ruled by the Japanese from 1910 until the end of World War II. In Korea, the Americans' South Korean allies were themselves heirs to an anti-Japanese, anticolonial heritage. Their credentials in this regard were at least as good as, if not better than, those of the opposing regime in the North. This gave them considerable domestic political legitimacy. Given this political strength, and the difficulty of conducting guerrilla operations in Korean terrain, the Americans found themselves defending a regime there that could only be seriously threatened by conventional military operations.

If we admit the distinction between Vietnam and Korea, could the Americans nevertheless have achieved military success if they had fought the war in Vietnam differently, if they had thrown off the restraints under which they operated?—restraints on the military means employed, on the geographic scope of military operations, on the targets against which they directed their attacks? Or would this approach have only produced increased risks, without bringing the United States any closer to military success?

As the war went on, President Nixon did indeed remove some of these constraints, which had been put in place by the Johnson administration. He carried the ground war into Cambodia and allowed the regime in Saigon to carry it into Laos. He expanded the scope of the air war against North Vietnam, mined the harbors in the North, and struck directly at Hanoi. The basic character of the policy driving strategy under the Nixon administration, however, remained the same as it had been under Johnson. Military force was to be used not to destroy the North Vietnamese capability to make war, but to coerce Hanoi into accepting a political settlement of the war that would ensure the indefinite independence of the South.

The American political leadership refrained from ordering the destruction of the North Vietnamese capability to make war for reasons arising from foreign policy and domestic politics. Externally, there was a fear that threatening Hanoi's capability to make war would be perceived in Moscow and Beijing as a threat to the very existence of the regime in Hanoi. This perception might, in turn, trigger direct intervention in the war by Russia, or China, or both. If the Russians did not intervene directly, they might engage American interests elsewhere on the globe. From a domestic perspective, there was a widespread belief in elite circles in Washington that the American people would not be prepared to bear the immense costs of a war in which Beijing or Moscow had thus intervened. They would not be prepared to accept the casualties or the material costs.

Whether or not there was direct intervention from the outside, however, it remains difficult to see how threatening Hanoi directly could have produced a decisive success for American arms. Even if there had been no outside intervention, a policy of striking directly at Hanoi could have produced a favorable outcome of the war only on the assumption that the United States would be prepared to sustain its military commitment indefinitely. Whatever the damage the Americans could inflict on Hanoi's political and military infrastructure, that damage would be reversible whenever the military pressure was lifted. In such a situation, Hanoi could, at any point, have made political concessions to gain relief or a reduction of the American presence. Once this had been achieved,

Hanoi could then have resumed its activities against the regime in the South at some lower level of violence. The Americans would not have had any effective sanction against this, short of maintaining a permanent garrison. It is difficult to accept that the maintenance of such a large-scale military commitment could ever have been politically feasible for the United States.

It might have been possible to sustain a minimal presence, especially if casualties were low and intermittent, as with the American presence in Korea since the Korean War. However, the nature of the terrain and the political background to the conflict would have required a large force, sustaining continual losses. There is little in American history to suggest that Americans would have been prepared to pay that sort of price indefinitely, with no end to such a commitment in sight. It is thus difficult to see how the United States could have achieved permanent political success in Vietnam, even if Washington had been prepared to fight what Clausewitz would have called a war for unlimited purposes—a war to destroy the regime in Hanoi.

Could they have fought the war they did fight—a war for limited purposes—in a more effective way? There are those who believe that a strategic defensive could have led to military success.[10] Such an approach would have concentrated upon protecting territory and population in the South. It would have combined the creation of barriers to facilitate interdiction of the battlefield with limited tactical offensives into the North to break up enemy concentrations. The object of such a campaign would have been to fight a war of attrition, as in Korea, in the belief that their enemies would wear down faster than would the Americans. Eventually the other side would be persuaded, by their inability to penetrate the screen and by the continued drain on their resources, to accept a political settlement in which they would give up their military attempts in the South.

Here again, interdiction of the battlefield would have proved difficult to accomplish because of the nature of the terrain and the relatively small quantities of supplies that would have been required to sustain guerrilla operations in the South. In any case the Americans could only have been successful for as long as they were prepared to keep up the pressure. Time is the crucial ingredient in such a contest in attrition. Which side is favored relatively by the passage of time? There is little in the proposal for a strategic defensive that provides convincing evidence that the Americans would have been able to hold out longer than the North Vietnamese—unless the latter cooperated by allowing the Americans to keep their casualties low.

The Americans entered the Vietnam War because of a mistaken assumption that they had an important stake in the outcome. Once at war, because of the history of the conflict and of the parties to it, because of the nature of the terrain and the battlefield, and because of the problems imposed by America's own domestic political structure and attitudes, it became a conflict in which Americans could not have hoped to achieve enduring political success, no matter how they conducted their military operations.

"DESERT STORM": RETURN TO DECISION?

Both Korea and Vietnam exhibited the frustrations encountered, even by a superpower, in effectively employing conventional war to achieve the goals of policy during the cold war. Both wars proved to be contests in attrition. In Korea the United States was forced to abandon its early expansive goal of changing the political order in the peninsula. It settled for the lesser goal of restoration of the status quo as it had been before the war, but even this achievement could only be bought at a high price in casualties and at major political cost to the administration in power. In Vietnam the Americans were unable to sustain the level of military effort necessary to attain even such a lesser goal. Operation Desert Storm, the Persian Gulf War the United States waged at the head of a coalition against Iraq in 1991 appears, however, to have been a different sort of conflict.[11] Coalition goals were achieved in full. Indeed, it seems almost to represent the archetype of the form Americans have thought a war properly should take. It was short, and it involved the massive application of force. It was, for coalition forces, astonishingly low in casualties.[12] Once the goals for which the war was undertaken had been accomplished, hostilities ceased. The great bulk of coalition forces left the area after the cease-fire, the political situation on the ground then remained stable and the remaining forces have not suffered appreciable casualties. Does Desert Storm represent a harbinger? Does it suggest that conventional warfare in the nuclear age has recaptured its potential for decisiveness as an instrument of policy?

Much of how this war was planned and conducted flows from the

American military leadership's assessment of the lessons of the Vietnam War. The dominant view of Vietnam in the Pentagon was not at all that presented earlier in this chapter. American military analysts denied the proposition that the Vietnam War was unwinnable under any conditions. They argued instead that Vietnam had been lost because it had been fought in the wrong way.[13] They were determined never again to repeat what they felt were the mistakes of the Vietnam War.

The American military leadership argued that military force should be used to destroy an opponent's capacity to wage war, not to coerce him. It should not be employed to convince him to engage in desired behavior, or to dissuade him from engaging in undesirable behavior. There should be a clear-cut and achievable military objective. If military force were to be used, it should be used in amounts sufficient to destroy the opponent's forces and accomplish the objective. Military power should be applied in great force from the outset; it should not be applied incrementally. Once the decision to use force had been made, strictly military considerations should be allowed to govern operational decisions. The political leadership should accept that, once the order to start fighting had been given, civilians should keep silent until informed by the military that the objectives set at the outset of the campaign had been accomplished.

The American military saw Vietnam as a war where these rules for the application of armed force had been violated. The military was never given a clear-cut mission. It was engaged in an attempt to coerce the North Vietnamese to cease their activities in the South. American forces were never allowed to apply sufficient force to do so, however, and they were only allowed to apply force in slow, incremental steps. In Vietnam, political considerations had been allowed to intrude to an extraordinary degree into decisions about military operations, the most egregious example of this, in the eyes of the military leadership, being President Lyndon Johnson's practice of personally choosing bombing targets in North Vietnam. The circumstances surrounding Desert Storm allowed the American military to plan and fight this war according to its notions of the requirements of successful military operations.

The Gulf War had its origins in an unambiguously aggressive act.[14] Iraq openly crossed a widely recognized international frontier with its regular armed forces, invading, occupying, and annexing another state. There was indeed a pretense at first by the Iraqis that dissident Kuwaitis had overthrown their government and then asked Iraq for help, but even the Iraqis themselves quickly gave up this pretense (in part because they found it so difficult to produce anyone willing to say publicly that he had invited them into Kuwait).

The Americans' first concern was how far Iraqi intentions went. Would the Iraqis move further and cross the Saudi Arabian frontier? Whatever the debates that raged later about Iraq's intentions, it was prudent at the time of the Iraqi invasion of Kuwait to be concerned that Iraqi forces might continue into Saudi Arabia. Therefore, the first American military deployments had as their purpose to discourage Iraq from making any further offensive moves.[15]

After the first few weeks, however, the administration of President George Bush was to establish a clear political objective from which it never departed throughout the war: to eject the Iraqis from Kuwait. The administration was to hint from time to time that it had greater ambitions; certainly a lot of rhetoric was expended encouraging the removal of Saddam Hussein as the head of the Iraqi government. While no doubt tempted to do so, however, the administration was never to make such a larger goal the objective of military activities. Indeed, when at the end of the war, the administration concluded that Saddam might only be removed at the cost of dismembering the Iraqi state, they explicitly refused to back rhetoric with military action and allowed the Iraqi regime to survive.

There was thus a clear political objective on which the military could base its planning. Although there may have been some hope that Saddam might have been persuaded to move out of Kuwait, by the threat of military force along with the operation of economic and other sanctions, this was not the military expectation. From the perspective of military planners, the military preparations to persuade Iraq to change its behavior were indistinguishable from preparations for forcible military operations themselves.

Whether this political objective could have been achieved without launching military operations was much debated at the time, with many, including former secretaries of defense and retired senior military officers, arguing for waiting. It appears in retrospect, however, that the administration had decided, well before this decision became publicly apparent, that military force would indeed be required. Those favoring the use of force argued that the wide and fragile allied political coalition against Iraq might not survive the extended period necessary to secure compliance by nonforcible means.

That President Bush was committed to the use of force became apparent when the administration announced, shortly after the 1990 congressional elections, that a large additional increment of troops was to be sent to the Gulf, doubling the forces already deployed there.[16] Before this, it might have been possible to consider keeping forces at existing levels indefinitely, by rotating new units in succession in and out of the theater. The significance of the new increment of force was that this option would no longer be available. Since so large a force could scarcely be kept there year round, and since unfavorable weather conditions would begin in the late spring, the president had in effect publicly put himself into a position where he either had to begin military operations by spring or publicly back down. Obviously Saddam did not understand the nature of Bush's commitment or, for domestic reasons, could not admit failure.

Hostilities began with a major air offensive that lasted some five weeks, and concluded with ground operations that lasted a hundred hours. Insofar as Iraqi intentions can be read, they were to exploit potential political points of vulnerability on the allied side. Iraq hoped to fracture the international coalition that gave legitimacy to—and, in large part, financed—the military effort. Since key coalition players were Arabs—the Saudis, Egyptians, and Syrians—Saddam tried measures that would paint the conflict as one of the West against the Arabs, thus hoping to provoke domestic pressure against coalition Arab governments. Saddam's attempt to provoke an Israeli attack on Iraq by launching ballistic missile attacks against Israeli cities was an important element in this approach. Whether the Arab governments in the coalition could have continued with action against Iraq if Iraq came under attack from Israel was questionable.

Saddam also hoped that he could force a war of attrition, in which he expected that western—and especially American—domestic tolerance for the high casualties that would follow would be exhausted. The eight-year war between Iran and Iraq that had just ended had given the Iraqi leadership no experience with the type of military operations that could be mounted by powers possessing great mobility and overwhelming air superiority. Yet it was Saddam's expectation that the conflict that was about to begin would be a slow-moving and costly contest between ground armies similar to the Iran-Iraq War.

The allied strategy had to be aimed to meet the difficulties that Saddam would seek to put in their path. Speed was essential. The longer the conflict lasted, the greater the potential for erosion of the political cohesion of the coalition. The military campaign also would have to be designed to minimize casualties. Saddam's calculations about the potential political weaknesses of the allies may have been correct. However, he never was to be allowed the opportunity to exploit these weaknesses.

Although the allied objective was the destruction or removal of Iraqi forces in Kuwait, this did not require, in the view of those planning the air campaign, that their military operations be confined to the Kuwait region. On the contrary, they took the view that achieving their objective required attacks on military support and supply activities and communications throughout Iraq, as well as upon military formations in and near Kuwait. Direct attack against civilians, however, was not part of the plan. Technical means to ensure accuracy were superior to those available in previous conflicts. Some targets, however, especially the electricity grid, had both civil and military functions. It appears now that an effort to shut down the electricity grid for the duration of the war was considerably more successful than anticipated, with the result that the system shut down for months, causing much wider and more long-lasting effects on the civil population than intended. We should emphasize, nevertheless, that the air campaign was not directed at civil morale but was aimed at destroying military capabilities as massively and as quickly as possible. The Iraqi air defense system collapsed almost immediately. Allied air attacks could thereafter be carried out in an almost ideal environment.

The ground attack was only launched when the theater commander, General Norman Schwartzkopf, was able to conclude that Iraqi ground forces were so disrupted, and so unable to maneuver, that a war of attrition was not likely. Even then, Schwartzkopf's main attack was not directly against Iraqi ground positions, as degraded by the air attack as the latter had been. Indeed, Saddam's heavy concentration of forces in southern Iraq and Kuwait must have looked to General Schwartzkopf very much like the British and French forces pushed up into Belgium looked to German commanders in 1940. By launching a turning movement to his left, Schwartzkopf was able to threaten to cut off the Iraqi forces in the South. Decimated and degraded by the air attacks, Iraqi forces were capable of little coherent resistance once the ground attack began. The result was a massive rout of Iraqi ground forces, and Iraqi acceptance of a cease-fire that left the allies in occupation of Kuwait, their principal war aim.

Before the war, many of those skeptical of military action based their opposition not on hostility to the use of armed force in general, but on doubts about the utility of force to achieve coalition aims. The analogy that worried many of the doubters was not Vietnam, but Korea. What if Saddam, having been ejected by force from Kuwait, chose to continue to wage a war along some line in Iraq north of Kuwait? If he were able to inflict continuing casualties on American and other coalition forces, would not this cause domestic pressures among the allies, either to end the war on Iraqi terms or to expand it? If the allies began extended ground operations in heavily populated regions of Iraq, they would risk both large casualties and intense pressures on the coalition.

As it happens, the allies were saved from this dilemma. It became apparent that the Iraqi state was more fragile than the Americans had anticipated before the onset of hostilities. As the scale of the military debacle Iraq had suffered in the south became known, widespread rebellions arose against the regime in Baghdad. The extent of these rebel movements came as a surprise, as much to coalition leaders as to the Iraqi government. Saddam was driven to accept a cease-fire on allied terms by the likelihood that, had he not, Iraq would have splintered into its three ethnically and religiously based components—the Kurds in the North, the Sunni Muslims in the Center, and the Shiites in the South. Since such a dismemberment of the Iraqi state would immediately have given great advantage in the region to Iran, hostile to Iraq, the West, and most Arab governments, it was an outcome neither the coalition nor Saddam could welcome.

The outcome of the Persian Gulf War apparently vindicated the proposition that the massive application of force directed against enemy military forces, and governed solely by technical military requirements, could still produce decisive political results in the contemporary world. We should be aware, however, of the various ways in which the conditions under which Desert Storm was fought were unique, and unlikely to be repeated in future conflict situations.

The coalition against Iraq was overwhelming. No power of any military or economic significance supported Iraq. Military contingents from countries in the Western alliance as well as Arab governments actively participated in hostilities against Iraq. Almost 90 percent of the costs of the American effort were borne by others.[17]

Because of the demise of the Soviet threat, the American government was able to move from Europe to the Gulf large forces previously acquired and trained for hostilities against the Red Army on the north German plain. These forces were now able to fight the Iraqis in the way they had planned to fight the Soviets, and under conditions better for fighting that sort of war than they would have been in Europe. Deserts are ideal places for air power to attack ground targets, especially armor. In Europe, it would have been much more difficult to target Soviet forces with such precision, not only because of the weather and the topography, but also because those forces would, in all probability, have been defending themselves against aerial attack and maneuvering against Western forces.

When American and allied forces arrived in Saudi Arabia, they found there a support structure, including air bases, as extensive and modern as any in the world, including those in Europe. In no other region of the world outside of Europe could the Americans have supported a force of this size and sophistication. If they had been dependent upon carrier-based aircraft and land-based aircraft flying from great distances, they could not have mounted anything like the massive and unhurried air offensive that was so crucial to devastating Iraq's capability to wage war.

At the beginning of hostilities, the coalition had easily destroyed Iraq's air defense system. Thereafter Iraqi forces were unable to maneuver or to reply effectively to aerial attack. Not only were Iraqi forces technologically inferior to coalition forces, but Saddam imposed on his military commanders tactics and deployments that further enhanced the coalition's advantages, relying on the hope, drawn from his experience with Iran, that the allies would bleed themselves in costly frontal assaults on static fortified Iraqi lines.

Nor should we exaggerate the political results of Desert Storm, or ignore the likelihood that they will prove short-lived. The American leadership sensibly confined themselves to the limited goal of ejecting Iraq from Kuwait. Had it given way to the temptation to do more, it would have risked a much more extended, costly, and drawn out involvement, in which domestic and alliance political cohesion would have been severely tested.

Had the war produced the dismemberment of Iraq, the Americans would have been drawn into an open-ended military involvement in the region to balance Iran. Furthermore, the difficulties faced by the United Nations in the years since the end of the Gulf War should suggest how hard it is to dismantle permanently the capabilities of Iraq to produce major military forces, including weapons of mass destruction, even when the conditions for mounting such an operation are close to ideal. These difficulties suggest that, while Iraqi military power has been gravely damaged, the war has not precluded the likelihood that this Iraqi regime, or a successor, would be in a position to pursue activities similar to Saddam's expansionism within a few years after the United Nations sanctions, imposed as a condition of the cease-fire, should cease to be strenuously enforced.

A great many conditions surrounding Desert Storm are unlikely to be repeated in the future. The clear cause of war, the wide political and financial support for American and allied efforts, the almost complete isolation of the opponent, the opportunity to fight the sort of war intended for Europe but under better conditions than in Europe, the technological asymmetry, the ineptness of the opponent—all these are unlikely to be repeated in concert. The American military in the Gulf War was able to fight under almost ideal conditions. Even under these conditions, the war produced only a limited and temporary result. It is doubtful, therefore, that Desert Storm has inaugurated a new era in world politics, an era in which military force will again prove useful for the decisive achievement of political purposes.

Much as nuclear weapons have proved elusive as usable tools of foreign policy, the American experience of conventional war after 1945 has provided scarce ground for confidence in a return to decisiveness in warfare. Nor have the experiences of others been different from those of the Americans.[18] The 1980–88 war between Iran and Iraq bore a distinct similarity to World War I.[19] It was a long contest between static entrenched lines, characterized by frontal attacks that produced small gains at great cost. The war concluded as a contest in exhaustion between the parties.

In the Falklands War of 1982, Argentina initially surprised and occupied undefended British colonial dependencies.[20] The British were eventually able to reconquer their territories at considerable cost in warships, only because Argentine defensive ground deployments were highly ill conceived and the Argentines had neglected to provide themselves with air cover based in the Falklands. The coverage they were able to provide from their mainland bases was at the limit of its operational range. Had the Argentines mounted effective air cover (or had the Falklands been a hundred miles closer to the mainland), the British fleet could not have sustained itself in the waters off the Falklands, and British hopes for military reconquest of the islands would have been doomed to failure.

After their intervention in Afghanistan in 1979, Soviet forces proved unable to exploit their technological edge to produce a settlement acceptable to Soviet interests.[21] The Soviets eventually withdrew in 1989, rather than continue bearing the costs. Israeli victories in successive wars with Arab states in 1956, 1967, and 1973 came only at progressively greater costs.[22] Its invasion of Lebanon in 1982 demonstrated its inability to convert military superiority into enduring political advantage.[23]

The wars that began in 1991 among the successor states to Yugoslavia, assisted by ethnic militia, display many of the same features.[24] Serbian forces, while inheriting the bulk of the military equipment of the former Yugoslav army, have not made swift conquests. The Serbian campaigns against Croatia and Bosnia have instead been characterized by incremental advances, preceded by lengthy artillery bombardment aimed largely at civil infrastructure and morale. In spite of their qualitative deficiencies, Bosnian and Croatian forces have shown impressive defensive strength against their better-armed opponents. When overrun, they have succumbed primarily to exhaustion and depletion of supplies.

Conventional wars in recent years have increasingly become contests in mutual attrition and exhaustion, in which quick movement has been difficult. In only a few instances have governments successfully secured decisive advantage through conventional warfare, and those apparent examples are the product of circumstances unlikely to be repeated, gross incompetence, or great disparities in military skill or technical endowment. The special circumstances surrounding the allied victory in the Persian Gulf War of 1991 only serve to underline the improbability that such a victory will be repeated elsewhere.

The Cold War, Arms, and the Obsolescence of War

12

The United States has it in its power to increase enormously the strains under which Soviet policy must operate, to force upon the Kremlin a far greater degree of moderation and circumspection than it has had to observe in recent years, and in this way to promote tendencies which must eventually find their outlet in either the breakup or the gradual mellowing of Soviet power.—"X" [George F. Kennan], 1947

The relationship between armaments and violent conflict is one of the central issues among those concerned with international politics. Is the acquisition of armaments itself at the root of conflict, producing otherwise needless fears and competitions? Or are the instruments of violence merely a symptom of the underlying differences on mutually important questions that arise between states and that cannot be effectively resolved by other means? Do weapons and arms races cause wars and conflicts, or are they only especially dramatic consequences of these conflicts? We have now seen the cold war, the great Soviet-American confrontation that dominated the world for more than four decades after the end of World War II, rise and fall. This experience of the origins and conclusion of the cold war gives us an opportunity to reexamine these questions about the relationship between weapons and international politics. We can assess the role that weapons played in the origins of the cold war. We can examine the role of attempts at disarmament and arms control in bringing the cold war to an end. Finally, we can assess the lessons that the experiences of the cold war hold for the utility of military force as an instrument of national policy.

The arms race after World War II between the United States and the Soviet Union was both qualitative and quantitative. The two powers competed with one another in building their arsenals and in developing new types of weapons. The weapons acquisition decisions of one affected those of the other. It was not, however, a mechanical relationship. Arms building did not follow a rigid formula in which one side reacted to the other in a precisely predictable manner. Although each power made the other an important element in its calculations about the numbers and types of weapons to build, other factors also played into these decisions. Considerations such as domestic political and bureaucratic interests, the psychological idiosyncrasies of leaders on both sides, the state of tension, and the character of the military doctrines each side entertained were all important. There was in addition a time lag between stimulus and response. One power, in a given decision to acquire some weapon, might well be reacting in significant measure to a decision the other had taken, but often it was to a decision taken many years previously.

The Czech coup of 1948, the Berlin crisis of the same year, and above all the Korean War and its frustrating final outcome catalyzed American domestic concern with the Soviet Union, even though it may now be possible to find nonthreatening interpretations for Soviet behavior in some of these incidents. These events evoked in the United States a widespread domestic sense of threat from the Soviet Union, in a public for whom the experience of the American entry into World War II was still vivid. The fear of sudden military attack had been validated in the most dramatic way by Pearl Harbor. Nuclear weapons raised these concerns to a higher order of magnitude. The mere Soviet possession of nuclear weapons, and the realization that the American homeland itself was now directly subject to massive external physical threat—to which Americans had long since convinced themselves that they were invulnerable—impelled them to forget the extreme improbability that any such threat, however horrendous in theory, would ever actually be carried out. The American nuclear arms buildup at the end of the Eisenhower years and at the beginning of the Kennedy presidency may thus have been a response not so much to what the Soviets were then actually doing but to what they had done in the 1940s and the early 1950s, to the menacing sound of Soviet rhetoric, and to the domestic political situation in the United States, which made fear of the Soviets paramount and American politicians vulnerable to the charge that they were allowing the United States to "fall behind" in the arms race.

Similarly, the Soviets undertook a great nuclear weapons buildup in the 1970s, during a period when American forces were growing much more slowly than Soviet forces. This led to widespread belief in the United States that the Soviets had embarked upon a campaign of military expansionism and intimidation. Reinforcing these American beliefs was a dramatic increase in Soviet military involvement in Third World conflicts, and an apparent Soviet program for the acquisition of widespread overseas bases for military operations, at points far removed from historic areas of Soviet security concern. The Soviets may well have been reacting, however, not to American programs of the 1970s but to the extensive American programs of the Kennedy period, and to the public humiliation the Soviets had experienced during the Cuban missile crisis. Once set in motion, Soviet armaments programs acquired powerful domestic political and bureaucratic support, which gave these programs an inertia that allowed them to continue on for many years. This domestic bureaucratic support combined with the historic Russian style in military matters, a style that stressed the importance of large numbers of weapons. Relative American quiescence after the Vietnam experience, and American domestic preoccupations in those years, may have also allowed Soviet leaders to indulge themselves in the illusion that their military programs were the source of America's restrained behavior, that their military expansion had allowed them to intimidate the United States and to make political gains at its expense. Such an illusion may have reinforced the importance of armaments programs in the Soviet domestic political debate, as it became increasingly obvious that other components of the Soviet economy were not yielding any tangible gains.[1]

It is thus not an easy matter to make a simple plot, a simple game of action and reaction, out of the arms relationship between the United States and the Soviet Union during the years of the cold war. There was a relationship, but decisions were made on the basis of a host of factors beyond the other side's latest move. The degree of outward rhetorical hostility in Soviet-American relations, furthermore, was not a simple product of their armaments programs, nor was it a good guide to the potential for those relations to become violent.[2]

Whatever else may have driven this relationship, was the competition in armaments itself responsible for the cold war? Many feel that this was indeed the case. Those who take this view draw implicitly from a more general understanding of the causes of wars, an account in which competitions in armament are themselves the cause of conflict.[3] As we have seen earlier, however, some arms races have historically led to wars and others have not.[4] On many occasions states have proved themselves able to settle their differences peacefully in spite of a history of competition in armaments. It is difficult therefore to accept the notion that arms competition itself creates an inevitable spiral of greater and greater tension, which must culminate ultimately in hostilities.

At worst, we might argue that some arms races contributed to a climate of opinion in which wars were made more likely, or more acceptable to those making decisions. This seems to have been the function played by the Anglo-German naval arms race in the years before the first world war. The naval race did not itself lead to war. The Germans had in effect capped their naval effort before the war, putting an end to the competition.[5] But the German High Seas Fleet, appearing as it did to the British as a weapon designed for use only against them, helped make Germany a plausible enemy in British eyes.

Many arms races never produced wars, because the parties involved ultimately decided they would be better off not fighting. The Anglo-French naval race in the nineteenth century became irrelevant once these two powers realized that their differences were less significant than the common danger each felt from Germany. As part of an agreement to cooperate in the event of war, each power put the defense of some of its most important interests in the hands of the other's navy. The political context was more important than the technical impact of the weapons themselves, in driving the decision between war and peace.

This view is borne out by our experience of the cold war and its conclusion. In the Soviet-American relationship, the geopolitical conflict, which grew out of disputes over spheres of control and influence in Europe in the wake of the defeat of Germany, produced the arms race, not the other way around. As World War II ended, both the Americans and the Soviets demobilized. Although the United States may indeed have reduced its troop levels much more precipitately than did the

Soviet Union, levels on both sides dropped off heavily, and the puny embryonic American nuclear stockpile of those days could hardly have counterbalanced the effects of American demobilization. American and Western concern with the implications of the remaining Soviet forces began with their concern over Soviet actions in eastern Europe in the early postwar years, actions such as the forcible Soviet installation of regimes congenial to Stalin.

American rearmament began only after concern over these Soviet actions became an important focus of policy. In the view of American leaders, Soviet actions created a serious potential for the Soviets to reap disproportionate benefit at American expense from the existing economic, political, and social disruption in western Europe. These benefits could eventually have enhanced significantly Soviet ability to make war against the United States.[6] Only at that point did the Americans become seriously concerned with the implications of the size and disposition of Soviet military forces. Only then did they begin a massive rearmament program, a program that included the great buildup in nuclear forces. Thus, it was the growing political dispute with the Soviets over the fate of eastern and central Europe, and the implications of that fate for western Europe, that produced the American concern with Soviet arms. Some would argue in hindsight that the American response may have been disproportionate to the military threats that the Soviets actually posed in these early years. However, this does not mean that we are justified in doubting that rearmament in itself was a prudent response to genuinely perceived dangers. Arms did not generate tensions. Rather, political disputes caused tensions that led to concern with the potential military implications of Soviet forces. American domestic interests, or American ideology, may have affected the balance between military and other means in the American response, as well as the size and character of the American military response, but did not in themselves determine that there would be such a response.[7]

How the cold war ended reinforces this conclusion.[8] The cold war effectively came to an end when the old Soviet Union allowed new governments to come to power in its former client states in eastern Europe, governments that not only proposed to pursue their own preferences in domestic economic and social policies, but also to pursue new foreign and security policies irrespective of Soviet preferences. Once the Soviet Union had signaled that it would no longer keep communist governments in power in these countries through use of the Red Army, or by threatening its use, these governments swiftly collapsed one after another in a cascade rather like a house of cards. Once the former Soviets had indicated that they would no longer require adherence to a pro-Soviet posture in foreign and defense policy on pain of military intervention, the Warsaw Treaty organization, through which the Soviets had dominated the security policies of their clients, ceased to function in any meaningful sense and its formal demise followed swiftly.

By indicating that they would no longer protect local communist governments by force, the Soviets signaled that they would no longer define their security, as they had defined it for forty-five years, as requiring a belt of subordinate governments to their west. It had been precisely this Soviet definition of security that had caused insecurity in western Europe and the United States, and the felt necessity in those quarters to find the means to resist a plausible military threat—even if that threat were not a probable one. Once the Soviets had moved away from this definition of their security requirements, political tensions with the West evaporated quickly, even before the Soviet Union itself collapsed in the wake of the abortive coup in August 1991. Tensions dissipated, though there was little actual change during this period in the numbers or disposition of Soviet weapons in central Europe. Weapons balances, which only shortly before had been regarded in the West as evidence of hostility or as threatening war because of arguably destabilizing technical characteristics, suddenly became irrelevant as obstacles to good relations. The end of the cold war was brought about by the end of the security conflict in the center of Europe that had given rise to the cold war in the first place.

Notably absent as contributors to the end of the cold war were formal negotiations to limit or regulate armaments.[9] Efforts at arms control have had little effect on the rise and fall of the cold war, or on its vicissitudes over the years in which it dominated international politics. Arms control agreements of one sort or another in the cold war years have been the product of favorable political circumstances, periods of reductions of tension when it has been felt useful in Washington and Moscow for the great powers to symbolize the relaxation of outward tensions in some formal manner. The Limited Test Ban Treaty of 1963, which prohibited nuclear weapons testing in the atmosphere, for example, was a product of such a period, as was the treaty regulating defenses against ballistic missiles in 1972 and the first strategic arms agreement (SALT) of the same year. Whether any of these agreements has had any independent effect on the likelihood of war, or on the likely destructiveness of war should it come about, can not be demonstrated. Certainly none of these agreements has prevented episodes of great public hostility between the superpowers from arising in the periods following their signing.

In 1972, each power felt that expansion of its capabilities to defend against ballistic missile attack would be immensely costly and would yield little military advantage. This mutual realization allowed an opening for an agreement to limit weapons that neither side was anxious to produce anyway.[10] It is doubtful, however, whether this process even allowed the powers to reduce what they might otherwise have spent on armaments. Offensive armaments and arms budgets continued to rise; any resources saved by not building antimissile defenses were diverted to the production of other kinds of weapons.

With the end of the cold war, the formal arms control process has been outstripped by reductions in armaments produced by mutually responsive but unilateral policy decisions by the governments concerned. Furthermore, these decisions have led, rather than followed, the elaborate process of negotiation and verification that had characterized earlier cold war arms control agreements. In the area of conventional arms control, for example, no sooner had governments begun to negotiate about how to bring about a reduction previously agreed, than that reduction itself was made obsolete by governments proclaiming new and still lower totals. As the conflicts that gave rise to the arms subsided, the arms themselves either dissipated in a process in which formal arms control regimes played little part, or they simply became regarded by governments as irrelevant to their concerns. The arms themselves might remain in place, but they no longer aroused the same level of alarm as they had previously.

A similar process can be seen if we turn to the area of nuclear weapons arms control. The Strategic Arms Reduction Treaty (START I), on which agreement had finally been reached in July 1991, provided for warhead reductions of approximately one-third from previous totals. Before the treaty had even been ratified, the Americans unilaterally removed their ground-based nuclear weapons from Europe without waiting for any further agreements. In January 1993, again before the

START I treaty had been ratified by all sides, the American and Russian presidents signed a START II treaty providing for reductions to half or less of the START I totals.[11] The later agreement was arrived at after only months of discussion, whereas the START I agreements— much more modest in the size and character of the reductions agreed to—took most of a decade to negotiate. The significance of the START II agreement, and of the speed with which it was reached, is emphasized if we note that START II provided for the total elimination on both sides of land-based multiple-warhead missiles, previously the mainstay of the Soviet strategic forces and long regarded as the weapons most capable of launching a first-strike by either side. Clearly the profound changes that had occurred in the interim in the political relationship between the two powers explains the ease with which arms reductions, of a character and degree that would have been unthinkable only a year or two previously, could now be agreed upon.

Armaments neither created the cold war, nor did their reduction play an important part in bringing it to an end. Weapons levels, for good or ill, were merely reflections of changes in political and security relationships. Changes in those relationships first caused the hostilities of the cold war, and then allowed them to subside.

THE COLD WAR AND THE OBSOLESCENCE OF WAR

The experience of the cold war, and especially how it ended, may suggest that a long-standing debate about the obsolescence of war as a means for achieving political goals has finally been resolved.[12] Perhaps war has become too costly and too unpredictable to be relied upon. Perhaps the important questions are increasingly those about which the use of violence is irrelevant or counterproductive. Perhaps the distinction between domestic and international politics that was drawn in the first chapter of this book may no longer be significant.

The geopolitical changes that accompanied the end of the cold war— the dismemberment of the Soviet Union and the collapse of its former system of political hegemony in central Europe—are of the sort that in previous eras could only have been accomplished in the wake of a major war. That these changes could have been brought about so far without major conflict suggests that other means have supplanted the function of warfare, a function that no other means previously could effectively discharge, of bringing fundamental change to the international system. Although changes in the economic relationships among states may previously have laid the basis for major changes in their political relationships, economic change has not up to now been sufficient in itself to bring about political change. Warfare has historically proved necessary to catalyze such change.[13] Austria-Hungary had been in decline for much of the nineteenth century, but it was only its defeat in World War I that produced its dissolution. In retrospect, we may perceive a steady Turkish decline from an apex in 1683, when it stood at the gates of Vienna, but that decline was registered outwardly only by numerous wars lasting into the nineteenth and early twentieth centuries. What has happened in the former Soviet Union and in eastern Europe since 1990 seems like a settlement that might have followed a Soviet defeat in a third world war; yet no such conflict was required to bring it about. Western containment of the Soviet Union without war has produced the results predicted by George Kennan at the outset of the cold war, in the quotation at the beginning of this chapter. No historical precedent exists for shifts in relationship of such magnitude without the assistance of major conflict. This is indeed a powerful argument that a decline has occurred in the historic importance of war among great states as the central agent of change in international politics.

Other evidence supports the view that war has lost much of its former usefulness. Great powers have recurrently experienced difficulty during the cold war in translating their military superiority to political advantage in peacetime and crisis. Quantitative superiority in the nuclear weapons balance did not reliably carry with it the ability to manipulate crises to the advantage of the superior party. Although the weaker party on occasion may have exhibited some measure of restraint, this has not been consistently so, and there is little ground for any claim that the stronger nuclear power has consistently been emboldened.[14] Neither have nuclear powers enjoyed any reliable advantage over smaller, non-nuclear, states in crises.

Desert Storm to the contrary notwithstanding, we can cite many cases where supposedly powerful states have found themselves unable to use their military advantages to secure outcomes that they desired. The Russians discovered this in Afghanistan, as the Americans learned it in Vietnam. Although Israel could produce a decisive military victory in 1967, it could not convert that victory into enduring political advantage.

It was forced to fight another, extremely costly war only six years later. Still later, in 1982, Israel was unable to translate an overwhelming military superiority in Lebanon into a lasting political settlement with that country. Serb nationalist forces in Bosnia inherited the full range of advanced military technology at the disposal of the army of the former Yugoslav federation in 1990. We should be struck, however, not by the swiftness by which they were able to emerge victorious in the ensuing wars, but by the slowness of their gains. Serbian attackers in the Yugoslav wars that began in 1991 have only been able to achieve small, incremental gains against organized Bosnian and Croatian defenders, even though the latter were quite inferior to the Serbs in the quality of the weaponry available to them.

It might well be argued that this decline in the utility of war is merely the culmination of what has been a long historic trend, with only episodic and brief interruptions. Thus, the exhausting melee of the seventeenth century was followed by a period in which war could be made manageable and affordable only at the cost of severely limiting the goals that could be attained through war. The Napoleonic period momentarily allowed warfare to resume a decisive role, but only for as long as it took other states to adopt the tactics and organizational forms that had been developed by the French. Some mid-nineteenth-century wars seemed to offer the prospect of decisive battles and quick victories, but in retrospect these prospects appear more as illusions fostered by momentary ineptness on the part of military leaders than as revealing any tendency of the new military technologies to make war again decisive. The slaughter of the American Civil War and then of World War I showed that warfare had returned to a condition of bloody attrition. The interwar years featured experimentation with new techniques that in 1940 seemed vindicated by Hitler's "lightning war" tactics. But once these techniques had been assimilated by the other belligerents, World War II became a long, costly slugging match in which easy solutions evaded all those engaged. After the war, nuclear weapons, once they were no longer an American monopoly, would become increasingly ineffective as instruments for the achievement of policy goals.

Much as some would argue that war has become too costly, others would argue that, with the demise of communism, no great conflicts of ideology among states remain.[15] Since democracies do not fight one another, military power among democracies has become increasingly irrelevant as a means to deal with the problems that face them.[16] These problems are increasingly economic, or ecological in character, it is argued. What these problems have in common is that they require everybody to cooperate in their solution.[17] If everyone does not cooperate, then everyone is worse off. Using force is not a very useful way to get cooperation in reducing carbon dioxide emissions, for example, or to open economies to imports. In a world characterized by problems of this sort, military force is no longer of much help in achieving goals.

Even if international problems are increasingly economic or ecological in character, however, this does not suggest that harmonious solutions to such problems will necessarily follow. While all may suffer from some anticipated ecological change, such as global warming, some may feel they will suffer relatively less than others, either from the problem or from particular proposed solutions to it. This leads to powerful differences of view about the policies that should be enacted. Policy differences that arose between industrialized and developing states at an environmental conference at Rio de Janeiro in 1992 over measures to be taken to counteract forest destruction and greenhouse gases are cases in point. Groups of states at the conference differed profoundly in their perception of relative loss from ecological destruction, as well as the balance they would strike between acceptance of such destruction in the long-term and willingness to forego economic advantage in the short-term.

Besides the apparently increasing role of international ecological and economic issues, it is not at all obvious that the world in other areas is hurtling into a condition of peace and harmony. The experience of conventional war in recent decades has shown that on occasion warfare can remain useful as an instrument of policy, or at least may seem preferable to the participants to accepting the situation that would result from the absence of war. India has derived distinct advantages from its wars with Pakistan. While its victory in 1967 was to be short-lived, few Israelis would argue that a decision not to go to war then would have been preferable. While Egypt's decision for war in 1973 did not result in military victory, it did produce a break in a stalemated diplomatic situation, a break that was to result in the return of the Sinai Peninsula to Egypt and a peace treaty with Israel. In this case, war certainly proved effective for achieving Egyptian policy goals.

Perhaps the trend to bloody attrition and indecisiveness in war will not continue indefinitely. Both Britain in the Falklands and the coalition in the 1991 war against Iraq were able to achieve their military objectives with minimal personnel casualties to the victors. It is not at all obvious that the application of new technology to warfare must forever favor the defense. Perhaps developing technologies will give a renewed advantage to speed and maneuver on the battlefield, as the development of armored warfare did at the end of World War I. Perhaps, contrary to those who believe it doomed to indecisiveness and thus uselessness, conventional warfare may be on the verge of a new renaissance as a cost-effective means to achieve goals in international politics.

A variety of conflicts has arisen in the wake of the cold war. These include conflicts that would have been unthinkable a few years ago. The dissolution of old states and old alliance systems has created new conflicts or revived old ones. Tensions have arisen, for example, between Hungary and Rumania over the Hungarian ethnic minority inside Rumania. In the former Soviet Union, conflict erupted between ethnic Russians in newly independent Moldova and the ethnic Rumanian majority in that state, many of whom apparently wish to amalgamate with Rumania. In the central Asia region of the former Soviet Union, a host of ethnic and national disputes has arisen, some of them resulting in large-scale violence and spilling over international borders. In the Caucasus, war has broken out between Armenia and Azerbaijan over ethnic minorities present within each state's old borders. Similar considerations have produced a series of wars among and within the states that have emerged out of the former Yugoslavia.

In many ways the cold war was a period of relative predictability. The superpowers knew who and where their opponents were, and kept conflicts among their client states from getting out of hand. With the end of the bipolar relationship between the United States and the Soviet Union, this predictability has vanished, and many newly autonomous governments have emerged, prepared to pursue their own goals, goals that previously they had been forced to suppress. When conflicts occur or threaten to occur among newly autonomous governments, the likelihood that outsiders can unite to encourage or impose settlements is limited. The difficulties encountered by outside governments, acting under European or United Nations auspices, in dealing effectively with conflicts among governments emerging from what was formerly the Soviet Union or Yugoslavia illustrate these limits. Whether the conflict is in the Balkans or the Caucasus or the Crimea, outsiders may have different preferences about how they prefer such conflicts to be resolved. A neighbor may prefer a solution to the advantage of one of the parties, or it may fear a solution that might give advantage to a party who might someday threaten its own interests. Thus, which groups gain and which groups lose in conflicts within the former Yugoslavia is of serious concern to such outside powers as Albania, Greece, Bulgaria, and Turkey. No mechanism exists to impose unity among these outside witnesses to the conflict. Indeed some neighbors may find themselves tempted to enter the conflict themselves to advance their own preferences, thus expanding the conflict beyond its original confines.

If united multilateral outside efforts to contain or settle such conflicts are difficult, it becomes likely that many of these conflicts will only be resolved—if at all—in contests between the parties involved, contests in their relative ability to mobilize resources and endure or resist punishment in pursuit of their goals. That these military contests persist only shows that those in power in many governments around the world still believe that military force may prove useful in getting them something they want, or in keeping something valued.

Historically, war has been a function not only of the existence of conflicts among states but of a shared belief that the consequences of warfare will be preferable to—or will at least be less unpleasant than—the consequences of remaining at peace.[18] Unless this belief is shared by the parties to a conflict, there can be no war between them. This belief has in turn been based in part on the expectation that warfare can be controlled, so that its costs are worth the anticipated gains. These beliefs are not of course infallible, as we have seen. In many periods governments have disastrously underestimated the cost of war, or overestimated their ability to control it. Disastrous miscalculations of this sort occurred during the religious wars of the seventeenth century, for example, and during the period that culminated in World War I. In both these periods governments were unable to extricate themselves from conflicts whose level and extent of destruction and drain on resources they had neither expected nor desired.

But in other periods governments have been conscious of the potential for warfare to get out of hand. This has not produced the end of war but a mutual inclination to limit it, to moderate its effects. Such a period we saw in the eighteenth century and again during the cold war.

The social and political structure of European states during the eighteenth century made governments reluctant to face the domestic costs
and risks that warfare for extensive aims would have involved. No doubt
the social dislocation that had been produced by the religious wars of
the seventeenth century, in which violence often escaped the control of
those who originally set it in train, provided an object lesson in what to
avoid. This motivation, and social structures unable or unwilling to
mobilize societal resources, combined to create the limited war regime
of the eighteenth century.

During the cold war, the role of conscious intent in causing the limitation of war must be assigned a greater weight. The potential for
nuclear weapons to remove violence from any meaningful relationship
to the ends of policy could scarcely be evaded. All efforts to find ways
to subordinate nuclear weapons to the constraints of policy in some
desirable way were ultimately unconvincing even to those who propounded them, dependent as these efforts were on the necessity to
assume collaboration on the part of the opponent. Yet the potential of
nuclear weapons was not alone in inducing restraint, at least among the
great powers.[19] The experience of the two world wars of this century
was one of long, hideously costly contests of endurance, whose costs to
the eventual victors—except for the United States—were scarcely less
than to the losers. If this were also to be the shape of warfare in the
future, even if such warfare could somehow be kept free of nuclear
weapons, this experience would continue to induce restraint scarcely
less than that imposed by the fear of uncontrollable violence represented by the new weapons.

The eclipse of nuclear weapons as direct considerations in a variety
of conflicts—generally conflicts at some remove from the central arenas
of superpower confrontation—allowed for the reemergence of expectations about conventional warfare as a means to resolve conflict. Thus
during the cold war there were, paradoxically, sharply different expectations about the controllability of different levels of violence. There was
a great fear that the biggest wars could not be controlled, combined
often with a considerable degree of confidence in the utility and controllability of small wars, or at least of some small wars.

Confidence in the utility of limited conventional wars as instruments
of policy has waxed and waned. In the United States, conventional war
was widely considered obsolete in the mid-1950s, as the army based its

formations and doctrines on the inclusion of nuclear weapons at all levels, only to be revived as a tool for policy at the end of the Eisenhower period, by those who feared that sole reliance on nuclear weapons would lead to paralysis. The Vietnam War ushered in a period of pessimism about conventional war's utility, only to be followed by the optimism engendered by American actions in Libya and Grenada under Reagan, and finally in Iraq in 1991 under Bush. The special circumstances surrounding these few victorious wars, however, make this optimism questionable. The experience of the small wars of the cold war era casts doubt on any sweeping assumption that warfare has been returned to its old position as a useful and controllable instrument of policy. Although some small wars can be cited as useful instruments in this way, many others have, as we have seen, only served to demonstrate the futility of force, even as an instrument of those possessing great superiority of resources over their opponents. There is thus little ground for expecting an early end to the costly indecisiveness of conventional warfare, an indecisiveness that had become increasingly evident even before the advent of the nuclear weapon.

Weapons did not cause the cold war, and efforts at the limitation of armaments were not significant in ending it. The end of the cold war has not put an end to conflict. Rather, occasions for conflict may well have increased. But the cold war years did witness the continuation of a long historical process in which the ability to translate military power into political results declined and the costs of attempting to do so increased. What is left for us is to speculate about the nature of the environment these contradictory conclusions suggest we now will face. What occasions for conflict will the world after the cold war present, and what role can we expect military power to play in attempts to resolve these conflicts? To what extent, and under what circumstances, may we expect that military power might still retain a role as a useful and controllable instrument of statecraft?

The Future Strategic Environment

13

It will be enough for me . . . if these words of mine are judged useful by those who want to understand clearly the events which happened in the past and which (human nature being what it is) will, at some time or other and in much the same ways, be repeated in the future.—Thucydides (trans. Rex Warner)

Let us assume that the cold war is over and that we are in the process of transition to a new era in international politics. The development of warfare in the modern state system, as it has been discussed in previous chapters, can help us to speculate on this new era and on the possible role of war and the threat of war. Before turning to these speculations, we should consider several changes occurring now in the enduring features of the international environment and in the character of the players involved in world politics.

The *structure* of international politics itself, the environment within which governments and other actors operate, as we have known it since 1945 is changing. Change is also occurring in the domestic *attributes* of the players in international politics, the motivations that drive their actions, and the capabilities widely shared among them.[1] Change in the fundamental structure of international politics has been historically infrequent. We can expect the outcome of the structural changes we are now witnessing to remain a feature of world politics indefinitely. However, we cannot be equally confident that the changes we now see in the widely shared attributes of the individual players in world politics will prove similarly long-lasting.

As to the structure of international politics, the identity of the players is changing. Economic change is affecting the position of the players in

relation to one another and bringing new and different issues to prominence. As to the attributes of the players, no great conflict of ideas
seems poised to divide governments and peoples into mutually hostile
groupings. However, the capability to produce and deliver weapons of
mass destruction is spreading. "Conventional" military technology with
capabilities orders of magnitude beyond what was used in recent wars is
becoming widely available. The impact of each of these developments
can be expected to affect the likelihood and character of warfare in the
post–cold war era.

CHANGES IN WORLD POLITICS

The identity of the players in international politics is changing. During the
cold war two superpowers could clearly be distinguished from lesser
states. Each superpower exercised a dominant influence over the external (and in some cases the internal) behavior of the other members of
its bloc or alliance system. We need not equate the dominance exercised
by one superpower with that of the other. The American alliance system
was largely voluntary, the product of the desires of the smaller states for
an American role in protecting their security. The Soviet system was
almost exclusively the product of coercion. It was a system created and
maintained by the threat and use of military force against Soviet client
states. Although these systems of dominance may have differed in their
organizing principles, they have each dissolved in the wake of the
decline of the Soviet-American geopolitical contest.

No longer do we have the old picture of two leaders and a host of
followers. Some states are disintegrating. Several states now occupy the
territory of what used to be called the Soviet Union. Yugoslavia has split
apart, as has Czechoslovakia. Also, attempts are under way to amalgamate some existing states into larger units. The most dramatic ambitions along these lines may be found in Europe, where plans have been
announced to produce not only common economic policies but also
common foreign and defense policies. As currently envisioned, these
foreign and defense policies would still require unanimous agreement, a
challenge to the European governments involved; but it is widely hoped
that common monetary and fiscal policies will have some "spillover"
effect.[2] Schemes for the creation of economic common markets and
free-trade zones abound in other regions, including North America; as

do plans for the coordination of foreign policy among regional states, as, for example, in Southeast Asia. The number of significant players has increased substantially over that during the cold war, a change that could affect patterns of war and conflict in the international system.

Economic change is affecting the position of the players in relation to one another. Some powers have declined in wealth relative to others, while others have advanced. The American economic position has declined with respect to that of many of her allies in Europe and Asia. The United States now imports products it previously supplied the world. Because new products and new methods of production are increasingly developed elsewhere, the United States has gone from a position of net creditor to one of net debtor internationally. This decline, to be sure, is in relative position only. In absolute terms, the American economy has been growing, albeit more slowly than other industrialized economies. Economic productivity in the former Soviet Union and in the states of eastern Europe, however, has undergone a decline in absolute terms.

These changes in economic position are important because of the historic relationship between national economic capability and the ability to exercise military and political influence. Economic development is uneven. All countries do not benefit equally or at the same time from the diffusion of new products and technologies throughout the international economic system.[3] Britain, Germany, and the United States, at various periods in the past, each developed great political and military influence because they were able to employ successfully the latest industrial processes. Britain was in a better position than anyone else— in part because of its reserves of coal and its development of a system of credit and finance more sophisticated than anywhere else—to exploit the new industrial technologies brought in by the industrial revolution of the late eighteenth century. Economic strength enabled Britain to dominate the international political structure for much of the nineteenth century. But in Britain's very success lay the seeds of its undoing.

Britain supported a free-trade and an international currency regime based upon the free convertibility of currencies into the pound and into gold. The net effect of this system was to allow others the capital to develop manufacturing industries of their own. Much of the industrial development of the United States in the years after the Civil War was due to the ready availability of British capital. Both Germany and the United States benefited, to a greater degree than powers that had arisen earlier, from the new manufacturing processes of the late nineteenth and early twentieth centuries, and were able to convert their dominance of these new processes into political and military influence.

In a similar fashion dominance over the latest manufacturing technologies in many areas has shifted from the United States to overseas. Innovation in the marketplace requires investment in activities without immediate economic payoff. Compared with other industrial democracies the United States has consistently saved and invested a lower proportion of its national product. Historical precedent suggests that this trend will lead to change in relative military and political influence. Should we expect such changes in military and political influence in the post–cold war era? Is this trend reversible? Who will dominate the technological processes of the future, and what effect will that dominance have on the relative ability of states to exercise military influence?[4]

No great conflict of ideas is poised to divide governments and peoples, as it divided them in the cold war, into mutually hostile groups. In the seventeenth century, differing conceptions of man's relationship to God and the nature of institutional authority, secular and theological, lent immense intensity to conflicts among states. As people felt that they were fighting for goals of transcendent importance, and against opponents who were literally instruments of the devil, actions that might otherwise have been regarded as impermissible became permissible. Sacrifices that previously would not have been borne seemed acceptable. The result was a period of warfare of singular brutality and extensive destructiveness.

The period of the cold war was also a period of ideological bifurcation. On both sides of the Iron Curtain, people—especially those in control of the instruments of government—were convinced that the conflict was over principles of human organization of universal significance. Each side viewed the other as totally untrustworthy and inherently aggressive. Although no great war broke out between the great powers during this period, the conflict between the superpowers became projected onto many local conflicts throughout the world, and tensions between the two systems often reached great heights.

No such ideological chasm now divides the world.[5] Unless a new clash of universal ideas should emerge, it is likely that international disputes will turn instead on particular issues, not on conflicting views of man, god, or society. International conflicts will not disappear, but they may change their form. Conflicts over particular issues may be intensely and brutally fought, as the barbarity among the ethnic groups and successor states to Yugoslavia illustrates. But a claim by a particular group to a particular territory is by its nature limited, and devoid of the potential to engage the intense enthusiasm of others, that a claim to a universally applicable mode of organizing society can evince.

The capability to produce nuclear weapons and other weapons of mass destruction, and to deliver those weapons by advanced means, will spread. Chemical weapons, the use of which in war had been banned internationally by treaty in 1925 under the Geneva Protocol, were employed by both sides in the Iran-Iraq War of 1980–88 (although Iraqi use was more widespread). Widespread reports of the development of bacteriological weapons (also banned under the Geneva Protocol) exist, although the use of such weapons has not been publicly confirmed. Various states are reported to be developing or in possession of nuclear weapons. Many states in the Third World have developed or acquired the ability to deliver such weapons by ballistic missile. Iraqi Scud missile attacks during the war in the Persian Gulf, while not in themselves militarily significant, are a harbinger.[6]

Attempts to acquire weapons of these sorts are fueled by a variety of motives. Governments are driven to acquire weapons that, they feel, will give them an advantage over regional competitors, or provide protection against threats from neighbors. They are also motivated to acquire such weapons to match capabilities that their regional rivals have, or that they believe their rivals have. Iraq employed chemical weapons to blunt Iranian attacks that threatened to break Iraqi lines in the Iran-Iraq War. Israel's widely reported nuclear capability is a response to the military threats of its neighbors. Pakistan's reported attempts to acquire nuclear weapons can be seen as a response to India's acquisition of a nuclear weapons capability, as India's acquisition can be seen as a response to China's acquisition of nuclear weapons still earlier. North Korea's nuclear weapons program may be fueled not only by the continuing competition with the more populous and economically powerful South Korean government, but also by a fear that the end of the cold war has left the regime in Pyongyang without a great power patron. The collapse of the Soviet Union has raised the possibility that Soviet successor states other than Russia will acquire control over nuclear weapons remaining on their territory; or even that such weapons might fall into the hands of factions in a civil war.

Attempts to acquire weapons such as these have not gone unresisted. The Nonproliferation Treaty (NPT) of 1968 prohibits the acquisition of nuclear weapons by signatory states not then having them and provides the framework for a system of international sanctions and inspections designed to reinforce these obligations. The NPT and the International Atomic Energy Agency (IAEA), the United Nations agency that carries out the inspections, are the centerpieces of an international regime designed to prevent the further spread of nuclear weapons.[7] Bacteriological and chemical weapons are regulated by other international legal structures with less elaborate institutional support.[8]

Under the cease-fire at the end of Operation Desert Storm in 1991, Iraq was forced to agree to eliminate its nuclear, chemical, and biological weapons capacity, and was required to accept wide-ranging and intrusive inspection of its territory to assure that this commitment was carried out. Inspection teams operating under United Nations authority were to be allowed complete freedom of movement throughout Iraqi territory and were to be allowed access to any facility they desired to see. The Iraqi case is instructive, because it represents perhaps the most favorable conditions under which a thoroughgoing effort to eliminate a nation's capacity to produce weapons of mass destruction might be carried out. Many would like to believe that the intrusive sanctions that have been carried out against Iraq represent a model for the sort of program that will, in coming years, be mounted against other potential proliferators. But we should understand clearly that this program could only be mounted against Iraq in the wake of its defeat in war. Unless we expect to see wars like the war against Iraq repeated, it is unlikely that we will see the imposition of inspections programs as intrusive as those attempted against Iraq repeated either.

The inspection program that we have seen brought into play against the Iraqi weapons programs is surely the most ambitious such program ever mounted. It can destroy existing physical facilities and stocks of sensitive materials. It can disrupt, scare off, and perhaps lead to the prosecution of some of Iraq's international network of suppliers of weapons materials. It can prevent Iraq from resuming the program for as long as the inspection teams are present and are allowed to carry out their work. But it cannot give permanent assurance that Iraq could not resume its programs at some future date when the Gulf War allies are no longer unanimous in supporting the inspectors with the threat of force if their work is impeded. Unless the allies are prepared to mount a permanent occupation of Iraqi territory there will come a time when Iraq will effectively be free to renew its efforts.

It is unlikely that future budding proliferators will be frustrated by the sort of political and military context that for a time frustrated the Iraqis. Thus, American efforts to secure effective inspection of North Korea's nuclear facilities have been hobbled by the reluctance of North Korea's neighbors to support the threat of economic sanctions against North Korea, and by the fear that Pyongyang might react to such threats by renewing the Korean War. It is equally unlikely that even sanctions like the unprecedented sanctions that have been mounted against Iraq will permanently strip such states of their capacity. It follows that we should expect that more of those regimes with active programs to acquire nuclear weapons and other weapons of mass destruction will be successful in their attempts. Thus, possession of weapons of mass destruction will, in the future, be more widely spread, and no longer restricted to a very few.

Conventional military technology with capabilities orders of magnitude beyond that used in World War II, Korea, or Vietnam is now available to armed forces around the world. It is not only weapons of mass destruction that will be widely disseminated around the world. Possession of conventional weapons with dramatically new capabilities is spreading.[9] Much of this weaponry is cheap, and does not require sophistication to operate. These new conventional weapons represent the by-product, in the sphere of military equipment, of the revolution in consumer electronics that has occurred in recent years. Computers and other electronic devices can make complex calculations quickly and accurately, can design optimal plans of action swiftly and can communicate information instantaneously to extensive networks of recipients. Devices are now available capable of detecting, targeting, and destroying targets with a speed, efficiency, and accuracy unheard of previously.

There will be far less room to hide on future battlefields. If a military vehicle moves, or even if it gives off more heat than the surrounding area, its location may become immediately apparent to hostile eyes. Once located it can be destroyed. Soldiers on the other side need have little more than video game skills to operate weapons systems capable of destroying sophisticated and expensive military vehicles or installations at great distances. If such a weapons system should malfunction, it can be fixed quickly by substituting a modular replacement for one of its components, without any requirement that soldiers present on the battlefield possess any great technical expertise. Weapons systems of this sort can, at times, be defeated. Technologies have been developed that enable prospective targets to hide themselves from surveillance, to interfere with the electronic communications of the potential attacker, or to defend themselves actively against attack. These technologies are generally expensive, available only to the most sophisticated and even then likely to be available only in small numbers, however.

Not all of the new military technologies will be cheap. Some, such as the so-called stealth technologies, which make a military vehicle far less visible to hostile electronic surveillance, are at the cutting edge of technology, are very expensive, and are likely to remain so. It is probable that such technologies will, for a long time, be available only to those few wealthy and sophisticated states that can command the latest technological and industrial innovations. Many other technologies, however, are mass-producible, are cheap, and require little maintenance. They are easy for the technically unsophisticated to operate and difficult for them to break. It is these latter technologies that we can expect to spread rapidly around the world, to be available to Third World armies and insurgent forces, as well as to the military forces of the wealthy industrial powers.

THE EFFECTS OF CHANGE

If these are the directions in which change has occurred in world politics, and if we can expect these changes to continue, what conclusions can be drawn as to their implications for the strategic environment of the future? Unfortunately, change in one area often implies conclusions different from, and contradictory to, what might be implied by change in another. Let us now examine the implications of these changes in world politics for the strategic environment, discussing the issues in the order in which they were presented in the preceding section.

The identity of the players in international politics is changing. The most likely effect of changing players is to make the world more complicated.

New conflicts are arising and old ones—believed dead for decades—have revived. If the world is becoming a more complicated place, the potential for surprise and miscalculation is increasing. In a more complicated world, each actor must watch and attempt to anticipate the actions of more players. Chances for miscalculation—for overlooking someone or predicting wrongly a government's reactions to some situation—are greater. Furthermore, the decline of empires and other dominant powers has often produced increased occasion for conflict arising out of the resulting succession struggle. The net effect of this change in the identities of the players is likely to be an increase in the incidence of conflict throughout the world.[10]

Economic change is affecting the position of the players in relation to one another. Economic change gives new advantages to some players and causes others to lose some advantages they formerly had. Thus, for example, the Japanese, the "Little Dragons" of Southeast Asia, and the Germans have each seen their share of world trade increase in recent decades, whereas that of the Americans has been in relative decline. We cannot, of course, be certain that this trend will continue. If it does, what effect is it likely to have on conflict and war? Theoretically, of course, it might have none, if the rising economic powers are satisfied with the world as it is. Insofar as they are not satisfied, they might be tempted to convert their economic potential into political influence or military power. The United States required vast subsidies from other governments to mount Operation Desert Storm against Iraq. Could it have mounted such an effort itself, if those others had not supported its policies?

In the decades immediately following World War II, military developments were largely separable from new industries in the civil sector. When there were connections, the demands of military requirements drove developments. These military developments then might find application in the civilian sector. To an increasing extent, advances in military technology now come from developments in technology originally designed for the civilian market. Technological development is increasingly driven by consumer demand.[11] The military sector thus reaps the fruit of developments originating elsewhere. In the early postwar years, for example, the development of electronic computers was almost wholly driven by the requirements of weapons development, especially of nuclear weapons developments. In today's world, however, weapons systems are increasingly dependent upon semiconductors developed for civil applications. Thus those who control the newest developments at the frontiers of civilian research and industrial application can increasingly derive military advantages from that control, if they wish to do so.

The international economic system is not automatically self-regulating. The proliferation of economic relations across national boundaries is no guarantee in itself of smooth international market operations, devoid of disruption. The international economic system, at least for most of the past two centuries, has required a dominant power to set the rules of the game and ensure the smooth running of the system.[12] Britain served this role for much of the nineteenth century, and the United States did so for the period immediately after World War II. During periods when no power was able or willing to play this role, growing protectionism and economic conflict was the result. Although the United States may be increasingly unable to play the dominant role any longer, owing to the decline in its relative economic position, no one else has come forward prepared to take its place. Neither the Germans nor the Japanese so far have demonstrated that they have the resources, or the interest, to set rules and bounds for the international economic system.

An international economy governed by a committee dominated by the United States, Japan, and Germany has been the result. The committee has cobbled together by consensus a series of ad hoc responses to major issues that have arisen in the international economic system. Sooner or later, however, committees deadlock, and there is thus a risk that the world economy might break down into mutually hostile protectionist trading blocs. Once such blocs are established, there is a further risk that hostility might spill over from economics into political and security affairs. That this risk has not been borne out in recent decades is due largely to the circumstance that economic change has thus far occurred within a structure of security presided over by the United States, a structure that has until now remained fundamentally unchanged. As the head of the international organization charged with overseeing the international trading system put it recently, "In a way, the Iron Curtain made the world economy more predictable because the free world was ultimately bound together by a political nexus against communism. Now you have more than 5 billion people competing for their share of the pie, and that makes conflict all the more inevitable."[13] Whether international economic ties will be sufficient to maintain a cooperative international economic system once those security structures have been fundamentally altered is questionable. Thus, economic change is likely to increase occasions for conflict, as well as simply to increase the number and change the relative position of the players, thereby making the world more complicated.

No great conflict of ideas is poised to divide governments and peoples, as it divided them in the cold war, into mutually hostile groups. The lack of grand ideological disputes in coming years is likely to moderate and limit conflict. If conflict occurs over material things, there may be a greater chance for compromise and accommodation. Tensions may be lower, because issues of an ultimate nature will less likely be perceived as being at stake. To be sure, there are many material issues over which compromise has historically proved to be difficult or impossible. Some territorial issues have appeared to the parties as incapable of a compromise solution. If one party should feel its security is irretrievably threatened by what another does to preserve its own, the two may find it difficult to reach accommodation. But the general tendency of a situation in which conflicts turn upon material rather than ideological issues will be to reduce the incidence of situations where the players in world politics feel that conditions essential to their existence are at stake, and thus that they cannot afford to compromise.

There are those who go further than this, arguing that the world is becoming more democratic, and that democratic states do not fight one another.[14] The relative lack of conflict among democracies, however, may be due simply to the very few states that could unquestionably be termed democracies before 1945, and to the fortuitous statistic that most of those few states that can be called "democratic" since then have benefited, whether directly or indirectly, from the security umbrella provided by the American alliance system. Thus, it can be argued, for example, that Sweden, while not part of the American alliance system, has benefited from the existence of the NATO alliance.[15] The small numbers and brief time for which this relative lack of conflict among democracies has arguably been a feature of world politics may thus merely be an artifact of the structure of alliance relationships in the cold war period. Will this relative lack of conflict among democracies survive the demise of cold war security structures? Only if democracies continue to avoid conflict among themselves even after they no longer share common overriding security concerns will the view that democracies are inherently peaceful become compelling.[16]

Furthermore, while communism may have been dismantled, this by no means implies that the successors to communist regimes must be democratic. In some few cases they do indeed appear to be so, or at least to be moving in that direction. We have little reason to believe, however, that democracy has been irreversibly established in any of these states, all of whom are subject to major economic and social stresses. In other formerly communist states, authoritarian regimes of a variety of stripes appear more likely. The crucial element here, however, is the absence of any new ideological movement under which many states might coalesce, a movement that could take on the role of philosophic adversary of democracy.

There has been no coalescence of states around religious, ethnic, economic or social principles. Thus, Islamic states have shown themselves more likely to respond to the differing interests that separate them as states than to the theoretical common interest that may unite them religiously. The recent war in the Gulf, which saw Islamic states on both sides of the conflict, as well as some adopting positions of neutrality, only confirms this. Nor has the Third World exhibited any success in pursuing common policies on economic, ecological, social, or cultural issues. Indeed, diversity in attitude among Third World states is increasingly more apparent than common feeling.

There may be a resurgence of nationalist sentiments on the part of peoples recovering their autonomy after many years, or perhaps gaining it for the first time. Popular hostility to other groups often will be the unfortunate concomitant of this nationalism.[17] But this nationalism will be particularist, appealing narrowly only to certain groups, and dealing with things of concern to them only. Serbian nationalism, for example, may be a powerful force among Serbs, and may provide motivation for considerable hostility toward their non-Serbian neighbors. But its influence is inherently self-limiting. Non-Serb peoples will not be tempted to enlist under a Serbian banner. Particularist nationalist sentiments, while widespread, will not provide the basis for a new bloc of states hostile to the democracies. A revival of "pan-Slavic" nationalist ideology could provide the basis for a nationalism with wider appeal. Because such a movement would doubtless be led by Russia, as it was in the nineteenth century, it could have the potential at some future date to present a renewed geopolitical threat to the democracies. However, while a revival of pan-Slavism cannot be ruled out for all time, there is now little evidence for its emergence as a politically significant force in the foreseeable future. As with followers of Islam, the differences among Slavic groups have so far outweighed their potential common interest. In the Balkans violent conflicts occur among Slavs. In the former Soviet Union the relationship between the two largest states where Slavs predominate—Russia and Ukraine—is tense and wary.

Insofar as the number of democracies does increase in coming decades, and the American security umbrella is increasingly furled, we may all witness what might well amount to a controlled experiment testing whether democracies are indeed more peaceful in their relationships one with another. One can argue that popular sentiment in the democracies in recent years has tended to oppose military involvement, although Desert Storm shows that the electorate can be brought around to support such activities by skillful political leadership, especially if cheap and quick results can be provided. On balance, we might be justified in expecting that the advance of democracy, and the absence of an ideological threat to it with wide appeal, will lower the virulence, if not the incidence, of conflict.

The capability to produce nuclear weapons and other weapons of mass destruction, and to deliver those weapons by advanced means, will spread. The spread of nuclear weapons and other weapons of mass destruction to new powers will tend over time to induce caution and to moderate conflict, as it has induced caution in the relations among the superpowers. Anyone contemplating an attack on a power possessing such capabilities will feel new constraints. Chemical and biological weapons' lack of military utility, except when used in surprise against unprotected opponents, will soon become apparent to new possessors of them. In the short run, while nuclear weapons are being introduced, when they are present in very small numbers and before they can be properly protected, they may exacerbate existing tensions. Some governments involved in a regional conflict, for example, acquiring a primitive nuclear capability and fearing their advantage might quickly disappear, could be tempted to use their nuclear weapons.

If nuclear weapons are used, it would be in the context of some regional conflict and would not be likely to spread more widely. While horrific for the peoples involved, it is extremely unlikely that such use could set off larger nuclear exchanges among those now possessing nuclear weapons.[18] Existing nuclear weapons states would have no reason to fear sudden nuclear disarmament by an attack from an emerging nuclear power, and thus would not react to such an attack with a massive nuclear response.

Conventional military technology with capabilities orders of magnitude beyond that used in World War II, Korea, or Vietnam is now available to armed forces around the world. New types of conventional military technology can make the attack more difficult in many combat situations.[19] The force that moves makes itself vulnerable. Furthermore, complex and expensive weaponry may be effectively neutralized by widely available equipment, costing only a tiny fraction of the cost of the weaponry it would destroy.

In general this will make the attack more difficult. An attacker must move, in order to gain ground. The relationship, however, is not a simple one. There are circumstances under which an attacker might make a sudden, surprise advance, and then rely on a tactically defensive posture to protect his gains. Even in such circumstances, however, the gains an attacker might hope to achieve will be inherently small and limited. Insofar as this relationship applies, we can expect that achieving decisive advantage in warfare, even by sophisticated armed forces, will become more and more difficult, and more and more costly.[20] As this occurs, the fear of sudden losses also will decline, and large powers will feel less incentive to intervene in conflicts between others to forestall such losses.[21] In general even small powers will have a greater capacity to impose major costs on large powers. We can expect that these constraints will make the use of force less attractive, will lower the incidence of violent conflict, or at least will tend to make those wars that do occur more limited and more localized.

CONCLUSION

Change in the identity of the players, and change in their relative position due to uneven economic development, are likely to increase the propensity for conflict. Conversely, the lack of great ideological divisions, the proliferation of weapons of mass destruction, and the spread of new types of conventional military technology will tend to moderate conflict, if not to reduce its incidence.

This raises the prospect that the uncertainties and dangers to be expected from a return to a multipolar world politically and economically may be balanced by the moderation in ambitions that would follow from a decline in ideological motives by players in international politics and from the spread of new military technologies. Any long-run tendencies of a multipolar international system toward uncertainty and conflict may be moderated by a lack of high motivation on the part of most actors to undertake major war, and a lack of great confidence in its utility. These attitudes in turn are a product of the particularist ideologies of the actors and the technology that they now have at their disposal. If powerful universalist ideologies arise among the actors, however, if military technology again appears to offer the potential for quick decisive gains at limited costs, the underlying tendency of a multipolar system to encourage conflict would resume.

Perhaps, at least for the immediate future, we are returning to an environment of limited, controllable warfare, where conflicts will, on occasion, lead to wars, but wars that will remain localized and unlikely to spread widely or quickly: wars in which decisive results, and sudden catastrophic reversals, are little to be feared. Perhaps then for a time it will also be a world in which external intervention in these local conflicts will be increasingly difficult, increasingly ineffective, and increasingly costly.

There are, to be sure, many disturbing parallels with 1914. Local conflicts abound and one must be concerned about the potential for outsiders to find themselves drawn into these conflicts, and thus for larger wars to result. Ironically, the Balkans, now as in 1914, are one major locus for conflicts with such potential. But there are crucial differences now. In 1914, most generals believed—and advised their governments—that a big war could be won cheaply and quickly, and that those who attacked first could gain an irreversible advantage. To allow an opponent the first blow was to court destruction. Fear that losses in a local conflict would impact adversely on the central relationship among the great powers encouraged belief in the necessity of outside intervention and discouraged localization of such conflicts. It is difficult to find similar beliefs today. Not only does the existence of nuclear weapons make it impossible to be certain that the costs could be kept in some meaningful relation to the gains, but conventional warfare itself makes major quick and decisive victories doubtful. The difficulty outside powers have shown in finding the will to intervene effectively in the Yugoslav wars may be due not only to their differing interests as to the outcome of those wars but also to the belief that, whatever the military outcome of the conflict, that outcome will not threaten outsiders with sudden and catastrophic change.

If these speculations about the new world strategic environment are correct, what implications do they carry for the policies of the United States and other powers? In such matters, predictions are suspect. The external environment within which policy makers operate does not determine, but only constrains or encourages, their responses. What policy makers actually do reflects not only these environmental considerations but also domestic politics, idiosyncrasies of personality, and peculiarities of approach, style, and tradition in foreign and military policy. In international politics—especially in today's world—a few examples of behavior contrary to that which the environment encourages, or even a single prominent example of such behavior, might carry fateful consequences for all of us.

In the American case, we may be entering an environment in which major geopolitical threats to our security are difficult to conceive. The world may not be an especially peaceful place, nor can we assume that Americans will be immune to terrorist attacks; but the conflicts that will exist will not have the potential to produce situations that will seriously or directly threaten us.[22] For the foreseeable future, no power threatens that domination of Europe or East Asia which drew us into the world wars and the cold war of this century. Furthermore, when threats to our interests do arise, a world with more actors also means that there will be others who would also feel threatened, would be motivated to deal with the problem in their own interest, and would be capable of doing so. Thus, we can expect more often to rely on others to take our irons out of the fire for us, and we will be less often confronted with the necessity to take direct action ourselves. Whether we will be inclined to accept this condition, or to resist it, will, of course, be a function of our domestic political attitudes. There might well be a revival of domestic political support for American military intervention overseas, but at present such a revival seems far-fetched.

In any case, the American ability to produce desired results externally by military force will be increasingly limited. If the assumption made earlier in this book that Desert Storm is not a harbinger proves correct, we will quickly discover the difficulties that new technologies put in the path of those attempting to project power at a distance, unless the qualitative differences between the sides are overwhelming. We may be tempted to repeat our success in Iraq elsewhere. If we succumb to this temptation, however, we are likely to encounter real costs and frustrations, which will quickly erode the domestic political basis for further military intervention.

In response to such frustrations, or in anticipation of them, the United States may instead adopt a military force based on the ability to inflict punishment cheaply and at a distance, not to conquer territory or destroy opposing armed forces.[23] The goal will be to achieve limited objectives by punishment, rather than by military victory. Thus, we may retain a capacity to make those who offend us suffer pain for their efforts, pain in the form perhaps of destruction of key assets, or particular military installations, launched by automated military systems—such as cruise missiles—with high accuracy and from great distances. In many ways this would be the modern equivalent of the nineteenth-century British navy's reliance on punitive expeditions, and the threat of coastal bombardments, to punish the obstreperous. The United States will maintain forces capable of small operations, such as the invasions of Grenada or Panama. But it will not be likely for long to retain large forces designed to take and hold territory against major opposition.

But is this expectation, that there will not be a geopolitical threat to American interests, justified? Future threats to deprive the United States or its friends of vital resources, most obviously oil, may be anticipated, as may terrorist attacks against American territory or American interests abroad. None of these considerations, however, invalidates the conclusions we have reached about the future strategic environment, or the policy implications that we have drawn from them. A future threat to disrupt international oil markets may arise from domestic political change in major oil-producing states, or it may arise from a new attempt to dominate oil-producing areas through international military conquest. A threat arising from domestic change is not inherently a threat for which major military operations are likely to provide a feasible solution. A threat arising from a renewal of Iraqi-like military expansionism is unlikely, however, to have more than short-term implications for oil markets. All those governments that might conceivably attempt such operations are governments for whom revenue considerations to defray growing domestic needs will be important. Indeed, this was the case with Saddam in 1990. Thus even successful military expansionism will not enable such a government to stem the flow of oil. Rather it is more likely instead to use its quasi-monopolistic position to raise prices; and experience has shown that the international economic system can adjust to major price rises without catastrophe. Finally, if military intervention is attempted, the recent war with Iraq may only serve to support the efficacy of air power; the relatively minor ground forces required for such a conflict, if the exceptional conditions that guaranteed air supremacy in that conflict can be repeated; and the lack of utility for major land forces, if those conditions cannot be repeated.

Terrorism may be a product of individual or small-group activities, or it may be inspired, financed, or directed by governments. If the former, prevention and defense against such activities are essentially police activities, in which military establishments have little role. If the latter, all that may be required of military forces is the capacity to punish the offender's sponsor and the political will to employ such means. The capacity to punish, in this context, may be less difficult to acquire than the political commitment to carry out such punishment. Protection of oil supplies and defense against terrorist attacks might indeed prove to be major problems, but it is not at all obvious that they are problems for which the retention of major interventionary forces provides solutions.

The considerations that will affect American policy will likely also affect other powers, all of whom are likely to experience difficulties in achieving lasting and significant political goals through the projection of major military power. Few governments will feel able to rely on the expectation that they could win a major war in a politically decisive way, although many will differ from the United States in that they will not enjoy the American freedom from direct geopolitical threat. These governments will likely retain military forces designed to make such threats increasingly costly, and to secure marginal gains for purposes of diplomatic bargaining.

These conclusions are heavily dependent upon the expectation that the trends that have been outlined here in the attributes of the players in world politics will continue. Interruption or reversal, even momentarily, of these trends could produce a profoundly different strategic environment. Thus, developments in military technology might occur that could hold out the possibility that inexpensive victories could again produce decisive results in warfare. Some may argue that Desert Storm could be repeated elsewhere, that it is feasible to maintain a technological edge that would allow governments to overwhelm opponents at little cost. The hope of quick victories—and the reciprocal fear of sudden and irreversible defeats—might increase the chances that political conflicts would run to war, and the likelihood that wars, once begun, would quickly spread.

Great ideological conflicts that might create broad popular support for costly military interventions could again arise. Religious movements, or nationalist movements—or some new political outlook, even now being polished in the halls of academe—could arise to produce widespread popular support for military sacrifice to achieve external goals. Such ideological fervor seems doubtful now; but the enthusiasms engendered by the French Revolution would have been inexplicable to the cool intellects of the eighteenth-century European Enlightenment, as would the passions exploited by twentieth-century totalitarianism to the mannered optimists of the post-Victorian twilight in 1914.

Finally, growing economic protectionism could lead to mutually hostile economic blocs. Economic issues and questions of environmental policy, far from tying nations together in a web of cooperative relationships, could lead to new occasions for conflict over relative advantage. Governments might prefer immediate advantage over competitors to the prospect of a long-run advantage for everyone. Economic hostility could lead to political and military confrontation.

Developments in any of these directions could swiftly reverse our expectation of a world in which warfare will not be widespread or threaten broad consequences, a world in which regional disputes will likely remain regional. If optimism about the continuance of present trends is justified, however, it is likely that the occasions on which the use of military force will appear more attractive, or less horrendous, than the alternative will increasingly be confined to limited and localized circumstances.

The role of war in international politics in the future will be a function of the things that determined it in the past: the goals for which people are willing to fight; the external context within which their actions take place; the technical means they have at their disposal; and their judgments about the degree to which those means will prove useful to achieve those goals. People could make colossal mistakes in the future. They have made some horrendous misjudgments in the past. But the mistakes of the past have generally been made out of honest, if willful, ignorance. We now carry a collective memory that makes similar ignorance in the future doubtful.

Notes

Chapter 1   The Role of War in International Politics

1. Jack S. Levy, *War in the Modern Great Power System, 1495–1975* (Lexington: University Press of Kentucky, 1983), 170. For a survey of organized violence in human society from prehistory through classical Greece, see Arthur Ferrill, *The Origins of War: From the Stone Age to Alexander the Great* (New York: Thames & Hudson, 1985).

2. See William H. McNeill, *The Pursuit of Power: Technology, Armed Force, and Society since A.D. 1000* (Chicago: University of Chicago Press, 1982). McNeill argues that the role of disease has been of comparable significance. See also his *Plagues and Peoples* (Garden City, N.Y.: Anchor Books, 1976).

3. Still unequaled in examining these matters, and in exploring their implications for the question of whether war in the modern era is becoming obsolete, is Robert E. Osgood and Robert W. Tucker, *Force, Order, and Justice* (Baltimore: Johns Hopkins Press, 1967). See also F. H. Hinsley, *Power and the Pursuit of Peace: Theory and Practice in the History of Relations between States* (Cambridge: Cambridge University Press, 1963). For an encyclopedic, if uncritical, survey of ideas on these topics up to the period between the two world wars of this century, see Frank M. Russell, *Theories of International Relations* (New York: Appleton-Century, 1936). See also Hedley Bull, *The Anarchical Society: A Study of Order in World Politics* (London: Macmillan, 1977); F. Parkinson, *The Philosophy of International Relations: A Study in the History of Thought* (Beverly Hills, Calif.: Sage Publications, 1977); John J. Weltman, "The American Tradition in International Thought: Science as Therapy," in Timothy Fuller, ed., *The Prospects of Liberalism: Nine Essays*, Colorado College Studies No. 20 (Colorado Springs: Colorado College, 1984), 124–45.

4. See Martin Wight, "Why Is There No International Theory?" in Herbert Butterfield and Martin Wight, eds., *Diplomatic Investigations* (Cambridge: Harvard University Press, 1966), 17–34.

5. Kenneth N. Waltz, *Man, the State, and War* (New York: Columbia University Press, 1954). The succeeding discussion in the text of the causes of war follows the analytical categories developed by Waltz in this classic work. See also John J. Weltman, "On the Interpretation of International Thought," *Review of Politics* 44, 1 (1982), 27–41.

6. Hans J. Morgenthau, *Politics among Nations: The Struggle for Power and Peace* (New York: Alfred A. Knopf, 1948).

7. See, e.g., Reinhold Niebuhr, *Moral Man and Immoral Society* (New York: Charles Scribner's Sons, 1960), and *The Structure of Nations and Empire* (New York: Charles Scribner's Sons, 1959).

8. See Robert Jervis, *Perception and Misperception in International Politics* (Princeton: Princeton University Press, 1976).

9. William H. McNeill points to the emotional solidarity produced by exercise in common of the large muscle groups, as in military drill: *The Pursuit of Power*, 13–43.

10. Kenneth N. Waltz, *Theory of International Politics* (Reading, Mass.: Addison-Wesley, 1979), 25.

11. See, e.g., Gordon A. Craig, *Germany, 1866–1945* (Oxford University Press, 1978), 116–24, 242–47.

12. Both Joseph Schumpeter and Max Weber argue in this fashion. See Joseph A. Schumpeter, *Imperialism and Social Classes* (Oxford: Blackwell, 1951); and Max Weber, *The Protestant Ethic and the Spirit of Capitalism* (New York: Charles Scribner's Sons, 1958). See also Reinhard Bendix, *Max Weber: An Intellectual Portrait* (Garden City, N.Y.: Doubleday, 1960), 49–64.

13. Schumpeter, *Imperialism*, 90–91.

14. See, e.g., Immanuel Wallerstein, *The Modern World-System* (New York: Academic Press, 1974). See also James A. Caporaso, ed., "Dependence and Dependency in the Global System," *International Organization* 32, 1 (1978); Tony Smith, "The Underdevelopment of Development Literature: The Case of Dependency Theory," *World Politics* 31, 2 (1979), 247–88.

15. See, e.g., Gordon A. Craig, "The Political Leader as Strategist," in Peter Paret, ed., *Makers of Modern Strategy: From Machiavelli to the Nuclear Age* (Princeton: Princeton University Press, 1986), esp. 481–91.

16. Waltz, *Man, the State, and War*, esp. 159–86.

17. See Waltz, *Theory of International Politics*, esp. 81–97.

18. For some arguments in the contrary tradition, that rules and rule making in the international arena do not differ in any fundamental sense from such processes in other arenas, see, e.g., Charles R. Beitz, *Political Theory and International Relations* (Princeton: Princeton University Press, 1979), and Nicholas G. Onuf, *World of Our Making* (Columbia: University of South Carolina Press, 1989).

19. Thomas Hobbes, *Leviathan* (Oxford: Basil Blackwell, 1960), esp. 80–145; John Locke, *Two Treatises of Government* (New York: Hafner Publishing, 1947), esp. 121–202.

20. Hobbes, *Leviathan*, 82.

21. Ibid., 83.

22. Cited in Waltz, *Man, the State, and War*, 167–69. For the original, see Jean Jacques Rousseau, *The Social Contract and Discourses* (New York: E. P. Dutton, 1950), 238.

23. The term was coined by John H. Herz. See his *International Politics in the Atomic Age* (New York: Columbia University Press, 1959), 230.

24. Waltz, *Man, the State, and War*, esp. 159–86.

25. Geoffrey Parker, *The Military Revolution: Military Innovation and the Rise of the*

West, 1500–1800 (Cambridge: Cambridge University Press, 1988), 4. See also McNeill, *The Pursuit of Power.*

26. B. H. Liddell Hart, *Strategy: The Indirect Approach* (London: Faber & Faber, 1968), 334.

Chapter 2   The Rise of Modern World Politics

1. On medieval warfare and military institutions, see Charles Oman, *A History of the Art of War in the Middle Ages,* 2d ed., 2 vols. (New York: B. Franklin, 1959); Archer Jones, *The Art of War in the Western World* (Oxford: Oxford University Press, 1989), 92–123; Bernard Brodie and Fawn M. Brodie, *From Crossbow to H-Bomb* (Bloomington: Indiana University Press, 1973), 28–40; Michael Howard, *War in European History* (Oxford: Oxford University Press, 1976), 1–19; Theodore Ropp, *War in the Modern World,* rev. ed. (New York: Collier, 1962), 19–25.

2. See, e.g., Martin van Creveld, *Technology and War* (New York: Free Press, 1989), esp. 81–110.

3. Ibid., esp. 99–109.

4. George Clark, *War and Society in the Seventeenth Century* (Cambridge: Cambridge University Press, 1958).

5. See George Clark, *The Seventeenth Century* (Oxford: Oxford University Press, 1961), 4–5. For some other accounts of the development of warfare through the seventeenth century, see Jones, *The Art of War in the Western World,* 214–66; Hans Delbrück, *History of the Art of War,* vol. 4, *The Dawn of Modern Warfare,* trans. Walter J. Renfroe, Jr. (Lincoln: University of Nebraska Press, 1990), 3–219; C. V. Wedgwood, *The Thirty Years War* (New Haven: Yale University Press, 1949); Brodie and Brodie, *From Crossbow to H-Bomb,* 41–99; E. B. Potter and Chester W. Nimitz, eds., *Sea Power: A Naval History* (Englewood Cliffs, N.J.: Prentice-Hall, 1960), 1–20; Howard, *War in European History,* 20–53; and Ropp, *War in the Modern World,* 25–44. See also Gunther E. Rothenberg, "Maurice of Nassau, Gustavus Adolphus, Raimondo Montecuccoli, and the 'Military Revolution' of the Seventeenth Century," in Peter Paret, ed., *Makers of Modern Strategy* (Princeton: Princeton University Press, 1986), 32–63; Martin van Creveld, *Command in War* (Cambridge: Harvard University Press, 1985), 17–57; John U. Nef, *War and Human Progress: An Essay on the Rise of Industrial Civilization* (New York: W. W. Norton, 1968), 3–270.

6. Voltaire, *Candide, or Optimism,* trans. John Butt (New York: Penguin Books, 1950), 23–24.

7. Walter L. Dorn, *Competition for Empire, 1740–1763* (New York: Harper & Row, 1963), 15.

8. See Potter and Nimitz, *Sea Power,* 21–65; Ropp, *War in the Modern World,* 70–75. Julian S. Corbett, ed., *Fighting Instructions, 1530–1816* (London: Navy Records Society, 1905); Alfred Thayer Mahan, *The Influence of Seapower upon History, 1660–1783* (New York: Hill & Wang, 1957).

9. On eighteenth-century land warfare, see Ropp, *War in the Modern World,* 44–59; Delbrück, *History of the Art of War,* 223–383; J. F. C. Fuller, *The Conduct of War, 1789–1961* (New Brunswick, N.J.: Rutgers University Press, 1961), 15–25; Spenser Wilkinson, *The Defence of Piedmont* (Oxford: Oxford University Press, 1927); Robert E. Osgood and Robert W. Tucker, *Force, Order, and Justice* (Balti-

more: Johns Hopkins Press, 1967), 41–53; Howard, *War in European History*, 54–74; Jones, *The Art of War in the Western World*, 267–319; Hans Speier, "Militarism in the Eighteenth Century," in *Social Order and the Risks of War: Papers in Political Sociology* (Cambridge: MIT Press, 1969), 230–52. See also Henry Guerlac, "Vauban: The Impact of Science on War," and R. R. Palmer, "Frederick the Great, Guibert, Bülow: From Dynastic to National War," both in Paret, *Makers of Modern Strategy*, 64–90, 91–119.

10. See William H. McNeill, *The Pursuit of Power: Technology, Armed Force, and Society since A.D. 1000* (Chicago: University of Chicago Press, 1982), esp. 117–43; Geoffrey Parker, *The Military Revolution: Military Innovation and the Rise of the West, 1500–1800* (Cambridge: Cambridge University Press, 1988), 103–45. The process of establishing this European dominance was not instantaneous, and took place at considerably different paces in different regions, depending on the characteristics of the societies with which Europeans came into contact, some of whom effectively resisted European military intrusion for extended periods of time.

11. On the eighteenth-century international system, see John B. Wolf, *The Emergence of the Great Powers, 1685–1715* (New York: Harper & Row, 1962); Penfield Roberts, *The Quest for Security, 1715–1740* (New York: Harper & Row, 1963); Dorn, *Competition for Empire*; Leo Gershoy, *From Despotism to Revolution, 1763–1789* (New York: Harper & Row, 1963); Max Beloff, *The Age of Absolutism, 1660–1815* (New York: Harper & Row, 1962); Edward Vose Gulick, *Europe's Classical Balance of Power* (Ithaca, N.Y.: Cornell University Press, 1955); Osgood and Tucker, *Force, Order, and Justice*, 96–104; F. Parkinson, *The Philosophy of International Relations: A Study in the History of Thought* (Beverly Hills, Calif.: Sage Publications, 1977), 43–60. See also the classic essay by David Hume, "Of the Balance of Power," in David Hume, *Essays, Moral, Political, and Literary* (Indianapolis: Liberty Fund, 1987), 332–41; Henry Brougham, "Balance of Power," in M. G. Forsyth, H. M. A. Keens-Soper, and P. Savigear, eds., *The Theory of International Relations* (New York: Atherton Press, 1970), 259–74; and Friedrich von Gentz, "Fragments upon the Present State of the Political Balance of Europe," in Forsyth et al., *The Theory of International Relations*, 275–304.

12. The Enlightenment of the eighteenth century was to give rise not only to such optimism about the controllability and utility of international conflict but also to a critical tradition that saw war as a species of irrational butchery. See Peter Gay, *The Enlightenment: An Interpretation* (New York: Norton, 1977), 2: esp. 401–7; Michael Howard, *War and the Liberal Conscience* (London: Temple Smith, 1978), esp. 13–51; John J. Weltman, "The American Tradition in International Thought: Science as Therapy," in Timothy Fuller, ed., *The Prospects of Liberalism: Nine Essays*, Colorado College Studies No. 20 (Colorado Springs: Colorado College, 1984), 124–45; Parkinson, *The Philosophy of International Relations*, 61–71.

Chapter 3   Nationalism and Savagery: The Wars of the French Revolution

1. For accounts of the politics, warfare, and diplomacy of the revolutionary and Napoleonic periods, see Steven T. Ross, *European Diplomatic History, 1789–1815: France against Europe* (Garden City, N.Y.: Anchor Books, 1969); Theodore Ropp, *War in the Modern World*, rev. ed. (New York: Collier, 1962), 98–139;

Hans Delbrück, *History of the Art of War,* vol. 4, *The Dawn of Modern Warfare,* trans. Walter J. Renfroe, Jr. (Lincoln: University of Nebraska Press, 1990), 387–456; Steven T. Ross, *Quest for Victory: French Military Strategy, 1792–1799* (South Brunswick, N.J.: A. S. Barnes, 1973); Peter Paret, "Napoleon and the Revolution in War," in Peter Paret, ed., *Makers of Modern Strategy: From Machiavelli to the Nuclear Age* (Princeton: Princeton University Press, 1986), 123–42; R. R. Palmer, *The World of the French Revolution* (New York: Harper & Row, 1971); R. R. Palmer, *Twelve Who Ruled* (Princeton: Princeton University Press, 1969); Steven T. Ross, ed., *The French Revolution: Conflict or Continuity?* (New York: Holt, Rinehart & Winston, 1971); J. F. C. Fuller, *The Conduct of War, 1789–1961* (New Brunswick, N.J.: Rutgers University Press, 1961), 26–58; Michael Howard, *War in European History* (Oxford: Oxford University Press, 1976), 75–93; Crane Brinton, *A Decade of Revolution, 1789–1799* (New York: Harper & Row, 1963); Geoffrey Brunn, *Europe and the French Imperium, 1799–1814* (New York: Harper & Row, 1963); David G. Chandler, *The Campaigns of Napoleon* (New York: Macmillan, 1966); Archer Jones, *The Art of War in the Western World* (Oxford: Oxford University Press, 1989), 320–86; James Marshall-Cornwall, *Napoleon as Military Commander* (London: Batsford, 1967); Gunther E. Rothenberg, *The Art of Warfare in the Age of Napoleon* (Bloomington: Indiana University Press, 1978); Peter Paret, *Clausewitz and the State* (Oxford: Oxford University Press, 1976), 3–77; Martin van Creveld, *Command in War* (Cambridge: Harvard University Press, 1985), 58–102.

2. Delbrück, *History of the Art of War,* 396.

3. See Jones, *The Art of War in the Western World,* 653–54.

4. Delbrück, *History of the Art of War,* 398.

5. For the Napoleonic battle experience, see John Keegan, *The Face of Battle: A Study of Agincourt, Waterloo and the Somme* (New York: Penguin Books, 1978), 117–206.

6. On nationalism, see, e.g., Hans Kohn, *The Idea of Nationalism: A Study in Its Origins and Background* (New York: Macmillan, 1956); E. J. Hobsbawm, *Nations and Nationalism since 1780: Programme, Myth, Reality* (Cambridge: Cambridge University Press, 1990); Eugene Kamenka, ed., *Nationalism: The Nature and Evolution of an Idea* (New York: St. Martin's Press, 1976), esp. 2–36; Elie Kedourie, *Nationalism* (London: Hutchinson, 1960); F. Parkinson, *The Philosophy of International Relations: A Study in the History of Thought* (Beverly Hills, Calif.: Sage Publications, 1977), 129–42.

7. For warfare at sea during this period, see E. B. Potter and Chester W. Nimitz, eds., *Sea Power: A Naval History* (Englewood Cliffs, N.J.: Prentice-Hall, 1960), 108–224; Ropp, *War in the Modern World,* 114–15, 120–32.

8. See Paul M. Kennedy, *The Rise and Fall of British Naval Mastery* (Malabar, Fl.: Krieger Publishing, 1982), esp. 117–47.

9. For a contemporary analysis of this campaign, see Carl von Clausewitz, *The Campaign of 1812 in Russia* (1843; reprint, translation, London: Greenhill Press; Novato, Calif.: Presidio Press, 1992).

10. Ropp, *War in the Modern World,* 135n.

11. H. Rothfels, "Clausewitz," in Edward Mead Earle, ed., *Makers of Modern Strat-*

egy: Military Thought from Machiavelli to Hitler (Princeton: Princeton University Press, 1943), 98.

12. Isaiah Berlin, "The Bent Twig: On the Rise of Nationalism," in *The Crooked Timber of Humanity: Chapters in the History of Ideas,* ed. Henry Hardy (New York: Alfred A. Knopf, 1991), 246.

13. On the diplomacy of the peace settlement and the early years of the Concert, see Henry A. Kissinger, *A World Restored: Metternich, Castlereagh and the Problems of Peace, 1812–22* (Boston: Houghton Mifflin, 1957). See also René Albrecht-Carrié, *A Diplomatic History of Europe since the Congress of Vienna* (New York: Harper, 1958), 3–58; René Albrecht-Carrié, ed., *The Concert of Europe* (New York: Walker, 1968), 1–128; Frederick B. Artz, *Reaction and Revolution, 1814–1832* (New York: Harper, 1963); Harold Nicolson, *The Congress of Vienna: A Study in Allied Unity, 1812–1822* (New York: Viking, 1961); Hajo Holborn, *The Political Collapse of Europe* (New York: Alfred A. Knopf, 1960), 21–36; F. H. Hinsley, *Power and the Pursuit of Peace: Theory and Practice in the History of Relations between States* (Cambridge: Cambridge University Press, 1963), 194–237; Edward Vose Gulick, *Europe's Classical Balance of Power* (Ithaca, N.Y.: Cornell University Press, 1955), 132–310.

14. Robert E. Osgood and Robert W. Tucker, *Force, Order, and Justice* (Baltimore: Johns Hopkins Press, 1967), 79.

Chapter 4   The Genesis of Strategic Thought: Jomini and Clausewitz

1. See Henry Guerlac, "Vauban: The Impact of Science on War," and R. R. Palmer, "Frederick the Great, Guibert, Bülow: From Dynastic to National War," both in Peter Paret, ed., *Makers of Modern Strategy: From Machiavelli to the Nuclear Age* (Princeton: Princeton University Press, 1986), 64–90, 91–119.

2. See especially his *Discourses on the First Decade of Titus Livius* (1513–17) and *Art of War* (1521), in *Machiavelli: The Chief Works and Others,* trans. Allan Gilbert, 3 vols. (Durham, N.C.: Duke University Press, 1989), 1:175–529; 2:561–726. See also Felix Gilbert, "Machiavelli: The Renaissance of the Art of War," in Edward Mead Earle, ed., *Makers of Modern Strategy: Military Thought from Machiavelli to Hitler* (Princeton: Princeton University Press, 1943), 3–25, and in Paret, *Makers of Modern Strategy,* 11–31. See also the superb recent intellectual biography of Machiavelli by Sebastian de Grazia, *Machiavelli in Hell* (Princeton: Princeton University Press, 1989), esp. 157–73; Herbert Butterfield, *The Statecraft of Machiavelli* (New York: Collier, 1962); Felix Gilbert, *Machiavelli and Guicciardini: Politics and History in Sixteenth Century Florence* (Princeton: Princeton University Press, 1965), esp. 105–200.

3. See also Michael Howard, "Jomini and the Classical Tradition in Military Thought," in Michael Howard, ed., *The Theory and Practice of War* (Bloomington: Indiana University Press, 1975), 3–20.

4. John Shy, "Jomini," in Paret, *Makers of Modern Strategy,* 160. See also Crane Brinton, Gordon A. Craig, and Felix Gilbert, "Jomini," in Earle, *Makers of Modern Strategy,* 77–92.

5. On the military reform movements, see, e.g., Theodore Ropp, *War in the Modern World* (New York: Collier, 1962), 143–60; Gordon A. Craig, *The Politics of the Prussian Army, 1640–1945* (Oxford: Oxford University Press, 1979), 37–81; Peter Paret, *Clausewitz and the State* (Oxford: Oxford University Press, 1976),

137–46; Peter Paret, *Yorck and the Era of Prussian Reform* (Princeton: Princeton University Press, 1966); Walter Goerlitz, *History of the German General Staff, 1657–1945* (New York: Praeger, 1953), 15–68; Gordon A. Craig, "Command and Staff Problems in the Austrian Army, 1740–1866," in Howard, *The Theory and Practice of War*, 43–67.

6. Antoine Henri de Jomini, *The Art of War* (1862 translation of *Précis de l'art de guerre*; reprint, London: Greenhill Press; Novato, Calif.: Presidio Press, 1992), 13–65. (Unless otherwise noted further references to the works of Jomini will refer to this edition. Although the translation is often strained and obtuse, this is the English version most easily available today.) While he admitted that wars might be made for different reasons, and that the military institutions of states might differ according to their differing constitutions, Jomini did not conceive that these matters would change the validity of the principles of strategy or the manner of their applicability.

7. Ibid., 70.

8. Ibid., 100–132.

9. The concept of "bases of operations" is developed in ibid., 77–84.

10. Ibid., 88–92.

11. Ibid., 102. Emphasis in the original.

12. Ibid., 114. Emphasis in the original.

13. Ibid., e.g., 178.

14. E.g., Howard, "Jomini and the Classical Tradition in Military Thought," 10.

15. Jomini, *The Art of War*, 176.

16. Ibid., 359–60. This passage was written after the outbreak of the Crimean War in 1854.

17. Ibid., 29–35.

18. A superb account of Clausewitz's life and the development of his thought is to be found in Paret, *Clausewitz and the State*; see also Peter Paret, "Clausewitz: A Bibliographical Survey," *World Politics*, 17, 2(1965), 272–85; Peter Paret, "Clausewitz," in Paret, *Makers of Modern Strategy*, 186–213; H. Rothfels, "Clausewitz," in Earle, *Makers of Modern Strategy*, 93–113; Michael Howard, *Clausewitz* (Oxford: Oxford University Press, 1983).

19. On misinterpretations of Clausewitz, see Michael Howard, "The Influence of Clausewitz," in Carl von Clausewitz, *On War*, ed. and trans. Michael Howard and Peter Paret (Princeton: Princeton University Press, 1976), 27–44 (unless otherwise noted, references to the works of Clausewitz will refer to this edition, which is the finest English translation and is accompanied by a number of very useful interpretive essays). Also see Peter Paret, "Clausewitz and the Nineteenth Century," in Howard, *The Theory and Practice of War*, 23–41.

20. "Two Notes by the Author on His Plans for Revising *On War*," in Clausewitz, *On War*, 69–71, indicates his intention to revise the entire work to reflect two major themes: the "dual nature" of war (see subsequent discussion) and the subordination of war to policy. At his death, only book 1, chapter 1, "What is War?" (75–89), had been fully revised to conform to these criteria, and book 8, "War Plans" (577–637), partially so. The unrevised remainder of *On War* should be read with Clausewitz's intentions in mind.

21. The term is Peter Paret's. See his essay, "The Genesis of *On War*," in ibid., 22–25; and Paret, *Clausewitz and the State*, esp. 378–81.

22. "Two Notes by the Author on His Plans for Revising *On War*," in Clausewitz, *On War*, 69. Emphasis in the original.
23. See Paret, *Clausewitz and the State*, 357ff.
24. Clausewitz, *On War*, 77.
25. Ibid., 78–79.
26. Ibid., 89.
27. Ibid., e.g., 76, 86–87, 585.
28. While "*the defensive form of warfare is intrinsically stronger than the offensive*," a merely passive defense will not allow the defender to achieve his object. At some point he must therefore assume the offensive. Ibid., 358. Emphasis in the original.
29. E.g., ibid., 523–73, passim.
30. Ibid., 605–10.
31. The influence of Clausewitz was not to be confined to those who accepted the primacy of the state. His emphasis on the political environment was to facilitate analysis of conflict in his terms by those in the revolutionary Marxist tradition who saw conflict primarily in class terms. See, e.g., Sigmund Neumann and Mark von Hagen, "Engels and Marx on Revolution, War, and the Army in Society," in Paret, *Makers of Modern Strategy*, 262–80; J. F. C. Fuller, *The Conduct of War, 1789–1961* (New Brunswick, N.J.: Rutgers University Press, 1961), 81–85; W. B. Gallie, *Philosophers of Peace and War* (Cambridge: Cambridge University Press, 1978), 66–99.
32. Clausewitz, *On War*, e.g., 226.

Chapter 5   False Victories: The Wars of the Mid-Nineteenth Century

1. For European politics and diplomacy from the mid-nineteenth century through World War I, see A. J. P. Taylor, *The Struggle for Mastery in Europe, 1848–1918* (Oxford: Oxford University Press, 1954). See also Hajo Holborn, *The Political Collapse of Europe* (New York: Alfred A. Knopf, 1960), 27–70; René Albrecht-Carrié, *A Diplomatic History of Europe since the Congress of Vienna* (New York: Harper, 1958), 65–295; Robert C. Binkley, *Realism and Nationalism, 1852–1871* (New York: Harper & Row, 1963); L. C. B. Seaman, *From Vienna to Versailles* (New York: Harper & Row, 1963), esp. 23–156.
2. For the wars of the mid-nineteenth century, see William McElwee, *The Art of War: Waterloo to Mons* (Bloomington: Indiana University Press, 1974); Theodore Ropp, *War in the Modern World*, rev. ed. (New York: Collier, 1962), 143–94; J. F. C. Fuller, *The Conduct of War, 1789–1961* (New Brunswick, N.J.: Rutgers University Press, 1961), 95–150; Robert E. Osgood and Robert W. Tucker, *Force, Order, and Justice* (Baltimore: Johns Hopkins Press, 1967), 53–64; Michael Howard, *War in European History* (Oxford: Oxford University Press, 1976), 94–115; Archer Jones, *The Art of War in the Western World* (Oxford: Oxford University Press, 1989), 387–433; Martin van Creveld, *Command in War* (Cambridge: Harvard University Press, 1985), 103–47.
3. On Bismarck, see A. J. P. Taylor, *Bismarck, the Man and the Statesman* (New York: Random House, 1967); Edward Crankshaw, *Bismarck* (New York: Viking, 1981); Henry A. Kissinger, "The White Revolutionary: Reflections on Bismarck," *Daedalus* 97 (Summer 1968), 888–924.

4. On German unification, see Gordon A. Craig, *Germany, 1866–1945* (Oxford: Oxford University Press, 1978), 1–37.

5. On changes in military technology, see McElwee, *The Art of War*, 106–46; Bernard Brodie and Fawn M. Brodie, *From Crossbow to H-Bomb* (Bloomington: Indiana University Press, 1973), 124–71; Martin van Creveld, *Technology and War* (New York: Free Press, 1989), 153–232; Trevor N. Dupuy, *The Evolution of Weapons and Warfare* (Fairfax, Va.: Hero Books, 1984), 169–216.

6. For the development of the general staff, see Walter Goerlitz, *History of the German General Staff, 1657–1945* (New York: Praeger, 1953); Gordon A. Craig, *The Politics of the Prussian Army, 1640–1945* (Oxford: Oxford University Press, 1979), esp. 82–254; Hajo Holborn, "The Prusso-German School: Moltke and the Rise of the General Staff," in Peter Paret, ed., *Makers of Modern Strategy: From Machiavelli to the Nuclear Age* (Princeton: Princeton University Press, 1986), 281–95; Gunther E. Rothenberg, "Moltke, Schlieffen, and the Doctrine of Strategic Envelopment," in ibid., 296–325.

7. For an extensive analysis of this conflict, see Michael Howard, *The Franco-Prussian War* (London: Methuen, 1981).

8. See Jay Luvaas, *The Military Legacy of the Civil War: The European Inheritance* (Chicago: University of Chicago Press, 1959).

9. James M. McPherson's *Battle Cry of Freedom: The Civil War Era* (Oxford: Oxford University Press, 1988) provides a comprehensive account of the war's background, genesis, and conduct in a single volume. See also David Donald, ed., *Why the North Won the Civil War* (Baton Rouge: Louisiana State University Press, 1960); Herman Hattaway and Archer Jones, *How the North Won: A Military History of the Civil War* (Urbana: University of Illinois Press, 1983); Richard E. Beringer, Herman Hattaway, Archer Jones, and William N. Still, Jr., *Why the South Lost the Civil War* (Athens: University of Georgia Press, 1986); Allan R. Millett and Peter Maslowski, *For the Common Defense: A Military History of the United States of America* (New York: Free Press, 1984), 153–232. Russell F. Weigley, *The American Way of War: A History of United States Military Strategy and Policy* (New York: Macmillan, 1973), 77–152.

10. McPherson, *Battle Cry of Freedom*, 854.

11. Hattaway and Jones, *How the North Won*, 243.

12. McPherson, *Battle Cry of Freedom*, 262.

13. Hattaway and Jones, *How the North Won*, 17–18.

14. E.g., McPherson, *Battle Cry of Freedom*, 771.

15. E.g., ibid., 546–67.

16. These arguments are rehearsed in Beringer et al., *Why the South Lost the Civil War*.

17. See also Alfred Vagts, *Defense and Diplomacy: The Soldier and the Conduct of Foreign Relations* (New York: King's Crown Press, 1956), 231–55, 377–412.

18. On arms races, see Samuel P. Huntington, "Arms Races: Prerequisites and Results," *Public Policy* 9 (1958), 41–83.

19. On naval warfare, see E. B. Potter and Chester W. Nimitz, eds., *Sea Power: A Naval History* (Englewood Cliffs, N.J.: Prentice-Hall, 1960), 225–393.

20. See Vagts, *Defense and Diplomacy*, 87–129.

Chapter 6   Military Surprise and Catastrophe: World War I

1. Direct combat deaths approached nine million. Marc Ferro, *The Great War, 1914–1918* (London: Routledge & Kegan Paul, 1973), 227.
2. For a study of literary imagery evoked by the war, see Paul Fussell, *The Great War and Modern Memory* (Oxford: Oxford University Press, 1975).
3. For the origins of World War I and diplomacy of the decades preceding it, see A. J. P. Taylor, *The Struggle for Mastery in Europe, 1848–1918* (Oxford: Oxford University Press, 1954), esp. 255–568; Fritz Fischer, *Germany's Aims in the First World War* (New York: W. W. Norton, 1967); V. R. Berghahn, *Germany and the Approach of War in 1914* (New York: St. Martin's Press, 1973); Raymond Aron, *The Century of Total War* (Boston: Beacon Press, 1955), 9–31; Hajo Holborn, *The Political Collapse of Europe* (New York: Alfred A. Knopf, 1960), 71–110; William L. Langer, *European Alliances and Alignments, 1871–1890* (New York: Random House, 1964); René Albrecht-Carrié, *A Diplomatic History of Europe since the Congress of Vienna* (New York: Harper, 1958), 299–384; L. C. B. Seaman, *From Vienna to Versailles* (New York: Harper & Row, 1963), esp. 157–211; Joachim Remak, *The Origins of World War I, 1871–1914* (New York: Holt, Rinehart & Winston, 1967); Zara S. Steiner, *Britain and the Origins of the First World War* (New York: St. Martin's Press, 1977). An introduction to the huge historical controversies on the causes of the war may be found in Dwight E. Lee, ed., *The Outbreak of the First World War: Causes and Responsibilities* (Lexington, Mass.: D. C. Heath, 1975). A popular revival of the claim that the machinery of mobilization overwhelmed statesmen can be found in Barbara W. Tuchman, *The Guns of August* (New York: Macmillan, 1962).
4. For an extensive development of this theme, see Geoffrey Blainey, *The Causes of War* (London: Macmillan, 1973).
5. Carl von Clausewitz, *On War*, ed. and trans. Michael Howard and Peter Paret (Princeton: Princeton University Press, 1976), 85. See also 90–99.
6. On arms races, see Samuel P. Huntington, "Arms Races: Prerequisites and Results," *Public Policy* 9 (1958), 41–83.
7. On the Franco-British naval competition, see Bernard Brodie, *Sea Power in the Machine Age* (Princeton: Princeton University Press, 1941), 38–69, 181–210, 283–95; Bernard Brodie and Fawn M. Brodie, *From Crossbow to H-Bomb* (Bloomington: Indiana University Press, 1973), 153–67.
8. See Taylor, *The Struggle for Mastery in Europe*, 479–82; Vagts, *Defense and Diplomacy*, 118–26.
9. On the Anglo-German naval race, see E. L. Woodward, *Great Britain and the German Navy* (London: Frank Cass, 1964); Robert K. Massie, *Dreadnought: Britain, Germany, and the Coming of the Great War* (New York: Random House, 1991).
10. See also Michael Howard, *The Continental Commitment: The Dilemma of British Defense Policy in the Era of the Two World Wars* (London: Maurice Temple Smith, 1972).
11. See George F. Kennan, *The Decline of Bismarck's European Order: Franco-Russian Relations, 1875–1890* (Princeton: Princeton University Press, 1979).
12. Vagts, *Defense and Diplomacy*, 126–29.

13. See, e.g., Theodore Ropp, *War in the Modern World*, rev. ed. (New York: Collier, 1962), 218–22.

14. See Gerhard Ritter, *The Schlieffen Plan: Critique of a Myth* (New York: Praeger, 1958). See also Gordon A. Craig, *The Politics of the Prussian Army, 1640–1945* (Oxford: Oxford University Press, 1979), 273–98.

15. On the evolution of German planning, see Jack L. Snyder, *The Ideology of the Offensive: Military Decision Making and the Disasters of 1914* (Ithaca, N.Y.: Cornell University Press, 1984), 125–47.

16. For the experience of combat on the western front, see John Keegan, *The Face of Battle: A Study of Agincourt, Waterloo and the Somme* (New York: Penguin Books, 1978), 207–89.

17. Ropp, *War in the Modern World*, 250.

18. For the course of the war, see Ferro, *The Great War*; B. H. Liddell Hart, *A History of the World War, 1914–1918* (London: Faber & Faber, 1936); Ropp, *War in the Modern World*, 239–74; J. F. C. Fuller, *The Conduct of War, 1789–1961* (New Brunswick, N.J.: Rutgers University Press, 1961), 151–82; Robert E. Osgood and Robert W. Tucker, *Force, Order, and Justice* (Baltimore: Johns Hopkins Press, 1967), 64–70; Michael Howard, *War in European History* (Oxford: Oxford University Press, 1976), 116–35; Archer Jones, *The Art of War in the Western World* (Oxford: Oxford University Press, 1989), 434–88; Martin van Creveld, *Command in War* (Cambridge: Harvard University Press, 1985), 148–88; Correlli Barnett, *The Swordbearers: Studies in Supreme Command in the First World War* (London: Eyre & Spottiswoode, 1963).

19. On the importance of the belief in the offensive, see Michael Howard, "Men against Fire: The Doctrine of the Offensive in 1914," in Peter Paret, ed., *Makers of Modern Strategy: From Machiavelli to the Nuclear Age* (Princeton: Princeton University Press, 1986), 510–26; Snyder, *The Ideology of the Offensive*; and Stephen van Evera, "The Cult of the Offensive and the Origins of the First World War," *International Security* 9, 1 (1984), 58–107.

20. The terms are drawn from those coined by the German historian Delbrück. Delbrück distinguished between two strategic approaches that could be found historically. Each had dominated certain periods. Neither should be construed as less legitimate a strategy than the other. They were *Niederwerfungsstrategie* (annihilation) and *Ermattungsstrategie* (exhaustion). The former's "sole aim was the decisive battle." In the latter, "the battle is merely one of several equally effective means of attaining the political ends of the war and is essentially no more important than the occupation of territory, the destruction of crops or commerce, and the blockade." Gordon A. Craig, "Delbrück: The Military Historian," in Paret, *Makers of Modern Strategy*, 341–42. For Delbrück's formulation of the distinction, see Hans Delbrück, *History of the Art of War*, vol. 4, *The Dawn of Modern Warfare*, trans. Walter J. Renfroe, Jr. (Lincoln: University of Nebraska Press, 1990), 108–9, 439–44. Delbrück himself drew upon a distinction made by Clausewitz between strategies emphasizing the decisive engagement in itself, and those which hope to gain their objectives by the cumulation of small gains. See Carl von Clausewitz, *On War*, ed. and trans. Michael Howard and Peter Paret (Princeton: Princeton University Press, 1976), e.g., 90–99.

21. Mahan's most influential work, *The Influence of Sea Power upon History, 1660–1783*, was first published in 1890 (reprint, New York: Hill & Wang, 1957). See

also Margaret Tuttle Sprout, "Mahan: Evangelist of Sea Power," in Edward Mead Earle, ed., *Makers of Modern Strategy: Military Thought from Machiavelli to Hitler* (Princeton: Princeton University Press, 1943), 415–45; Philip A. Crowl, "Alfred Thayer Mahan: The Naval Historian," in Paret, *Makers of Modern Strategy*, 444–77.

22. On the *Jeune Ecole*, see Theodore Ropp, "Continental Doctrines of Sea Power," in Earle, *Makers of Modern Strategy*, 446–56.

23. This was the essence of Delbrück's critique. See Craig, "Delbrück: The Military Historian," 344–53.

24. For the retreat of the political leadership, see, e.g., Craig, "The Political Leader as Strategist," in Paret, *Makers of Modern Strategy*, 481–91.

Chapter 7   Fear and Hope: Military Power between the Wars

1. On the Versailles settlement, see esp. Harold Nicolson, *Peacemaking, 1919* (New York: Grosset & Dunlap, 1965).

2. See esp. Arnold Wolfers, *Britain and France between Two Wars: Conflicting Strategies of Peace from Versailles to World War II* (New York: W. W. Norton, 1966). For some accounts of politics and strategic developments in the interwar period, see E. H. Carr, *International Relations between the Two World Wars (1919–1939)* (London: Methuen, 1947); A. J. P. Taylor, *The Origins of the Second World War* (Greenwich, Conn.: Fawcett Publications, 1961), 13–101; René Albrecht-Carrié, *A Diplomatic History of Europe since the Congress of Vienna* (New York: Harper, 1958), 385–496; Hajo Holborn, *The Political Collapse of Europe* (New York: Alfred A. Knopf, 1960), 111–37; Akira Iriye, *After Imperialism: The Search for a New Order in the Far East, 1921–1931* (Cambridge: Harvard University Press, 1965); Sally Marks, *The Illusion of Peace: International Relations in Europe, 1918–1933* (New York: St. Martin's Press, 1976); Arnold A. Offner, *The Origins of the Second World War: American Foreign Policy and World Politics, 1917–1941* (New York: Holt, Rinehart & Winston, 1975); Theodore Ropp, *War in the Modern World*, rev. ed. (New York: Collier, 1962), 275–313; Barry Posen, *The Sources of Military Doctrine: France, Britain, and Germany between the World Wars* (Ithaca, N.Y.: Cornell University Press, 1984).

3. In 1931 Japan began a campaign of military expansion into Manchuria, then formally a province of China. The League of Nations condemned this, but took no more forcible action. No power was prepared to risk Japanese attacks against its colonial territories in East Asia. League action led to Japanese withdrawal from the league, but Japanese military action continued, and was broadened in 1937 into a major invasion of southern China. In 1935, Italy invaded Ethiopia, then widely recognized as an independent state. League action this time included economic sanctions, but Britain and France, hoping to enlist Italy as an ally against Germany, shrank from including oil. Italy's invasion succeeded, and Italy soon aligned itself with Germany anyway.

4. For a study of American domestic politics during this period and the limits politics imposed on the conduct of foreign policy, see Robert Dallek, *Franklin D. Roosevelt and American Foreign Policy, 1932–1945* (Oxford: Oxford University Press, 1979), esp. 3–168.

5. See again Wolfers, *Britain and France between Two Wars*.

6. On Douhet and other early air power advocates, see Giulio Douhet, *The Com-

mand of the Air (New York: Coward-McCann, 1942); Edward Warner, "Douhet, Mitchell, Seversky: Theories of Air Warfare," in Edward Mead Earle, ed., *Makers of Modern Strategy: Military Thought from Machiavelli to Hitler* (Princeton: Princeton University Press, 1943), 485–503; David MacIsaac, "Voices from the Central Blue: The Air Power Theorists," in Peter Paret, ed., *Makers of Modern Strategy: From Machiavelli to the Nuclear Age* (Princeton: Princeton University Press, 1986), 624–647; Bernard Brodie, *Strategy in the Missile Age* (Princeton: Princeton University Press, 1959), 3–106.

7. See Norman Gibbs, "British Strategic Doctrine, 1918–1939," in Michael Howard, ed., *The Theory and Practice of War* (Bloomington: Indiana University Press, 1975), 185–212.

8. See George H. Quester, *Deterrence before Hiroshima: The Airpower Background of Modern Strategy* (New York: John Wiley & Sons, 1966), esp. 1–104; Noble Frankland, *The Bombing Offensive against Germany: Outlines and Perspectives* (London: Faber & Faber, 1965), 21–46.

9. For the advocates of armored warfare, see Michael Geyer, "German Strategy in the Age of Machine Warfare, 1914–1945," in Paret, *Makers of Modern Strategy*, 527–95; Brian Bond and Martin Alexander, "Liddell Hart and De Gaulle: The Doctrines of Limited Liability and Mobile Defense," ibid., 598–623; John J. Mearsheimer, *Conventional Deterrence* (Ithaca, N.Y.: Cornell University Press, 1983), esp. 30–52; J. F. C. Fuller, *The Conduct of War, 1789–1961* (New Brunswick, N.J.: Rutgers University Press, 1961), 242–47; Trevor N. Dupuy, *The Evolution of Weapons and Warfare* (Fairfax, Va.: Hero Books, 1984), 230–40. Also see Edward N. Luttwak, "The Operational Level of War," *International Security*, 5, 3 (1980–81), 61–79.

10. Beginning with the first Hague Peace Conference of 1899, attempts had been made to achieve multilateral agreement on the *means* permissible in waging war, with little notable success. From time to time previously, states had attempted with a few local successes to reach *bilateral* agreement on the limitation of arms in specific areas. The most well known was the Rush-Bagot Agreement of 1817 between Britain and the United States restricting warships on the Great Lakes. For the early history of disarmament, see Merze Tate, *The Disarmament Illusion: The Movement for a Limitation of Armaments to 1907* (New York: Macmillan, 1942).

11. See Roger Dingman, *Power in the Pacific: The Origins of Naval Arms Limitation, 1914–1922* (Chicago: University of Chicago Press, 1976); Thomas H. Buckley, *The United States and the Washington Conference, 1921–1922* (Knoxville: University of Tennessee Press, 1970); Raymond G. O'Connor, *Perilous Equilibrium: The United States and the London Naval Conference of 1930* (Lawrence: University of Kansas Press, 1962).

12. On the World Disarmament Conference at Geneva, 1932–34, see John W. Wheeler-Bennett, *The Pipe Dream of Peace: The Story of the Collapse of Disarmament* (New York: W. Morrow, 1935). See also Robert E. Osgood and Robert W. Tucker, *Force, Order, and Justice* (Baltimore: Johns Hopkins Press, 1967), 108–18; Taylor, *The Origins of the Second World War*, 66–78.

13. E.g., Offner, *The Origins of the Second World War*, 144.

Chapter 8   Return to Attrition: World War II

1. See George H. Quester, *Deterrence before Hiroshima: The Airpower Background of Modern Strategy* (New York: John Wiley & Sons, 1966).
2. On Hitler, see Alan Bullock, *Hitler: A Study in Tyranny,* rev. ed. (New York: Harper & Row, 1964). For a contemporary psychoanalytic study of Hitler, see Walter C. Langer, *The Mind of Adolf Hitler: The Secret Wartime Report* (New York: Basic Books, 1972).
3. On the rise of the Nazis, see Gordon A. Craig, *Germany, 1866–1945* (Oxford: Oxford University Press, 1978), esp. 534–601; William L. Shirer, *The Rise and Fall of the Third Reich: A History of Nazi Germany* (New York: Simon & Schuster, 1960), esp. 3–230; and F. L. Carsten, *The Rise of Fascism*, 2d ed. (Berkeley: University of California Press, 1980), 82–159.
4. For an English translation, see Adolf Hitler, *Mein Kampf,* trans. Ralph Manheim (Boston: Houghton Mifflin, 1943).
5. On Germany policy after Hitler came to power and the allied response (or lack of it) through the outbreak of war, see, e.g., A. J. P. Taylor, *The Origins of the Second World War* (Greenwich, Conn.: Fawcett Publications, 1961); Gordon A. Craig and Felix Gilbert, eds., *The Diplomats* (New York: Atheneum, 1963), vol. 2; Klaus Hildebrand, *The Foreign Policy of the Third Reich* (Berkeley: University of California Press, 1979); Craig, *Germany,* 673–713; E. H. Carr, *International Relations between the Two World Wars (1919–1939)* (London: Methuen, 1947), 197–278. René Albrecht-Carrié, *A Diplomatic History of Europe since the Congress of Vienna* (New York: Harper, 1958), 461–540; Martin Gilbert and Richard Gott, *The Appeasers* (Boston: Houghton Mifflin, 1963); Martin Gilbert, *The Roots of Appeasement* (New York: New American Library, 1966); James L. Richardson, "New Perspectives on Appeasement: Some Implications for International Relations," *World Politics,* 40, 3 (1988), 289–316; Gordon A. Craig, *The Politics of the Prussian Army, 1640–1945* (Oxford: Oxford University Press, 1979), 468–503; Robert J. O'Neill, *The German Army and the Nazi Party, 1933–1939* (London: Cassell, 1966).
6. On Munich, see Williamson Murray, *The Change in the European Balance of Power, 1938–1939: The Path to Ruin* (Princeton: Princeton University Press, 1984); John W. Wheeler-Bennett, *Munich: Prologue to Tragedy* (London: Macmillan, 1966); Dwight E. Lee, ed., *Munich: Blunder, Plot, or Tragic Necessity?* (Lexington, Mass.: D. C. Heath, 1970). Also see Christopher Thorne, *The Approach of War, 1938–1939* (New York: St. Martin's Press, 1968).
7. For the origins of the war in the Pacific, see Dorothy Borg and Shumpei Okamoto, eds., *Pearl Harbor as History: Japanese-American Relations 1931–1941* (New York: Columbia University Press, 1973); Arnold A. Offner, *The Origins of the Second World War: American Foreign Policy and World Politics, 1917–1941* (New York: Holt, Rinehart & Winston, 1975); Herbert Feis, *The Road to Pearl Harbor: The Coming of the War between the United States and Japan* (Princeton: Princeton University Press, 1950); Robert J. C. Butow, *Tojo and the Coming of the War* (Stanford: Stanford University Press, 1969); Stephen E. Pelz, *Race to Pearl Harbor* (Cambrige: Harvard University Press, 1974). For a firsthand account, see the diaries of the American Ambassador in Japan from 1931 to 1941: Joseph C. Grew, *Ten Years in Japan* (New York: Simon & Schuster, 1944).

8. Paul Schroeder, *The Axis Alliance and Japanese-American Relations* (Ithaca, N.Y.: Cornell University Press, 1958).

9. See Akira Iriye, *Power and Culture: The Japanese-American War, 1941–1945* (Cambridge: Harvard University Press, 1981), esp. 82–83.

10. On the Pearl Harbor attack and its origins, see the exhaustive analysis by Gordon W. Prange, *At Dawn We Slept: The Untold Story of Pearl Harbor* (New York: McGraw-Hill, 1981). Also see Roberta Wohlstetter, *Pearl Harbor: Warning and Decision* (Stanford: Stanford University Press, 1962). Since the American government and military leadership had agreed with the British on the primacy of the European theater, claims periodically advanced that the Pearl Harbor attack was the product of a deliberate conspiracy to force the United States into the war "by the back door" are patently absurd. But for Germany's declaration of war on the United States on December 11, the Americans could easily have found themselves drawn by domestic opinion into a conflict focused on the Pacific, precisely the situation that the Roosevelt administration wished to avoid. If there was indeed a conspiracy, it must be assumed, therefore, to have included Hitler. See also Robert Dallek, *Franklin D. Roosevelt and American Foreign Policy, 1932–1945* (Oxford: Oxford University Press, 1979), esp. 269–313; and Robert A. Divine, *The Reluctant Belligerent: American Entry into World War II*, 2d ed. (New York: John Wiley & Sons, 1979), esp. 108–64.

11. For the course of the war, see B. H. Liddell Hart, *History of the Second World War* (New York: Paragon Books, 1979); Theodore Ropp, *War in the Modern World*, rev. ed. (New York: Collier, 1962), 314–390; Archer Jones, *The Art of War in the Western World* (Oxford: Oxford University Press, 1989), 508–95; Kent Roberts Greenfield, *American Strategy in World War II: A Reconsideration* (Baltimore: Johns Hopkins Press, 1963); J. F. C. Fuller, *The Conduct of War, 1789–1961* (New Brunswick, N.J.: Rutgers University Press, 1961), 248–309.

12. See also John J. Mearsheimer, *Conventional Deterrence* (Ithaca, N.Y.: Cornell University Press, 1983), 99–133.

13. See also Samuel M. Osgood, ed., *The Fall of France, 1940: Causes and Responsibilities* (Boston: D. C. Heath, 1965).

14. For the war in the Pacific generally, see Ronald H. Spector, *Eagle against the Sun: The American War with Japan* (New York: Free Press, 1985). See also E. B. Potter and Chester W. Nimitz, ed., *Sea Power: A Naval History* (Englewood Cliffs, N.J.: Prentice-Hall, 1960), 628–841. For an interpretation stressing the symbolic aspects of the war, and its cultural significance for the two major belligerents, see Iriye, *Power and Culture: The Japanese-American War, 1941–1945*.

15. Spector, *Eagle against the Sun*, xiv.

16. On the military technologies of World War II, see Bernard Brodie and Fawn M. Brodie, *From Crossbow to H-Bomb* (Bloomington: Indiana University Press, 1973), 200–232; Martin van Creveld, *Technology and War* (New York: Free Press, 1989), 153–232, passim; Trevor N. Dupuy, *The Evolution of Weapons and Warfare* (Fairfax, Va.: Hero Books, 1984), 230–66.

17. For the abortive German plan to invade England, see Ronald Wheatley, *Operation Sea Lion: German Plans for the Invasion of England, 1939–1942* (Oxford: Clarendon Press, 1958).

18. See also Uri Bialer, *The Shadow of the Bomber: The Fear of Air Attack and British Policies, 1932–1939* (London: Royal Historical Society, 1980); and Williamson

Murray, *Strategy for Defeat: The Luftwaffe, 1933–1945* (Maxwell, Al.: Air University Press, 1983), esp. 321–39.

19. See Noble Frankland, *The Bombing Offensive against Germany: Outlines and Perspectives* (London: Faber & Faber, 1965). See also Charles K. Webster and Noble Frankland, *The Strategic Air Offensive against Germany, 1939–1945* (London: HMSO, 1961), 3, 207–311.

20. See Bernard Brodie, *Strategy in the Missile Age* (Princeton: Princeton University Press, 1959), 107–44.

21. See Herbert Feis, *Churchill Roosevelt Stalin: The War They Waged and the Peace They Sought* (Princeton: Princeton University Press, 1967).

22. See Craig, *Germany*, 663–72; Craig, *Politics of the Prussian Army*, 496–503; Robert J. C. Butow, *Japan's Decision to Surrender* (Stanford: Stanford University Press, 1954).

Chapter 9 The Emergence of Nuclear Weapons

1. On the American wartime intelligence effort to determine the character and accomplishments of the German nuclear program, see Samuel A. Goudsmit, *Alsos* (Los Angeles: Tomash Publishers, 1983).

2. Thomas Powers, *Heisenberg's War: The Secret History of the German Bomb* (New York: Knopf, 1933), argues that Werner Heisenberg, Nobel laureate and Germany's most distinguished physicist, deliberately set out to prevent German development of a nuclear weapon. Whether or not this is accepted—and Heisenberg's actions remain open to the interpretation that he simply misjudged the feasibility of producing a bomb that could be used in the current war—this does not alter the conclusion that, from the perspective of the reasonable observer in the British or American government, the danger that the Germans might be engaged in a bomb project appeared highly plausible.

3. For the life and career of Robert Oppenheimer, see Alice Kimball Smith and Charles Weiner, ed., *Robert Oppenheimer, Letters and Recollections* (Cambridge: Harvard University Press, 1980); James W. Kunetka, *Oppenheimer: The Years of Risk* (Englewood Cliffs, N.J.: Prentice-Hall, 1982); Peter Goodchild, *J. Robert Oppenheimer: Shatterer of Worlds* (Boston: Houghton Mifflin, 1981); Herbert F. York, *The Advisors: Oppenheimer, Teller, and the Superbomb* (Stanford: Stanford University Press, 1989); Nuel Pharr Davis, *Lawrence and Oppenheimer* (New York: Simon & Schuster, 1968).

4. In order to ascertain the characteristics of fissile materials from the extremely small quantities that were at first the only samples available, the scientists developed novel computational techniques, techniques that would later drive the postwar development of the electronic computer.

5. For the atomic bomb development program, see the contemporaneous report by Henry DeWolf Smyth, *Atomic Energy for Military Purposes: The Official Report on the Development of the Atomic Bomb under the Auspices of the United States Government, 1940–1945* (Stanford: Stanford University Press, 1945; reprint, 1989). See also Richard Rhodes, *The Making of the Atomic Bomb* (New York: Simon & Schuster, 1986); Martin J. Sherwin, *A World Destroyed: The Atomic Bomb and the Grand Alliance* (New York: Knopf, 1975); James W. Kunetka, *City of Fire: Los Alamos and the Birth of the Atomic Age, 1943–1945*, rev. ed. (Albuquerque: Uni-

versity of New Mexico Press, 1979); John J. Weltman, "Trinity: The Weapons Scientists and the Nuclear Age," *SAIS Review*, 5, 2 (1985), 29–39.

6. In enriched uranium the highly fissionable isotope U-235 is concentrated, by means of chemical separation, into relative quantities far greater than those found in nature. The level of enrichment in U-235 required for weapons is considerably higher than that required for most reactors.

7. Plutonium is an element not found in nature, produced artificially by transmutation from uranium in a nuclear reactor.

8. For a detailed account, see Robert J. C. Butow, *Japan's Decision to Surrender* (Stanford: Stanford University Press, 1954), esp. 142ff.

9. The Nagasaki bomb—the implosion device—was actually more powerful, but it caused less damage than the Hiroshima bomb because hilly terrain shielded some areas of the city from the effects of the explosion.

10. See, e.g., Ronald H. Spector, *Eagle against the Sun: The American War with Japan* (New York: Free Press, 1985), 503–6.

11. See, e.g., B. H. Liddell Hart, *History of the Second World War* (New York: Paragon Books, 1979), 589–613; and Noble Frankland, *The Bombing Offensive against Germany: Outlines and Perspectives* (London: Faber & Faber, 1965), 102, 114–20.

12. See, e.g., Spector, *Eagle against the Sun*, 497–503, 532–50; Liddell Hart, *History of the Second World War*, 683–86.

13. A major historian of the war seems to regard this argument as having some weight. Spector, *Eagle against the Sun*, 558–59.

14. See Butow, *Japan's Decision to Surrender*, 210–27; Herbert Feis, *The Atomic Bomb and the End of World War II* (Princeton: Princeton University Press, 1966), 147; Spector, *Eagle against the Sun*, 557–58.

15. For a study of the conference, see Herbert Feis, *Between War and Peace: The Potsdam Conference* (Princeton: Princeton University Press, 1960).

16. For this "revisionist" position on the origins of the cold war, see, e.g., Gar Alperowitz, *Atomic Diplomacy: Hiroshima and Potsdam: The Use of the Atomic Bomb and the American Confrontation with Soviet Power* (New York: Random House, 1965). For a selection of readings covering the main interpretations of the origins of the cold war, see Thomas G. Paterson, ed., *The Origins of the Cold War* (Lexington, Mass.: D. C. Heath, 1974). For an interpretation of cold war origins skeptical of the revisionist approach, see John L. Gaddis, *The United States and the Origins of the Cold War, 1941–1947* (New York: Columbia University Press, 1972); on the question of nuclear intimidation of the Soviet Union, see ibid., esp. 244–81. On Soviet motives, see Vojtech Mastny, *Russia's Road to the Cold War: Diplomacy, Warfare and the Politics of Communism, 1941–1945* (New York: Columbia University Press, 1979), and Vojtech Mastny, "Stalin and the Militarization of the Cold War," *International Security*, 9, 3 (1984–85), 109–29.

17. For some public estimates, see, e.g., Lawrence Freedman, *The Evolution of Nuclear Strategy*, 2d ed. (New York: St. Martin's Press, 1989), 27, 50; Bernard Brodie, "The Weapon: War in the Atomic Age and Implications for Military Policy," in Bernard Brodie, ed., *The Absolute Weapon: Atomic Power and World Order* (New York: Harcourt, Brace, 1947), 41; Thomas B. Cochran, William M. Arkin, and Robert S. Norris, "History of the Nuclear Stockpile," *Bulletin of the Atomic Scientists* 41 August (1985), 106–9; and "U.S., Soviet Nuclear Weapons

Stockpile, 1945–1989: Number of Weapons," *Bulletin of the Atomic Scientists* 45 (November 1989), 53.

18. See, e.g., Arnold Kramish, *Atomic Energy in the Soviet Union* (Stanford: Stanford University Press, 1959); and York, *The Advisors,* 29ff.

19. Igor Golovin, formerly deputy to the director of the Soviet atomic bomb program, as quoted in Dan Charles, "Soviet Union 'Copied' American Atom Bomb," *New Scientist* 136, 1843 (October 17, 1992), 6.

20. Recently there has been substantial public confirmation of the role of intelligence agents in providing information about the early American nuclear weapons development program. See, e.g., "1st Soviet A-Bomb Built from U.S. Data, Russian Says," *New York Times,* January 14, 1993, A12. See also York, *The Advisors,* 69; Sherwin, *A World Destroyed,* 102–04; David Holloway, *The Soviet Union and the Arms Race* (New Haven: Yale University Press, 1983), 23; Michael Dobbs, "How Soviets Stole US Atom Secrets," *Washington Post,* October 4, 1992; Charles, "Soviet Union 'Copied' American Atom Bomb." The second known agent, David Greenglass, had functioned as a draftsman. Although Greenglass did not have the technical knowledge of Fuchs, his drawings could well have provided support and detail for Fuchs's reports. Greenglass would later escape execution by turning upon his sister and brother-in-law, Julius and Ethel Rosenberg, who had apparently recruited him for the Soviets and who served as a communications link with Soviet intelligence. While Fuchs and Greenglass received prison sentences, the Rosenbergs were executed. On the Rosenbergs, see Ronald Radosh and Joyce Milton, *The Rosenberg File: A Search for the Truth* (New York: Holt, Rinehart & Winston, 1983). While the Soviets were fully capable of producing nuclear weapons by their own unaided efforts, the fruits of espionage enabled them to do so more quickly and cheaply than would have been the case otherwise. Empirical information derived from espionage, on the feasibility and utility of various alternative approaches in the American program to the design of weapons and the production of fissionable materials, would have directed Soviet scientists and engineers to the courses of action most likely to prove fruitful, and allowed them to avoid the diversion of resources in directions that the American experience had shown to be "dead ends."

21. George F. Kennan's article, which is generally held to represent the first public formulation of the containment policy, was originally published, under the pseudonym, "X," in *Foreign Affairs* in the summer of 1947. It has recently been reprinted: George F. Kennan, "The Sources of Soviet Conduct," *Foreign Affairs* 65 (1987), 852–68.

22. For the evolution of the alliance, see Robert E. Osgood, *NATO: The Entangling Alliance* (Chicago: University of Chicago Press, 1962).

23. On the variety of ways in which the policy of containment was carried out, see John L. Gaddis, *Strategies of Containment* (New York: Oxford University Press, 1982). For Kennan's later views, see, among his other works, George F. Kennan, *Russia, the Atom and the West* (New York: Harper, 1958).

24. For the development of thermonuclear weapons in the United States and in the Soviet Union, see York, *The Advisors,* esp. 23, and 41–96. The Soviet thermonuclear program was not merely a response to the American. It had begun independently. Ibid., 88–89.

25. Ibid., 93.

26. See, e.g., Bernard Brodie, *Strategy in the Missile Age* (Princeton: Princeton University Press, 1959), 160–65.

27. Brodie, *Absolute Weapon*, 76.

28. Carl von Clausewitz, *On War*, ed. and trans. Michael Howard and Peter Paret (Princeton: Princeton University Press, 1976), 79.

Chapter 10 Nuclear Weapons: Uses and Uselessness

1. The armed services differed in the degree to which they accepted the centrality of the deterrent role. The new United States Air Force, which would, until the navy's submarine-launched ballistic missiles (SLBMs) began deployment in 1960, have control of the great bulk of the nuclear weapons meant for use against the Soviet homeland, embraced this outlook most enthusiastically. The United States Army was most skeptical, most army officers being inclined to take the view that war aims could in the end only be accomplished by the engagement of armies on the ground. The navy's position shifted over time and varied among the differing weapons platform "communities" within the navy. With deployment of SLBMs the submarine community became enthusiastic supporters of deterrence, while naval aviators and surface warfare officers saw a greater role for the direct clash between armed forces.

2. For the general development of nuclear strategic thought, see Lawrence Freedman, *The Evolution of Nuclear Strategy*, 2d ed. (New York: St. Martin's Press, 1989).; Robert W. Tucker, *The Nuclear Debate: Deterrence and the Lapse of Faith* (New York: Homes & Meier, 1985); Robert E. Osgood, *The Nuclear Dilemma in American Strategic Thought* (Boulder, Colo.: Westview Press, 1988); Fred Kaplan, *The Wizards of Armageddon* (New York: Simon & Schuster, 1983). For some discussions of early war-planning, see Samuel F. Wells, Jr., "Sounding the Tocsin: NSC 68 and the Soviet Threat," *International Security* 4, 2 (1979), 116–58; Marc Trachtenberg, "Strategic Thought in America, 1952–1966," *Political Science Quarterly* 104 (1989), 301–34; Marc Trachtenberg, "A 'Wasting Asset': American Strategy and the Shifting Nuclear Balance, 1949–1954," *International Security* 13, 3 (1988–89), 5–49; Steven T. Ross and David A. Rosenberg, eds., *The Atomic Bomb and War Planning: Concepts and Capabilities* (New York: Garland, 1989); David A. Rosenberg, "'A Smoking Radiating Ruin at the End of Two Hours': Documents on American Plans for Nuclear War with the Soviet Union, 1954–55," *International Security* 6, 3 (1981–82), 3–38; David A. Rosenberg, "The Origins of Overkill: Nuclear Weapons and American Strategy, 1945–1960," *International Security* 7, 4 (1983), 3–71; Richard H. Kohn and Joseph P. Harnahan, "U.S. Strategic Air Power, 1948–1962: Excerpts from an Interview with Generals Curtis E. LeMay, Leon W. Johnson, David A. Burchinal, and Jack J. Catton," *International Security* 12, 4 (1988), 78–95.

3. For an explanation of nuclear weapons targeting, see Desmond Ball, "Targeting for Strategic Deterrence," *Adelphi Papers* 185 (1983).

4. Henry A. Kissinger argued for the utility of a strategy based upon limited nuclear war in *Nuclear Weapons and Foreign Policy* (New York: Harper, 1957). He retracted this argument only a few years later in *The Necessity for Choice: Prospects of American Foreign Policy* (New York: Harper, 1961). See also Chapter 11.

5. For the background of strategic defenses against both bombers and missiles, and

a discussion of such defenses, see Ashton B. Carter and David N. Schwartz, eds., *Ballistic Missile Defense* (Washington, D.C.: Brookings, 1984).

6. See also Robert W. Tucker, *SDI and US Foreign Policy* (Boulder, Colo.: Westview Press, 1987).

7. The terms "escalation ladder" and "escalation dominance" are Herman Kahn's inventions. See Herman Kahn, *On Escalation: Metaphors and Scenarios* (New York: Praeger, 1965); and *On Thermonuclear War* (Princeton: Princeton University Press, 1961).

8. See Rosemary J. Foot, "Nuclear Coercion and the Ending of the Korean Conflict," *International Security* 13, 3 (1988–89), 92–112; and Roger Dingman, "Atomic Diplomacy during the Korean War," *International Security* 13, 3 (1988–89), 50–91.

9. On this see John L. Gaddis, *The Long Peace: Inquiries into the History of the Cold War* (Oxford: Oxford University Press, 1987), 104–46.

10. For an analysis of the role of nuclear weapons in Cold War crises, see Richard Betts, *Nuclear Blackmail and Nuclear Balance* (Washington, D.C.: Brookings, 1987). See also Barry M. Blechman and Stephen S. Kaplan, *Force without War: U.S. Armed Forces as a Political Instrument* (Washington, D.C.: Brookings, 1978); and Stephen S. Kaplan, *Diplomacy of Power: Soviet Armed Forces as a Political Instrument* (Washington, D.C.: Brookings, 1981).

11. The classic analysis of the Cuban missile crisis was Graham T. Allison, *Essence of Decision: Explaining the Cuban Missile Crisis* (Boston: Little, Brown, 1971). Since then a considerable amount of material has come to light which has changed our understanding of this crisis in important ways. For some accounts of these new understandings, see James G. Blight and David A. Welch, *On the Brink: Americans and Soviets Reexamine the Cuban Missile Crisis* (New York: Hill & Wang, 1989); and Marc Trachtenberg, "The Influence of Nuclear Weapons in the Cuban Missile Crisis," *International Security* 10, 1 (1985), 137–203.

12. Recent recollections by Soviet participants attribute importance, as a Soviet motive, to the protection of Cuba from an American invasion. See Blight and Welch, *On the Brink*.

13. See Raymond L. Garthoff, *Deterrence and the Revolution in Soviet Military Doctrine* (Washington, D.C.: Brookings, 1990); and Raymond L. Garthoff, *Soviet Strategy in the Nuclear Age*, rev. ed. (New York: Praeger, 1962). For a selection of Soviet writings, see Harriet Fast Scott and William F. Scott, eds., *The Soviet Art of War: Doctrine, Strategy, and Tactics* (Boulder, Colo.: Westview Press, 1982), esp. 123–295. See also Derek Leebaert and Timothy Dickinson, eds., *Soviet Strategy and the New Military Thinking* (Cambridge: Cambridge University Press, 1992); and Michael MccGwire, *Military Objectives in Soviet Foreign Policy* (Washington, D.C.: Brookings, 1987).

Chapter 11   The Revival of "Conventional War"

1. For a recent examination of the reasons why nuclear weapons were not used in Korea and other early cold war encounters, see John L. Gaddis, *The Long Peace: Inquiries into the History of the Cold War* (Oxford: Oxford University Press, 1987), 104–46.

2. An argument for the use of nuclear weapons in limited war was made by Henry A. Kissinger in *Nuclear Weapons and Foreign Policy* (New York: Harper,

1957), and retracted by him in *The Necessity for Choice: Prospects of American Foreign Policy* (New York: Harper, 1961). The classic work on limited war is Robert E. Osgood, *Limited War: The Challenge to American Strategy* (Chicago: University of Chicago Press, 1957). See also Robert E. Osgood, *Limited War Revisited* (Boulder, Colo.: Westview Press, 1979).

3. On the Korean war, see Bernard Brodie, *War and Politics* (New York: Macmillan, 1973), 57–112; James L. Stokesbury, *A Short History of the Korean War* (New York: W. Morrow, 1988); John W. Spanier, *The Truman-MacArthur Controversy and the Korean War* (New York: W. W. Norton, 1965); David Rees, *Korea: The Limited War* (New York: St. Martin's Press, 1965); Callum A. MacDonald, *Korea, the War before Vietnam* (New York: Free Press, 1987); Max Hastings, *The Korean War* (New York: Simon & Schuster, 1987); Clay Blair, *The Forgotten War: America in Korea, 1950–1953* (New York: Times Books, 1987).

4. Quoted in Spanier, *Truman-MacArthur Controversy*, 222.

5. See Rosemary J. Foot, "Nuclear Coercion and the Ending of the Korean Conflict," *International Security* 13, 3 (1988–89), 92–112, and Roger Dingman, "Atomic Diplomacy during the Korean War," *International Security* 13, 3 (1988–89), 50–91.

6. On the Vietnam war, see George C. Herring, *America's Longest War: The United States and Vietnam, 1950–1975*, 2d ed. (New York: Alfred A. Knopf, 1986); Leslie H. Gelb and Richard K. Betts, *The Irony of Vietnam: The System Worked* (Washington, D.C.: Brookings, 1979); Brodie, *War and Politics*, 113–222; William S. Turley, *The Second Indochina War: A Short Political and Military History, 1954–1975* (New York: Penguin Books, 1987); and Michael Maclear, *The Ten Thousand Day War: Vietnam, 1945–1975* (New York: St. Martin's Press, 1981).

7. Herring, *America's Longest War*, 141.

8. For a prominent statement of this view, see Harry G. Summers, Jr., *On Strategy: A Critical Analysis of the Vietnam War* (Novato, Calif.: Presidio Press, 1982).

9. See, e.g., Samuel Eliot Morison, Frederick Merk, and Frank Friedel, *Dissent in Three American Wars* (Cambridge: Harvard University Press, 1970).

10. See Summers, *On Strategy*.

11. On the Gulf War, see Lawrence Freedman and Efraim Karsh, *The Gulf Conflict, 1990–1991: Diplomacy and War in the New World Order* (Princeton: Princeton University Press, 1993); Lawrence Freedman and Efraim Karsh, "How Kuwait Was Won: Strategy in the Gulf War," *International Security* 16, 2 (1991), 5–41; U.S. News & World Report, *Triumph without Victory: The Unreported History of the Persian Gulf War* (New York: Times Books, 1992); Norman Friedman, *Desert Victory: The War for Kuwait* (Annapolis, Md.: Naval Institute Press, 1991); Roland Dannreuther, "The Gulf Conflict: A Political and Strategic Analysis," *Adelphi Papers* 264 (1992).

12. Battle casualties for coalition forces were no greater than the casualties suffered by the forces involved before the outbreak of the ground war. See, e.g., Freedman and Karsh, *The Gulf Conflict*, 408–9.

13. See again Summers, *On Strategy*.

14. We will leave aside questions about American policy before the Iraqi invasion of Kuwait—whether the United States in any way encouraged Iraqi president Saddam Hussein in the belief that he could launch his attack with impunity, by in-

advertently giving him false signals that led him to believe that the United States would be indifferent if he decided forcibly to settle his territorial dispute with Kuwait. For an argument that the invasion of Kuwait was "unstoppable," and "irreversible, short of the use of force," see Janice Gross Stein, "Deterrence and Compellence in the Gulf, 1990–1991: A Failed or Impossible Task?," *International Security* 17, 2 (1992), 147–79.

15. Freedman and Karsh, *The Gulf Conflict*, 92–94.
16. Ibid., 201–10.
17. Ibid., 358, 361.
18. For some overviews, see John Shy and Thomas W. Collier, "Revolutionary War," in Peter Paret, ed., *Makers of Modern Strategy: From Machiavelli to the Nuclear Age* (Princeton: Princeton University Press, 1986), 815–62; and Michael Carver, "Conventional Warfare in the Nuclear Age," in ibid., 779–814.
19. See Efraim Karsh, "The Iran-Iraq War: A Military Analysis," *Adelphi Papers* 220 (1987).
20. See Max Hastings and Simon Jenkins, *The Battle for the Falklands* (New York: Norton, 1983), and Lawrence Freedman, *Britain and the Falklands War* (Oxford: B. Blackwell, 1988).
21. See Roy Oliver, "The Lessons of the Soviet/Afghan War," *Adelphi Papers* 259 (1991).
22. On the Arab-Israeli wars, see Nadav Safran, *From War to War: The Arab-Israeli Confrontation, 1948–1967* (New York: Pegasus, 1969); Michael Howard and Robert Hunter, "Israel and the Arab World: The Crisis of 1967," *Adelphi Papers* 41 (1967); Chaim Herzog, *The War of Atonement, October 1973* (Boston: Little, Brown, 1975); Mohamed Heikal, *The Road to Ramadan* (New York: Quadrangle/New York Times, 1975).
23. See Richard A. Gabriel, *Operation Peace for Galilee: The Israeli-PLO War in Lebanon* (New York: Hill & Wang, 1984); also see Thomas L. Friedman, *From Beirut to Jerusalem* (New York: Farrar, Straus, Giroux, 1989).
24. See John Zametica, "The Yugoslav Conflict," *Adelphi Papers* 270 (1992), and Misha Glenny, *The Fall of Yugoslavia: The Third Balkan War* (New York: Penguin, 1992).

Chapter 12   The Cold War, Arms, and the Obsolescence of War

1. For an extensive analysis of Soviet military programs and the motivations for them, see David Holloway, *The Soviet Union and the Arms Race* (New Haven: Yale University Press, 1983). See also Michael MccGwire, *Military Objectives in Soviet Foreign Policy* (Washington, D.C.: Brookings, 1987).
2. See also John J. Weltman, "Détente and the Decline of Geography," *Jerusalem Journal of International Relations* 4, 2 (1979), 75–94.
3. For an argument along these lines, see two articles by Michael D. Wallace, "Arms Races and Escalation: Some New Evidence," *Journal of Conflict Resolution* 23 (March 1977), 3–16; and "Armaments and Escalation," *International Studies Quarterly* 26 (March 1982), 37–56. See also J. David Singer, "Threat Perceptions and the Armament-Tension Dilemma," *Journal of Conflict Resolution* 2 (March 1958), 90–105.
4. See again, e.g., Samuel P. Huntington, "Arms Races: Prerequisites and Results," *Public Policy* 9 (1958), 41–83.

5. Bernadotte E. Schmitt, *The Coming of the War* (London: Routledge & Paul, 1958), 1:72–73; Sydney B. Fay, *The Origins of the World War* (New York: Macmillan, 1929), 1:299ff. See also E. L. Woodward, *Great Britain and the German Navy* (London: Frank Cass, 1964), esp. 323ff.; and Michael Howard, "The Edwardian Arms Race," in *The Lessons of History* (New Haven: Yale University Press, 1991), 81–96.

6. For recent interpretations that give weight to the importance of Soviet behavior in the origins of the Cold War, see John L. Gaddis, "The Emerging Post-Revisionist Synthesis on the Origins of the Cold War," *Diplomatic History* 7 (Summer 1983), 171–190; Vojtech Mastny, *Russia's Road to the Cold War: Diplomacy, Warfare and the Politics of Communism, 1941–1945* (New York: Columbia University Pres, 1979); and Vojtech Mastny, "Stalin and the Militarization of the Cold War," *International Security* 9, 3 (1984–85), 109–29. For an earlier interpretation along these lines, see Louis J. Halle, *The Cold War as History* (New York: Harper & Row, 1967). See also Wilfrid Knapp, *A History of War and Peace 1939–1965* (London: Oxford University Press, 1967), esp. 83–140, 265–319; and Melvyn P. Leffler, "National Security," in Michael J. Hogan and Thomas G. Paterson, eds., *Explaining the History of American Foreign Relations* (Cambridge: Cambridge University Press, 1991), esp. 210–12.

7. See John L. Gaddis, *Strategies of Containment* (New York: Oxford University Press, 1982).

8. See also John L. Gaddis, *The United States and the End of the Cold War* (New York: Oxford University Press, 1992). For an often prescient earlier view, see John L. Gaddis, *The Long Peace: Inquiries into the History of the Cold War* (New York: Oxford University Press, 1987). For a recent journalistic acount, see Michael R. Beschloss and Strobe Talbott, *At the Highest Levels: The Inside Story of the End of the Cold War* (Boston: Little, Brown, 1993).

9. For general analyses of arms control through the early years of the cold war, see Hedley Bull, *The Control of the Arms Race: Disarmament and Arms Control in the Missile Age* (New York: Praeger, 1966); Donald G. Brennan, ed., *Arms Control, Disarmament and National Security* (New York: George Braziller, 1961); Thomas C. Schelling and Morton H. Halperin, *Strategy and Arms Control* (New York: Twentieth Century Fund, 1961). For some later accounts, see John Newhouse, *Cold Dawn: The Story of SALT* (New York: Holt, Rinehart & Winston, 1973); Strobe Talbott, *Endgame: The Inside Story of Salt II* (New York: Harper & Row, 1979); and Thomas C. Schelling, "What Went Wrong with Arms Control?" *Foreign Affairs* 64 (1985–86), 219–33. See also Michael Nacht, "Strategic Arms Control and American Security," in John J. Weltman, Michael Nacht, and George H. Quester, *Challenges to American National Security in the 1990s* (New York: Plenum Press, 1991), 93–106.

10. See, e.g., Lawrence Freedman, *The Evolution of Nuclear Strategy*, 2d ed. (New York: St. Martin's Press, 1989), 261, 271, 355. For an extensive discussion of the ballistic missile defense question, see Ashton B. Carter and David N. Schwartz, eds., *Ballistic Missile Defense* (Washington, D.C.: Brookings, 1984).

11. START I provided that each side would reduce its warhead totals from a range publicly estimated at 11,000–12,000 to approximately 6,000 for the Soviets and 8,000 for the United States. START II provided for further reductions to 3,500 for the United States and 3,000 for Russia by the year 2003. Carrying the trea-

ties into force, however, was complicated by the breakup of the Soviet Union, which left some of these forces in successor states to the Soviet Union other than Russia. See, e.g., *New York Times*, January 4, 1993, A8–9.

12. For analysis and critique of this debate, see Robert E. Osgood and Robert W. Tucker, *Force, Order, and Justice* (Baltimore: Johns Hopkins Press, 1967); John J. Weltman, "On the Obsolescence of War: An Essay in Policy and Theory," *International Studies Quarterly*, 18, 4 (1974), 395–416.

13. See Robert Gilpin, *War and Change in World Politics* (Cambridge: Cambridge University Press, 1981).

14. See Richard Betts, *Nuclear Blackmail and Nuclear Balance* (Washington, D.C.: Brookings, 1987). See also Barry M. Blechman and Stephen S. Kaplan, *Force without War: U.S. Armed Forces as a Political Instrument* (Washington, D.C.: Brookings, 1978), and Stephen S. Kaplan, *Diplomacy of Power: Soviet Armed Forces as a Political Instrument* (Washington, D.C.: Brookings, 1981).

15. For a recent restatement of this view, see Francis Fukuyama, *The End of History and the Last Man* (New York: Free Press, 1992).

16. This view, of course, goes back at least to Kant and is at the core of liberal and progressive thinking about war and peace. For a recent revival of this view, see Michael W. Doyle, "Liberalism and World Politics," *American Political Science Review* 80 (December 1986), 1151–69.

17. See, e.g., Robert O. Keohane and Joseph S. Nye, *Power and Interdependence* (Glenview, Ill.: Scott, Foresman, 1989).

18. See Geoffrey Blainey, *The Causes of War* (London: Macmillan, 1973), for a brilliant exposition of this theme.

19. For an argument that nuclear weapons were largely irrelevant to this retreat from war, see John Mueller, *Retreat from Doomsday: The Obsolescence of Major War* (New York: Basic Books, 1989). For a critique of this argument, see Carl Kaysen, "Is War Obsolete?" *International Security*, 14, 4 (1990), 42–64.

Chapter 13 The Future Strategic Environment

1. The distinction between "system-level" and "unit-level" features in international politics is of course from Kenneth N. Waltz, *Theory of International Politics* (Reading, Mass.: Addison-Wesley, 1979).

2. "Spillover" is the central notion in the "Functionalist" and "Neo-Functionalist" school of international relations. See, e.g., Ernst Haas, *Beyond the Nation-State* (Stanford: Stanford University Press, 1964), and Joseph S. Nye, *Peace in Parts: Integration and Conflict in Regional Organization* (Boston: Little, Brown, 1971).

3. See Robert Gilpin, *War and Change in World Politics* (Cambridge: Cambridge University Press, 1981); see also Paul M. Kennedy, *The Rise and Fall of the Great Powers: Economic Change and Military Confict from 1500 to 2000* (New York: Random House, 1987), and William H. McNeill, *The Pursuit of Power: Technology, Armed Force, and Society since A.D. 1000* (Chicago: University of Chicago Press, 1982).

4. See John Zysman, "Security and Technology," in John J. Weltman, Michael Nacht, and George H. Quester, eds., *Challenges to American National Security in the 1990s* (New York: Plenum Press, 1991), 219–36; Michael Borrus and John Zysman, "Industrial Competitiveness and National Security," in Graham Allison

and Gregory F. Treverton, eds., *Rethinking America's Security* (New York: W. W. Norton, 1992), 136–75.

5. This was of course the central premise in Francis Fukuyama, "The End of History," *National Interest* 16 (Summer 1989), 3–18. We need not, however, accept the conclusion he draws from this premise: that international peace will follow. Lack of ideological intensity may affect the *character* of international conflicts without affecting their *existence*.

6. For a survey of the proliferation of weapons of mass destruction and ballistic missile technology, and attempts at control of this proliferation, see Lewis A. Dunn, "New Weapons and Old Enmities: Proliferation, Regional Conflict, and Implications for U.S. Strategy in the 1990s," in Weltman et al., *Challenges to American National Security,* 179–203. See also Leonard S. Spector, *Nuclear Ambitions* (Boulder, Colo.: Westview Press, 1990); Lewis A. Dunn, "Containing Nuclear Proliferation," *Adelphi Papers* 263 (1991); Martin Navias, "Ballistic Missile Proliferation in the Third World," *Adelphi Papers,* 252 (1990); and George H. Quester, *The Politics of Nuclear Proliferation* (Baltimore: Johns Hopkins University Press, 1973).

7. For an analysis of this regime, see Lawrence Scheinman, *The Nonproliferation Role of the International Atomic Energy Agency* (Washington, D.C.: Resources for the Future, 1985). See also Joseph F. Pilat and Robert E. Pendley, eds., *Beyond 1995: The Future of the NPT Regime* (New York: Plenum Press, 1990).

8. A treaty prohibiting the development, production, or stockpiling of bacteriological weapons was signed in 1972. In 1987, a number of Western governments and Japan began to cooperate to restrict the spread of ballistic missiles, under the aegis of the international Missile Technology Control Regime agreement. In 1990 the Soviets indicated that they would abide by this agreement. In 1993 a treaty was opened for signature that would ban the production or stockpiling of chemical weapons and prohibit their use, even in retaliation for an attack with such weapons, as early as 2005. The treaty would also establish a regime of intrusive inspections, supervised by a new international monitoring organization. See also Dunn, "New Weapons and Old Enmities," 195–98.

9. For some surveys of new technologies and their impact on warfare, see Seymour J. Deitchman, *New Technology and Military Power* (Boulder, Colo.: Westview Press, 1979); Robert J. O'Neill, ed., *New Technology and Western Security Policy* (Hamden, Conn.: Archon Books, 1985); Andrew J. Pierre, ed., *The Conventional Defense of Europe: New Technologies and New Strategies* (New York: Council on Foreign Relations, 1986); Richard Burt, "New Weapons Technologies: Debate and Directions," *Adelphi Papers* 126 (1976); Robert L. Pfaltzgraff, Jr., Uri Ra'anan, Richard H. Shultz, and Igor Lukes, eds., *Emerging Doctrines and Technologies: Implications for Global and Regional Political-Military Balances* (Lexington, Mass.: Lexington Books, 1988), esp. 141–250; B. T. Feld, T. Greenwood, G. N. Rathjens, and Stephen Weinberg, *Impact of New Technologies on the Arms Race* (Cambridge: MIT Press, 1971). For a historical account of the effects of technological development upon war, and of war upon technological development, see Martin van Creveld, *Technology and War* (New York: Free Press, 1989). See also John U. Nef, *War and Human Progress: An Essay on the Rise of Industrial Civilization* (New York: W. W. Norton, 1968).

10. The relationship between numbers and conflict in the international system has

been the topic of long-standing scholarly debate. That in a world of many powers the opportunity for miscalculation, and thus the potential for war, is greater than in a world of only two major actors is classically argued by Kenneth N. Waltz, "The Stability of a Bipolar World," *Daedalus* 93 (Summer 1964), 881–909. See also Kenneth N. Waltz, "International Structure, National Force, and the Balance of World Power," *Journal of International Affairs* 21 (1967), 215–31. For the opposing view, see Karl Deutsch and J. David Singer, "Multipolar Power Systems and International Stability," *World Politics*, 16 (April 1964), 390–406. See also Richard N. Rosecrance, "Bipolarity, Multipolarity and the Future," *Journal of Conflict Resolution*, 10 (September 1966), 314–27; J. David Singer and Melvin Small, "Alliance Aggregation and the Onset of War," in J. David Singer, ed., *Quantitative Approaches to International Politics: Insights and Evidence* (New York: Free Press, 1968), 246–86. See also Alan Ned Sabrosky, ed., *Polarity and War: The Changing Structure of International Conflict* (Boulder, Colo.: Westview Press, 1985). For a recent discussion in which strategic beliefs and the military balance between the offense and the defense are given greater explanatory importance than the number of powers in the system, see Ted Hopf, "Polarity, the Offense-Defense Balance and War," *American Political Science Review* 85, 2 (1991), 475–93; see also the exchange between Manus I. Midlarsky and Ted Hopf, "Polarity and International Stability," *American Political Science Review* 87, 1 (1993), 173–81. An empirical study of the last five centuries concludes "there is no relationship between the number of Powers in the system and the frequency or destructiveness of the wars that occur." Jack S. Levy, *War in the Modern Great Power System, 1495–1975* (Lexington: University Press of Kentucky, 1983), 170.

11. For the distinction between yesterday's "spin-off" technologies, in which consumers found applications for technologies originally developed for the military, and today's "spin-on" technologies, in which the military sphere is increasingly dependent upon consumer-driven technological developments, see Zysman, "Security and Technology." See also B. R. Inman and Daniel F. Burton, Jr., "Technology and U.S. National Security," in Allison and Treverton, *Rethinking America's Security*, 117–35.

12. See also Robert Gilpin, *The Political Economy of International Relations* (Princeton: Princeton University Press, 1987), esp. 341–408.

13. Peter Sutherland, General Director of the General Agreement on Tariffs and Trade (GATT), as quoted in William Drodziak, "Historic Trade Pact Signed, but Global Tensions Persist," *Washington Post*, April 16, 1994.

14. For example, Michael W. Doyle, "Liberalism and World Politics," *American Political Science Review* 80 (December 1986), 1151–69.

15. The major exception to this generalization that democracies have been beneficiaries of the American alliance system is of course India, which for much of the cold war period was allied with the Soviet Union, largely because the Indian government saw the principal threats to its security in America's ally, Pakistan, and the Soviet Union's antagonist, China.

16. For an exchange of views on the likelihood that the end of the cold war will return Europe to its former condition of endemic intramural conflict, see John Mearsheimer, "Back to the Future: Instability in Europe after the Cold War,"

International Security 15, 1 (1990), 5–56; and Jack L. Snyder, "Averting Anarchy in the New Europe," *International Security* 14, 4 (1990), 5–41.

17. For a brilliant recent discussion of the origins and varieties of nationalism, see Isaiah Berlin, "The Bent Twig: On the Rise of Nationalism," in *The Crooked Timber of Humanity: Chapters in the History of Ideas*, ed. Henry Hardy (New York: Alfred A. Knopf, 1991), 238–61.

18. See also John J. Weltman, "Nuclear Devolution and World Order," *World Politics* 32, 2 (1980), 169–93; and "Managing Nuclear Multipolarity," *International Security* 6, 3 (1981–82), 182–94. See also Kenneth N. Waltz, "The Spread of Nuclear Weapons: More May Be Better," *Adelphi Papers* 171 (1981).

19. See also George H. Quester, *Offense and Defense in the International System* (New Brunswick, N.J.: Transaction Books, 1988).

20. The view that, over the long perspective of Western history, periods of decisiveness in warfare have been the exception and periods of indecisiveness the norm is the major theme in Archer Jones, *The Art of War in the Western World* (Oxford: Oxford University Press, 1989); see, e.g., 648–62, 666–68, 704–10. See also Levy, *War in the Modern Great Power System, 1495–1975*, 148–49.

21. The relationship between the characteristics of military technology and the felt necessity of security concerns is also discussed by Robert Jervis in "Cooperation under the Security Dilemma," *World Politics* 30, 2 (1978), 167–214.

22. See Richard Clutterbuck, *Guerillas and Terrorists* (Athens: Ohio University Press, 1980).

23. For another view of the tendencies of American policy, see Robert W. Tucker and David C. Hendrickson, *The Imperial Temptation: The New World Order and America's Purpose* (New York: Council on Foreign Relations, 1992). See also Steven E. Miller, ed., *Conventional Forces and American Defense Policy* (Princeton: Princeton University Press, 1986).

Index

Albrecht-Carrié, René, 232 n, 234 n, 236 n, 238 n, 240 n
Alexander, Martin, 239 n
Alexander the Great (king of Macedonia), 6
Allison, Graham T., 246 n, 250 n, 252 n
Alperowitz, Gar, 243 n
American Civil War, 76–79
  Antietam, battle of, 77–78
  Bull Run, first battle of, 76
  Emancipation Proclamation, impact of, 78
  European misreading of, 76, 79–80
  Gettysburg, battle of, 77
Anglo-Japanese alliance (1902), 115
annihilation in warfare, xi–xii, 15–16, 253 n
  defined, 237 n
  and expectations about World War I, 90–91, 93, 100
  and expectations about World War II, 108–13, 117, 135
  in French Revolutionary war, 16, 40–41, 47–49
  in mid-nineteenth century European wars, 70–71, 73
  in opening of World War II, 16–17, 118, 128–29
  in post–Cold War era, 224–25
  search for, in American Civil War, 76–79
  See also Persian Gulf war (1991); technological change in war
Anti-Ballistic Missile (ABM) Treaty (1972), 158, 197–98
Antietam, battle of. See American Civil War
Arab-Israeli wars, 164, 191, 200–202
Arkin, William M., 243 n
Armenia-Azerbaijan war, 203–4. See also Soviet Union succession conflicts
arms control
  and Cold War, 197–99, 206, 212, 251n
  early attempts, 239 n
  inter-war period, 113–17, 211
  political context dominates technical, 116–17
arms races, 81–82
  and Cold War, 193–97, 206
  and origins of World War I, 85–86, 195

military uselessness, 18, 156–57, 167–68, 205, 250 n

and political bargaining in peacetime, 162–65

Soviet nuclear strategy, 165–67

uniqueness affirmed, as deterrence, 149–51

uniqueness denied, 148–49

See also strategic defense; war, limited

numbers and international conflict, x, 251–52 nn. *See also* complexity and international conflict

Nye, Joseph S., 250 n

O'Connor, Raymond G., 239 n

Offner, Arnold A., 238–40 nn

Okamoto, Shumpei, 240 n

Oliver, Roy, 248 n

Oman, Charles, 229 n

O'Neill, Robert J., 240 n, 251 n

Onuf, Nicholas G., 228 n

Oppenheimer, J. Robert, 136, 139, 141, 242 n

Osgood, Robert E., 169, 227 n, 229–30 n, 232 n, 234 n, 237 n, 239 n, 244–45 n, 247 n, 250 n

Osgood, Samuel M., 241 n

Ottoman Empire, decline of, 66, 86, 102, 200

Palmer, R. R., 230–232 nn

"Pan-Slavism," 218–19. *See also* ideology and conflict

Paret, Peter, 228–35 nn, 237–39 nn, 248 n

Parker, Geoffrey, 228–229 n

Parkinson, F., 227 n, 230–31 n

Paterson, Thomas G., 243 n, 249 n

Pearl Harbor attack. *See* World War II

Peloponnesian War (431–404 B.C.), 1

Pelz, Stephen E., 240 n

Pendley, Robert E., 251 n

Persian Gulf war (1991), 18, 170, 183–91, 203, 206, 211–12, 215, 218

American pre-war policy, 247–48 n

casualties, 247 n

compared with Korean war, 188

compared with Vietnam war, 183–84, 188

unlikely to be repeated, 188–91

Persian War (490–478 B.C.), 1

Pfaltzgraff, Robert L., Jr., 251 n

Piedmont, kingdom of, and unification of Italy, 67, 70

Pierre, Andrew J., 251 n

Pilat, Joseph F., 251 n

Posen, Barry, 238 n

Potsdam conference, 142

Potter, E. B., 229 n, 231 n, 235 n, 241 n

Powers, Thomas, 242 n

Prange, Gordon W., 241 n

professionalization of warfare, 27–28, 51

and Prussian (later German) general staff, 71–72, 82

and war plans, 82, 87–88, 91–92, 128, 236 n

progress in domestic and international politics, compared, 2–4

proliferation, weapons. *See* technological change after Cold War

Prussia, kingdom of, and unification of Germany, 67–70

Pusan. *See* Korean War

Quester, George H., 239–40 n, 249–51 nn, 253 n

Ra'anan, Uri, 251 n

Radosh, Ronald, 244 n

Rathjens, G. N., 251 n

Reagan, Ronald, 158, 160, 206

Rees, David, 247 n

Remak, Joachim, 236 n

Rhineland, German remilitarization of (1936), 121

Rhodes, Richard, 242 n

Richardson, James L., 240 n

Ritter, Gerhard, 237 n

Roberts, Penfield, 230 n

Ropp, Theodore, 229–32 nn, 234 n, 237–38 n, 241 n

Rosecrance, Richard N., 252 n

Rosenberg, David A., 245 n

Rosenbergs, Ethel and Julius, 244 n

Ross, Steven T., 230–31 n, 245 n

Rothenberg, Gunther E., 229 n, 231 n, 235 n

Rothfels, H., 231–33 nn

Rousseau, Jean Jacques, 13, 228 n

Royal Air Force (RAF), 110, 113, 131

Ruhr, French occupation of (1923), 106